PRAISE FOR *AWARE*

"Dan Siegel brings us a precious gift that will transform your mind, life, and relationships in a most wonderful way, using an easy-to-learn and revolutionary new system for meditation—one that beginners and experts alike will cherish!"

—Dr. Rudolph Tanzi, professor of neurology,
Harvard University, coauthor of *The Healing Self*

"Dan has produced a masterpiece containing invaluable knowledge in the fields of psychiatry, therapy, interpersonal neurobiology, meditation, and more. Very few people understand the intricacies of the human mind and how it can be channeled to achieve true well-being as Dan does. The Wheel of Awareness is a simple yet profound way for all to learn and advance in their practice of being aware."

—Menas C. Kafatos, Fletcher Jones Endowed Professor of
Computational Physics, Chapman University, coauthor with Deepak
Chopra of the *New York Times* bestseller *You Are the Universe*

"Dan is a brilliant integrator and *Aware* is a visionary blend of neuroscience, physics, and cutting-edge psychology combined with creative approaches to mindfulness and compassion. The practice of the Wheel brings together many skillful and wise elements of meditation, all rolled into one."

—Jack Kornfield, author of *The Wise Heart*

"A life-changing journey into the deep nature of our consciousness, what it means to be human, and how to truly thrive."

—Arianna Huffington, founder and CEO of Thrive Global and
founder of *The Huffington Post*

"Dan's ability to distill and clarify insights from fields as diverse as neurobiology, psychology, philosophy, and spirituality is a gift to us all relationally, socially, and soulfully. In *Aware*, he plumbs the depths of his profound knowledge to uncover what it means to be truly alive and present."

—Alanis Morissette

"Daniel Siegel counts among the most aware people I know—and now he's shared with us all a brilliant, practical tool for us all to sharpen our awareness."

—Daniel Goleman, author of *Altered Traits: Science Reveals How Meditation Changes Your Mind, Brain, and Body*

"Growing a strong mind in our lives is the scientifically proven pathway for cultivating more well-being, emotional intelligence, and social connection. Dan Siegel's new approach of the Wheel of Awareness offers us a powerful tool to do just that—bring more health, resilience, and caring into our lives throughout the lifespan."

—Goldie Hawn, author of *A Lotus Grows in the Mud* and *Ten Mindful Minutes*

"*Aware* enables you to successfully search inside yourself to cultivate well-being and a deeper understanding of the mind with an exciting new approach to meditation. The Wheel of Awareness provides a comprehensive, science-based way to develop the focused attention, open awareness, and kind intention that research reveals can help bring health and resilience into your life."   —Chade-Meng Tan, *New York Times* bestselling author of *Joy on Demand* and *Search Inside Yourself*

"In *Aware*, Dan Siegel combines insights from a range of traditional practices into an original method of practicing mindfulness: one that fully integrates mind-and-embodied experience and guides us towards health and happiness for all. Grounded in the research-based practice of the Wheel of Awareness, Dr. Siegel reveals just how multisensory and holistic awareness practices lead to relationally robust presence, harmony, and peaceful living in diverse communities. Read *Aware* to unlock a new way of being awake to the infinite possibility of being and loving in our lives and communities, embracing our differences and moving joyfully from 'Me' to 'MWe.'"

—Rhonda V. Magee, professor of law, University of San Francisco

"Dr. Dan Siegel has an extraordinary gift: to describe patterns and make accessible in a powerful way the insights and practices that are fundamental to well-being and awakening. In his book *Aware*, we are introduced to the power of presence. Using science and psychology, he opens for us his Wheel of Awareness, a way of perceiving and working with the mind that is both practical and liberating."

—Joan Halifax, PhD, Abbot, Upaya Zen Center

"Dan Siegel brings a fresh look and creative imagination to provide a roadmap of the mind and make mindfulness practices more accessible and applicable in everyday life. *Aware* provides a way to grow our skills in self-awareness, self-monitoring, and self-regulation—enhancing our capacity for joy, flourishing, and peace."

—Ronald Epstein, MD, professor of family medicine, psychiatry,
oncology, and medicine, University of Rochester School of
Medicine and Dentistry, author of *Attending*

"We know so much about what's outside in the cosmos, billions of light-years away, but very little about what's going on inside our heads right now. We know about dark matter but not so much about grey matter, which, I would think, matters most. Daniel Siegel finally gives us insight into who we are, how we work, and, most important of all, how to retrain and change our minds. For me, almost every line is an 'aha' moment. At long last, someone nails what it is to have a healthy mind, and if you don't have one, how to get one."

—Ruby Wax, author of *Sane New World*

"Daniel Siegel is truly one of a kind. His ability to blend no-nonsense neuroscience with accessible techniques for training the mind is masterful. Anyone wanting to be less distracted and more present in their life will want to read this book."

—Andy Puddicombe, cofounder of Headspace

"Dan Siegel, a brilliant and compassionate clinician and master translator of research and complex topics, offers this wise and practical guide on the Wheel of Awareness. Inspired by science and decades of clinical and teaching experience, combined with Dan's unique insights, *Aware* opens our minds to a transformative mental practice that can serve as a valuable resource to living fully in the ups and downs of everyday life."

—Susan Bauer-Wu, president of the Mind & Life Institute,
author of *Leaves Falling Gently*

"This is the first time I have seen the integration of the three core meditation practices (concentration, loving kindness, open awareness) into a scientifically supported theory . . . while also linking self-inquiry to our need for community. From Tibetan text to quantum theory, Dan takes our understanding of the mind to the next level."

—Jeffrey C. Walker, retired vice chairman, JPMorgan Chase & Co.

"With warmth and humanity, Dr. Siegel gives us a brilliant summary of the new sciences of the mind that is fascinating, sometimes jaw-dropping, and always wonderfully useful. This is a remarkable integration of cutting-edge neuroscience, profound contemplative insights, and down-to-earth experiential practices. A tour de force from a master of this field."

—Rick Hanson, PhD, author of *Resilient: How to Grow an Unshakable Core of Calm, Strength, and Happiness*

ALSO BY DANIEL J. SIEGEL, MD

The Developing Mind

Parenting from the Inside Out
(with Mary Hartzell)

The Mindful Brain

Mindsight

The Mindful Therapist

Pocket Guide to Interpersonal Neurobiology

The Whole-Brain Child
(with Tina Payne Bryson)

Brainstorm

No-Drama Discipline
(with Tina Payne Bryson)

Mind

The Yes Brain
(with Tina Payne Bryson)

AWARE

THE SCIENCE AND PRACTICE OF PRESENCE

THE GROUNDBREAKING MEDITATION PRACTICE

Daniel J. Siegel, MD

A TarcherPerigee Book

tarcherperigee

An imprint of Penguin Random House LLC
penguinrandomhouse.com

First trade paperback edition 2020

Most TarcherPerigee books are available at special quantity discounts for bulk purchase for sales promotions, premiums, fund-raising, and educational needs. Special books or book excerpts also can be created to fit specific needs. For details, write: SpecialMarkets@penguinrandomhouse.com.

LIBRARY OF CONGRESS CATALOGING-IN-PUBLICATION DATA

Names: Siegel, Daniel J., author.
Title: Aware : the science and practice of presence : the groundbreaking meditation practice / Dr. Daniel Siegel, M.D.
Description: New York : TarcherPerigee, 2018. |
Includes bibliographical references and index. |
Identifiers: LCCN 2018016987 (print) | LCCN 2018027672 (ebook) |
ISBN 9780143111788 | ISBN 9781101993040 (hardback)
Subjects: LCSH: Self-actualization (Psychology) | Mindfulness (Psychology) |
Meditation. | BISAC: SELF-HELP / Personal Growth / General. |
BODY, MIND & SPIRIT / Meditation.
Classification: LCC BF637.S4 (ebook) | LCC BF637.S4 S54 2018 (print) |
DDC 158.1/2—dc23
LC record available at https://lccn.loc.gov/2018016987
p.   cm.

ISBN 9780143111795 (paperback)

Printed in the United States of America
ScoutAutomatedPrintCode

Book design by Daniel Lagin

CONTENTS

A mind that is stretched to a new idea
never returns to its original dimension.

Oliver Wendell Holmes

To Caroline Welch
The magnificent mindful woman who shows me every day
the power and potential of presence in our
personal and professional lives

and

In Memory of John O'Donohue:

A decade
does not diminish
the
love
laughter
and
light
your life
brings to us
still
truth and
transformation
meaning and
your mind
with us
for
now
forever

AWARE

PART I

THE WHEEL OF AWARENESS: IDEA AND PRACTICE

AN INVITATION

There is an old saying that consciousness is like a container of water. If you take a tablespoon of salt and place it in a small container, say, the size of an espresso cup, the water most certainly will be too salty to drink. But if your container is much larger—say it is capable of holding many, many gallons of water—that same tablespoon of salt, now placed into this vast amount of liquid, will taste fresh. Same water, same salt; simply a different ratio, and the experience of drinking is totally different.

Consciousness is like that. When we learn to cultivate our capacity for being aware, the quality of our life and the strength of our mind are enhanced.

The skills you'll learn in this book are really quite simple: You will learn to increase the mind's capacity for being aware so that you will be able to adjust the ratio of the experience of awareness itself (the water) to the object of your awareness (the salt). You might call this cultivating consciousness; you might call it strengthening your mind. Research reveals that you would be correct in even calling this integrating your brain—growing the linkages among its different regions, strengthening the brain's ability to regulate things such as emotion, attention, thought, and behavior, learning to live a life with more flexibility and freedom.

Learning this skill of distinguishing awareness from that which you are aware of will enable you to expand the container of consciousness and empower you to "taste" so much more than just a salty glass of water. You will be able to immerse yourself fully in whatever experiences arise, regardless of how many tablespoons of salt life throws your way.

To enable these abilities to become a part of your life, this book will teach you a practice I developed called the Wheel of Awareness. As you become adept at using this tool, you may come to find that you'll be able to weather life's storms more easily and live life more fully, opening to whatever experiences arise, be they positive or negative. This skill of cultivating consciousness by expanding awareness, like transforming the small espresso cup into a vast container of water, will not only help you enjoy life more, it can also bring a deeper sense of connection and meaning to everyday experience, and even make you healthier.

CULTIVATING WELL-BEING BY DEVELOPING ATTENTION, AWARENESS, AND INTENTION

In the pages of this book we will dive deep into three learnable skills that have been shown in carefully conducted scientific studies to support the cultivation of well-being. When we develop *focused attention*, *open awareness*, and *kind intention*, research reveals we:

1. *Improve* **immune function** to help fight infection.
2. *Optimize* the level of the enzyme **telomerase**, which repairs and maintains the ends of your chromosomes, keeping your cells—and therefore *you*—youthful, functioning well, and healthy.
3. *Enhance* the **"epigenetic" regulation** of genes to help prevent life-threatening inflammation.

4. *Modify* **cardiovascular factors**, improving cholesterol levels, blood pressure, and heart function.

5. *Increase* **neural integration** in the brain, enabling more coordination and balance in both the functional and structural connectivity within the nervous system that facilitates optimal functioning, including self-regulation, problem solving, and adaptive behavior, which are at the heart of well-being.

In short, the scientific findings are now in: your mind can change the health of your body and slow aging.

In addition to these concrete discoveries, we have the more subjective yet equally powerful findings that cultivating these aspects of mind—how you focus attention, open awareness, and guide intention toward kindness and caring—also increases a sense of well-being, connection to others (in the form of enhanced empathy and compassion), emotional balance, and resilience in the face of challenges. Studies reveal that these practices nurture an overall ease of being—what some call equanimity—and increase a sense of meaning and purpose.

These are all outcomes of strengthening your mind by expanding the container of consciousness.

The word *eudaimonia*, a term from ancient Greek, beautifully describes the deep sense of well-being, equanimity, and happiness that comes from experiencing life as having meaning and connection to others and the world around you. Does cultivating eudaimonia seem like something you'd like to place on your to-do list in life? If you experience this *quality of being* already in your day-to-day living, these practices of training attention, awareness, and intention may enhance and reinforce where you already are in life. Wonderful. And if it feels like these features of eudaimonia are distant or perhaps unfamiliar to you, and you'd like to make these more near and dear to your everyday existence, you've come to the right conversation, here in this book.

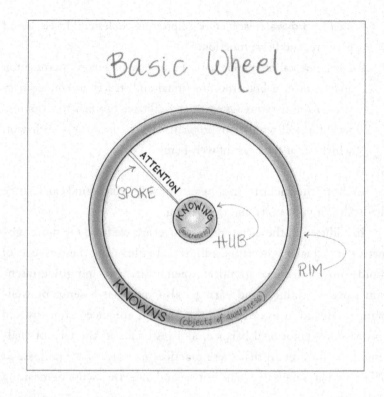

A PRACTICAL TOOL

The Wheel of Awareness is a tool I've developed over many years to help expand the container of consciousness.

I've offered the Wheel to thousands of individuals around the world, and it's proven to be a practice that can help people develop more well-being in both their inner and interpersonal lives. The Wheel practice is based on simple steps that are easy to learn and then apply in your everyday experiences.

The Wheel is a very useful visual metaphor for the way the mind works. The concept came to me one day as I stood looking down at a circular table in my office. The tabletop consists of a clear glass center surrounded by a wooden outer rim. It occurred to me that our awareness could be seen as lying at the center of a circle—a hub, if you will—from which, at any given moment, we can choose to focus on a wide array of thoughts, images, feelings, and sensations circling us on the rim. In other words, what we could be aware of could be represented on the wooden rim; the experience of being aware we could place in the hub.

If I could teach people how to expand that container of consciousness by more freely and fully accessing the Wheel's hub of awareness, they'd be able to change the way they experience life's tablespoons of salt, and perhaps even learn to savor life's sweetness in a more balanced and fulfilling way, even if there were a lot of salt present at the time. As I looked down at this table, I saw that the clarity of that glass hub might represent how we become aware of all of these tablespoons of life, each of the varied experiences we could become aware of, from thoughts to sensations, which we might now visualize as being placed on the circle around this hub—the table's outer wooden rim.

The central hub of that table, of what we were now calling the Wheel of Awareness, represents the experience of being aware, of *knowing* that one is surveying the knowns of life. The rim came to represent that which is known; for instance, at this moment, you are aware of the words you are reading on this page, and now perhaps you've become aware of the associations you are having with the words—the images or memories that come to mind.

Consciousness can be simply defined as our subjective sense of knowing—like your awareness now of my writing the word *hello*. In this book, we'll use a perspective that *consciousness includes both the knowing and the known*. You know I wrote *hello*. "You knowing" is awareness; "hello" is the known. The knowing is in the hub; the knowns are on the rim. When we speak of expanding the container of consciousness, we are then strengthening the experience of knowing—strengthening and opening our capacity to be aware.

Now imagine what might happen if, from the starting point of the hub, our attention were directed out to any of the various knowns on the rim, focused on one point or another—on a given thought, a perception, or a feeling; any single one of the wide range of knowns of life that rest on the rim of the wheel. Extending the metaphor of the wheel, one might envision these moments of focusing attention as a spoke on the wheel.

The spoke of attention connects the hub of knowing to the rim of the knowns.

In the practice, I invite my patients or students to imagine their minds to be like the Wheel. We envision next how the rim could be divided into four parts or segments, each of which contains a certain category of knowns. The first segment contains the category of knowns of our first *five senses*: hearing, sight, smell, taste, and touch; the second segment represents another category of knowns, one that includes the *interior signals of the body*, such as sensations from our muscles or from our lungs. The third segment contains the *mental activities* of feelings, thoughts, and memories, while the fourth holds our *sense of connection* to other people and to nature, our *relational sense*.

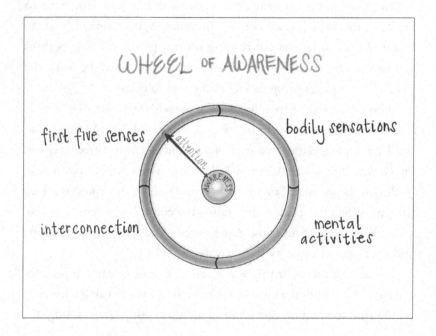

We slowly move that singular spoke of attention around the rim, bringing into focus, one by one, each of the elements of that segment, and then move the spoke of attention to the next segment, and review those points as well. Systematically we take in rim element by rim element, moving the spoke of attention around the rim of knowns. As the practice unfolds in a given session, and as individuals continue to practice on a regular basis, there is a common description of feeling more clarity and calm, a deeper sense of stability and even vitality, not just during the practice itself, but during the rest of the day.

The Wheel practice is a way to open awareness and cultivate a larger, more expansive container of consciousness. People who participate in the practice seem to be strengthening their minds.

The Wheel was designed as a practice that could balance our lives by integrating the experience of consciousness. How? By distinguishing the wide array of knowns on the rim from each other and from the knowing of awareness in the hub itself, we can differentiate the components of consciousness. Then, by systematically connecting these knowns of the rim to the knowing of the hub with the movement of the spoke of attention, it becomes possible to link the differentiated parts of consciousness. This is how, by differentiating and linking, the Wheel of Awareness practice integrates consciousness.

Another useful perspective for understanding consciousness and mind comes from the study of complex systems and their emergent properties, including one property called self-organization. That's a term you might think someone in psychology might have created—but it is a mathematical term. The form or shape of the unfolding of a complex system is determined by this emergent property of self-organization. This unfolding can be optimized, or it can be constrained. When it's not optimizing, it moves toward chaos or toward rigidity. When it is optimizing, it moves toward harmony and is flexible, adaptive, coherent, energized, and stable.

At the time I came across the theory of complex systems I had been observing in my patients (and my friends and myself when things weren't going so well), I began to wonder if the mind might be some kind of self-organizing process. A strong mind might optimize self-organization and create an experience of harmony in life; a compromised mind might lean away from that harmony and toward chaos or rigidity. If this were true, then cultivating a strong mind might be aided by asking how optimal self-organization occurs. There is an answer to that question.

The linking of differentiated parts of a complex system is how the emergent self-organizing property that regulates how that system unfolds over time—how it self-organizes—enables optimal functioning. In other words, integration (as we are defining it with the balancing of differentiation and linkage) creates optimal self-organization with its flexible and adaptive functioning.

The essential idea behind the Wheel is to expand the container of consciousness and, in effect, balance the experience of consciousness itself. *Balance* is a common term that we can understand scientifically as coming from this process that we are calling integration—the allowing of things to be different or distinct from each other on the one hand, and then connecting them to each other on the other. When we differentiate and link, we integrate. We become balanced and coordinated in life when we create integration. Various scientific disciplines may use other terminology, but the concept is the same. Integration—the balancing of differentiation and linkage—is the basis for optimal regulation that enables us to flow between chaos and rigidity, the core process that helps us flourish and thrive. Health comes from integration. It's that simple, and that important.

A system that is integrated is in a flow of harmony. Just as in a choir, with each singer's voice both differentiated from the other singers' voices but also linked, harmony emerges with integration. What is important to note is that this linkage does not remove the differences, as in the notion of blending; instead it maintains these unique contributions as it links them together. Integration is

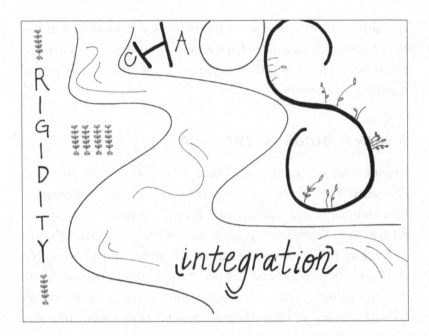

more like a fruit salad than a smoothie. This is how integration creates the synergy of the whole being greater than the sum of its parts. Likewise, this synergy of integration means that the many aspects of our lives, like the many points on the rim, can each be honored for their differences but then brought together in harmony.

In my own journey as a clinician, working within the framework of a multidisciplinary field called interpersonal neurobiology, reflecting on our mind as a self-organizing way we regulate energy and information flow inspired me to try and find strategies to create more integration in my patients' lives in order to create more well-being in their bodies and in their relationships. The many books I've written or cowritten have integration at their core.

When we integrated consciousness with the Wheel of Awareness, people's lives improved.

Many individuals have found the Wheel of Awareness a skill-building practice that empowers them in quite profound ways. It transformed how they came to experience their inner, mental lives—their emotions, thoughts, and memories—opened new ways of interacting with others, and even expanded a sense of connection and meaning in their lives.

A TRAVEL GUIDE TO THE MIND

My hope for our conversation in this book is that the Wheel of Awareness will become a part of your life, as both an idea and a practice, and that it will enhance well-being in your body, mind, and relationships. While this practice is inspired by science and bolstered by feedback from thousands of individuals who have explored it, you and I need to keep in mind that *you* are a particular individual with your own history, proclivities, and ways of being in the world. We are each unique. So while there are generalizations we will be discussing, your own experience of this material will be a one-of-a-kind unfolding.

Like others in the health-care profession, I try my best to build on scientific data and general findings and then apply them carefully and openly to a particular person. I aim to remain open—seeking, receiving, and responding to feedback from those who are taking in these ideas and trying out these practices. We as clinicians cannot guarantee an outcome for any specific patient or client; we can simply build on science and prior experience to offer steps that have a *high likelihood* of helping. With this perspective, our approach can be to offer the best we can and remain open to the wide ways in which any given person may in fact respond.

This is a book, not psychotherapy or even an educational workshop. Our connection here with this set of words is not a live, in-the-moment, give-and-take relationship, and so direct, real-time, ongoing feedback and exchange between you and me is naturally not possible. But as a reader you are invited to have an ongoing moment-to-moment dialogue with yourself. You as the reader can take in these ideas and try out the practices and *see how they work for you*. I, as the author, can simply share my experiences and perspectives, offering you words that cannot lead to direct feedback from you but can hopefully offer something that is helpful. In this sense, the book can be seen as a travel guide, discussing the details of a possible journey that only you can take. The author of the guide has the responsibility to make suggestions; the travelers' role is to take these in, consider what is being offered, and then responsibly create their own journey. I can act in the role of a Sherpa, someone who supports your travels, but as the traveler, you need to take the steps and modify them as necessary along the way.

I have kept the importance of your subjective experience in the front of my mind both in creating the Wheel of Awareness itself, as well as in constructing this book that explores its conceptual ideas and its practical potentials. No offering can guarantee benefits. But please use this as, hopefully, a useful and accessible travel guide to the ideas and practices that are of potentially powerful benefit to your life.

This will *not* be a detailed, research-project-summarizing accounting of all of the fascinating and relevant fields' discoveries, but it will be a scientifically inspired, practical travel guide to the mind and mental health that offers ideas and practices as a structured framework for your specific journey ahead.

Helpful reviews of the scientific studies affirming the kinds of practices that cultivate well-being can be found in a number of publications, including a very accessible exploration of the science of meditation by Daniel Goleman and Richie Davidson, called *Altered Traits*. Another example of rigorous researchers who've taken scientific findings and carefully outlined their practical use is *The Telomere Effect* by the Nobel Laureate Elizabeth Blackburn and her scientific colleague Elissa Epel. Since I've previously published references relevant to this science in a number of books, such as *The Developing Mind* and *Mind*, here in *Aware* we will get right to the ideas and practices

that are supported by that science to offer a potential path for cultivating more resilience and well-being in your life. A listing of general references and suggested reading can be found on my website,
DrDanSiegel.com, as introduced at the end of this book.

In the pages that follow, we'll be dipping into the waters and
having some deep dives and fun hikes along a range of trails that
explore and strengthen your mind. I'll be there with you for every
step on the path ahead.

STORIES OF USING THE WHEEL OF AWARENESS: HARNESSING THE POWER OF PRESENCE

I would now like to offer some concrete examples of how the Wheel of Awareness—as an idea and as a practice—has been useful in the lives of a range of people. Here I'll introduce you to specific individuals and how they used the Wheel to strengthen their minds and improve their lives. After you begin your own explorations of the Wheel in this first part of the book, we'll be ready to build on your personal practice to deepen our exploration into the mechanisms of the mind in part II. We'll next return, in part III, to these same individuals and see how we can apply these new insights in expanding our understanding of how the Wheel may have helped them, and how the mind itself might function. In part IV, we'll harness these new notions about the mind and the Wheel as we continue to explore how you might usefully weave these ideas and practices into your own life. Perhaps you'll come to find, as I and many others have, that utilizing these new insights into the nature of what the mind is and of what an expanded awareness is all about, and the direct experiences with how the Wheel practice integrates consciousness, may help you strengthen your own mind and cultivate more well-being in your life.

BILLY AND HIS RETURN TO THE HUB

Billy, a five-year-old boy expelled from one school for beating up another kindergarten student on the playground, was transferred to Ms. Smith's class in a new elementary school. This teacher had learned about the Wheel from my books. In her class she asks her students to draw a wheel figure with a large outer circle and a smaller inner circle connected with a line as the spoke. She then describes how the hub is our awareness, the rim is the various things that we are aware of, and the spoke is how the children could determine where their attention could go. A few days after learning the Wheel as a drawing, Billy came to her and said the following, which she quoted in an email she wrote to me: "Ms. Smith! I need to take a break—I am about to punch Joey because he took my block out on the yard. I'm stuck on the rim, I need to get back to my hub!" Billy took the time he needed to distance himself from the impulse to hit—something he undoubtedly had learned earlier as a rigid response with chaotic results—and with the Wheel image, he was able to articulate what he needed and then develop an alternative, more integrated way of responding. He could respect another child's behavior and acknowledge his own impulse but choose not to react impulsively. Weeks later, Ms. Smith wrote back to me that Billy had become a welcome addition to her class.

JONATHAN'S RESPITE FROM HIS EMOTIONAL ROLLER COASTER

And consider this example of someone using the Wheel not only as an *idea* in the form of a visual metaphor, as with Billy, but also as a practice that offers an *experience* that can transform attention, awareness, and intention. If you've read my book *Mindsight*, you may recall that a sixteen-year-old patient, a young man I call Jonathan, used the Wheel practice to deal with severe mood swings that were creating great suffering in his life. With the intentional creation of a particular *state*, practicing the Wheel over time, Jonathan was able to cultivate a new *trait* of emotional equilibrium in his life. In his own words, "I just don't take all those feelings and thoughts so seriously—and they don't take me on such a wild ride anymore." What the ideas and practices of the Wheel did for Jonathan was enable him to intentionally apply the learned concepts and the skills he developed to regularly create a state of mind that likely involved a particular set of brain firings. This repeated pattern of *functional* neural activation can then become a change in *structural* neural connection. This is a concrete example of how we can transform an intentionally created state into a healthy trait in our lives.

MONA AND THE SANCTUARY OF THE HUB

Mona was a forty-year-old mother of three children, each of them under the age of ten, who often found herself at the end of her rope. She was raising her children without much help from her spouse or family and friends, and was becoming easily irritated with her children, and then irate with herself for feeling this way.

Mona came to one of my workshops and began to implement the Wheel of Awareness as a regular practice. She found that over time, her ability to access the hub of awareness gave her both the experience of choice in her behavior and more resilience in facing the day-to-day challenges of raising three kids. Integrating her consciousness transformed Mona's parenting from being repeatedly *reactive* to becoming reliably *receptive*. In reactivity she'd become chaotic or rigid in her inner life or outer behavior; with receptivity she could be flexible in creating a more integrated way of being with her children, and herself. Mona could now be more present and loving with her children—and kinder and more caring toward herself as well.

TERESA, TRAUMA, AND HEALING WITH
THE INTEGRATION OF THE WHEEL

Developmental trauma is a term we use for significantly stressful events happening early in life; for instance, abuse or neglect of young children. Some people use a related term for a broader set of early challenges in life: *adverse childhood experiences*, or ACEs. The overall impact of such developmental trauma, and likely even less intense adverse childhood stress, is to impair the growth of integration in the brain—an effect that, fortunately, can usually be healed. Integration in the brain, what we are calling neural integration, is needed to give us balance in life in the form of a range of executive functions that regulate things like emotion and mood, thinking and attention, and even relationships and behavior. Teresa struggled with each of these areas and came to me for help. Her experiences as a twenty-five-year-old struggling with the aftermath of a traumatic childhood exemplify this important principle of chaos or rigidity in relationships leading to compromised neural integration. After she slowly connected with me, building the trust to open up about what being vulnerable as a child with abusive parents was like for her, I introduced her to the ideas and practice of the Wheel.

For many who've experienced overwhelming and terrifying events, especially at the hands of people who should have protected and cared for them, the experience of distinguishing being aware (in the hub) from what we are aware of (on the rim) can be both new and upsetting at first. Why? One reason may be that when we enter the state of being aware of our own awareness, the metaphoric hub of the Wheel, we can experience a state of openness and expanded possibility that can be quite different from the feeling of certainty that arises when we are aware of only the metaphoric rim of the knowns of life. Getting "lost in familiar places" on the rim—even if these sensations or thoughts or feelings arise from trauma and receiving suboptimal care—can ironically be more reassuring than entering a state of uncertainty and freedom, the experience of the hub. This pattern of being drawn to the abused state of mind, those repeated rim elements, may involve what for some is a passive victim stance and for others may be an active angrily fighting back state. These states reveal how we can become *reactive* in response to threat. For Teresa, being reactive meant sometimes being frightened and in the state of mind to flee from challenges, while at other times it meant fighting even those who were hoping to connect with and be supportive of her. What Teresa needed was to shift from being reactive to becoming *receptive*. Being open and available to connect is not a passive stance, but for a traumatized person, it can seem like giving up and being even more at risk of being hurt and let down. Put in Wheel terms, Teresa's reactivity could be seen as a set of the familiar knowns of fighting, fleeing, freezing, and even fainting, the legacy of repeated reactive states of her childhood that had now become traits or automatic tendencies of her adulthood.

This is an important general principle. What is practiced repeatedly strengthens brain firing clusters or patterns. With repetition, neural structure is literally altered. This is how repeated states become enduring traits.

You may have noted that in each of these examples, a simple scientific reality is revealed. I summarize this fundamental principle of mind integration in this way:

Where attention goes, neural firing flows, and neural connection grows.

For Teresa, as with many others, the Wheel offered a chance to get out of autopilot states of reactivity and awaken her mind to new possibilities of being and doing. Having an awakened mind means using the mental processes of attention, awareness, and intention to activate new states of mind that, with repeated practice, can become intentionally sculpted traits in a person's life. When that trait is an integrated mind, this means that we can move from automatic reactivity without choice to the freedom of responsiveness with choice. This is how integrating consciousness could transform Teresa's life: With repeated practice, she could shape her attention, awareness, and intention to create a more integrated way of living—the basis of eudaimonia.

The hub of the Wheel represents the knowing of awareness and is the source of receptive consciousness, of being open and available to connect to anything arising on the rim and not becoming lost or stuck on that rim, consumed by the knowns of life. In this way, the metaphor of the Wheel, both as an idea and, for Teresa, as a practice she'd soon learn, could help her become aware of the prison her own mind had been trained to become. If experience could teach her to exist as if in a prison, an intentional and repeated integrative experience—such as the Wheel practice—might teach her how to free herself from that prison.

Ideas are wonderful, but sometimes, in fact quite often, practice is also needed to begin experiencing new ways of being and behaving and to build these liberating ideas deeply into us as we live their meaning in our day-to-day lives.

When Teresa experienced a state of panic when she first explored the Wheel's hub in part of the practice we will discuss later, we spent time pausing and reflecting on what that experience of fear was all about. As with many other people who've experienced some form of trauma, the initial focus on the body, on emotions in general, or on the hub by itself can sometimes be distressing. That upsetting experience, taken in with patience and support, can be simply "grist for the mill," meaning it is an uncomfortable feeling, yes, but an invitation to further explore what may be going on. Every challenging feeling or image can be an opportunity to learn and grow. That is ultimately a lesson the Wheel offers as it strengthens the mind and frees us from the prisons of the past.

With repeated practice, Teresa learned many things from these experiences. One lesson was that what initially created anxiety, such as focusing on parts of her body that had been hurt by her parents, could be shifted and she'd come to feel at ease with such a focus of her attention. Remember that where attention goes, neural firing flows and neural connection grows: Teresa could now shift more nimbly between focusing on one or another point along the rim versus her previous reactive focus on the same points of pain or the active strategies to avoid them. She developed an integrated state of hub-based receptivity. Her memories and prior traits of reactivity could be experienced now simply as rim points as her hub became a source of reflection, awareness, choice, and ultimately change.

Another important lesson for Teresa was in the realization that her hub had been inhabited by such a sense of not being in control of what was going on that she initially viewed the hub itself with fear. As her practice continued, that fear shifted first into a more moderate cautionary stance, and then into one that developed to the point that she could view her hub with curiosity—a true relief for her after so many years of guarding herself against her own receptive awareness. In her life, Teresa had never been allowed to simply rest in the spaciousness of *being present* and open to whatever arose, and instead as a child had to be on guard for the next onslaught of unpredictable and terrifying behaviors from her parents. As she came to enjoy a new state of being present, one in which she was wide open to the vast terrain in front of her, she felt more and more at peace and joyful.

What Teresa's transformation tells us is that it is never too late in life to develop, grow, and transform. Through the Wheel of Awareness and other meditation and mindfulness practices, it is possible to develop the state of receptive presence that can form the basis for a deep sense of well-being and a greater ease in connecting compassionately with others. Sadly, many of us learn to be wary of others, and even of our own inner life, and the resulting prison of our own mental adaptations to survive creates a belief that we are helpless to make a change. In contrast, when we are present for life, we are open to deeply joining others, and even joining with our inner experience. Teresa's courage to immerse herself in the ideas and practices of the Wheel helped her develop an inner strength and resilience that will last the rest of her life.

ZACHARY: FINDING MEANING, CONNECTION, AND RELIEF FROM PAIN

Zachary was a participant who chose to dive into the Wheel practice at a workshop his brother had invited him to attend. Though Zachary's business was thriving and his family life was busy and full, he felt at fifty-five that something wasn't quite right, something was missing that he couldn't name. During the Wheel practice, he reported that a pain in his hip that he had experienced almost constantly for over ten years somehow seemed to dissolve away. As we repeated the Wheel practice several times throughout the weekend, each time he noticed where the pain had been, the soreness that had before been a sharp, distracting painful sensation would lessen and lessen. By the fifth and final Wheel immersion that weekend, the feelings from his hip felt like just one of a large set of sensations he could dip into and let go.

Zachary described the relief from the physical pain at that meeting with a sense of joy and mastery. I invited him to keep in touch with me by email and let me know how it went following the workshop. I heard from him only once during that year, with the very positive news that, with continued practice, the pain had not returned.

Surprisingly, this finding of the release from chronic pain was something very common in the Wheel workshops around the world. Studies using meditative interventions had found that training the mind in these ways of focused attention, open awareness, and kind intention could have many benefits, among them not only the reduction of the subjective experience of pain but also an objective diminishment of the representation of pain within the brain.

One way to understand this phenomenon is to return to our analogy of consciousness as a container of water. In this case, physical pain is the salt that in too small a vessel can make the water too salty to comfortably drink, even undrinkable altogether. But if we increase the amount of water from a cup to one hundred gallons, then that new, expanded container can hold the tablespoon of salt and the huge quantity of water will dilute it so much that it remains fresh to the taste. Doing a mind-training practice can be seen as expanding the hub of our metaphoric Wheel of Awareness, making the container of awareness, the receptive knowing of consciousness, so much larger. With this expanded container, this expanded hub, the same tablespoon of pain—a single point on the rim—becomes diluted as merely one of an infinite number of points along the whole rim of knowns. We experience relief from what before was a singular focus on the pain. In Wheel terms, we'd say that Zachary's experience was to free himself from a rim point that had become excessively differentiated and dominated his hub. If the brain studies of meditation apply, we'd suggest that even Zachary's brain was having much less neural firing in the region that represents pain and our awareness of it. This view of water and salt helps explain the efficacy of the Wheel as visual image, idea, and practice, and perhaps of mind-training practices in general, to help alleviate the suffering of chronic pain.

Beyond helping with physical pain, the Wheel experience invites other changes in how life unfolds. I was pleasantly surprised to find Zachary at a lunch the following year (the same organization had asked me to come back and do another three-day Wheel workshop). Beyond the diminishment of physical pain, Zachary also experienced another kind of relief. He told me, as a small group gathered before the meeting began, that the experience of the Wheel at the first workshop had opened his mind to a new way of experiencing meaning in his life, helping him feel a richer connection to himself, to others, and to the larger world around him. Beyond just feeling grateful to have his physical pain reduced, he had been introduced to a new sense of meaning and purpose in his life. He told us at the lunch about his experience with focusing the spoke of attention on the hub of awareness in the more advanced Wheel practice (which we'll get to soon!). He said that when he had first "bent the spoke of attention around and back into the hub, the sense of being wide open and filled with joy and love" gave him a new sense of being "real and alive," an experience that came to change his life and the direction of his professional and personal path. It was, he said, what had been missing that he could never quite name—a sense of meaning, purpose, and connection. His brother, also at the lunch, joked with me that Zachary's wife was going to send me a bill for the meditation-training program that he was now enrolled in. Zachary quickly added, "It's your fault—I now have a sense of being alive that I'd like to learn how to share with others, not just keep to myself." He said that he was even considering becoming a minister in his faith or a mental health practitioner. Zachary's choice was to pivot away from the world of his particular business, in which he felt these new visions of what mattered to him could not find a home; he now wanted to develop his own mind and learn how he might be of service to others.

PREPARING YOUR MIND FOR THE WHEEL OF AWARENESS: FOCUSED ATTENTION

A s you prepare to experience the Wheel firsthand, let's now explore some basic practices and ideas that will help ready your mind for what lies ahead. As I have mentioned, in the Wheel practice you'll be learning basic skills that enable you to integrate consciousness and strengthen your mind. Integration is the linking of different elements—and the Wheel supports this integration by differentiating elements of the rim as the knowns of consciousness from one another and from the knowing of the hub, and then systematically linking these to each other with the movement of the spoke of attention around the wheel. With practice, you'll be enriching not only your attentional skills, but your experience of consciousness and of the mind itself.

BUILDING THE REGULATORY ASPECT OF THE MIND

The mind can be seen as having one facet that is a *regulatory process* engaged in the business of determining how energy and information flow in our lives. A process is a verblike unfolding, and so the mind in this way is more like a verb than a noun. Regulation has two aspects. One is monitoring. The other is modifying. Developing a mind-strengthening practice such as the Wheel of Awareness enables you to build your mind's regulatory facet and become better able to optimize its functioning. Before we try out the Wheel in the next section, here we'll begin with stabilizing the monitoring function of the mind as we build the skill of focused attention—the first pillar of mind training.

When you ride a bicycle, you watch where you are going, feel the balance of the bike, and listen for oncoming traffic. Watching, feeling, and listening are how you soak in various forms of energy within perception. That's all *monitoring*. And then you also *modify* by pedaling, steering, and braking. This is how you change the position and motion of the bicycle by altering energy flow, the movement of the bike in space. In order to become a better, more capable cyclist, you sharpen these monitoring and modifying skills. In the same way that you can hone your bike-riding skills, you can cultivate a stronger mind by honing how you monitor and modify energy and information flow—the essence of the system of the mind.

One way to strengthen how we monitor energy flow is to stabilize the lens with which we sense that flow. A practice that teaches us how to stabilize attention exercises how we aim attention like the beam of a flashlight on a chosen focus. A very useful focus for this practice, one found in many cultures around the world, is the breath. When we do a basic breath-awareness practice, we are strengthening the monitoring capacity of the mind so that we stabilize attention. With the extension of the more elaborate Wheel practice itself, as we'll soon see, we will be furthering that stabilizing of attention and then also adding other aspects of strengthening to both the monitoring and the modifying of that energy flow.

What you are about to learn is how to stabilize *monitoring* so that you can sense energy and information flow with more focus, depth, clarity, and detail. Once you can stabilize the monitoring function of the mind, you can learn to *modify* toward integration.

SOME STARTING TIPS

Before we do our Wheel practice in the next section, it is important to have some experience with stabilizing attention. If you've done a lot of reflective practices or "meditation," a term that essentially means practices that train the mind that come in many forms, you've likely had some experience with a breath-awareness practice and may choose to skip over this initial section and go directly to the Basic Wheel practice in the next section. But if you haven't done much inner reflection, then doing this breath practice to stabilize attention can be quite useful. For instance, in our Mindful Awareness Research Center at UCLA, our first study of a MAP (a mindful awareness practice) was to explore how mindfulness practice based on the breath as a focus might support adults and adolescents with challenges in their tendency to focus and sustain their attention. Our pilot study revealed that the participants achieved more improvements in these attentional skills with their mindfulness practice than

individuals on medications for attention deficit issues (see Lidia Zy-
lowska's summary of that work in *The Mindful Prescription for Adult
ADHD*).

Here are a few starting ideas.

First, try to stay awake. When you reflect inwardly, such as focusing on the breath as a sensation of the body, you are letting go of
attention directed toward the outside world. For some, this inward
focus is so different from an outward focus that it can feel unfamiliar,
awkward, or even uncomfortable. Some people find this inner focus
dull and boring. The tendency in this situation can be to lose focus,
become less alert, get sleepy, and to even fall asleep. While napping
is perhaps one of the most underrated of human activities, staying
awake for the practice may be something you want to do to gain its
benefits. Staying alert is in fact part of learning to strengthen the
mind's focus of attention by noticing when you are getting groggy
and then waking yourself up. Monitoring your state of alertness is
part of learning to strengthen how you monitor energy and information flow. Now you can take this information about your sleepiness
and modulate energy in ways to keep yourself awake, and even to
become more alert.

For example, if you've closed your eyes you might consider
opening them a bit to let light in and stimulate your brain. You can
do this whole practice with eyes wide open. If that doesn't work to
keep you awake, try sitting up if you're lying down. If you're sitting
down, you can try standing, and if you're standing, try walking
around. You can do something to change energy flow and enliven
the mind to stabilize attention. The key is to monitor your own state
of energy and alertness and then do something about it. If you need
a nap, sometimes it's just better to intentionally let the reflective practice go, for now, and simply let the nap happen and enjoy the rest!

A second tip: If you are doing this as a group practice, it may be
helpful to establish some collective agreement that if someone does
indeed go into the sleep state, and that person starts snoring, other

members of the group have permission to wake up the snoring individual. It's really hard for others to ignore a snore. Better to agree ahead of time and give permission for a respectful, gentle prod to awaken the sleeper.

A third pointer: There is a difference between relaxation and reflection. Relaxation techniques are great for getting calm, but they have been shown to be quite different from the effects of a meditative mindfulness practice. So while you may get relaxed doing this reflective breath exercise, or later doing the Wheel practice, it is equally possible that you will not come to feel relaxed at all, and that's perfectly fine. Reflection is not the same as relaxation—neither in the doing, nor in the results. Reflection is more like becoming stable and clear, even in the face of a lot of chaos around you—or inside you. The state of mindful awareness is about monitoring with stability whatever is arising as it arises. That's the receptive awareness that we are calling presence. This is the clarity that reflection builds as it enables things to arise and simply be experienced within awareness, the hub of our Wheel.

A fourth notion: There is a difference between *observing* something and *sensing* it. When we open awareness to sensation, such as that of the breath, we become a *conduit* directing the flow of something into our awareness; for instance, enabling the sensation of the breath at the nostrils to flow into consciousness. Attention here is more like a hose letting the water flow through it rather than freezing the water and then building an igloo out of the constructed blocks of ice. When we observe something, there is a quality of being more like a witness *constructing* a perception, rather than a conduit directing a stream. And as we'll see, when we begin to witness and narrate from that observational stance, we construct a story about something—even about the breath—rather than simply sensing the conduit flow of that sensory stream. If energy flow is like soapy water, then the mind is like the loop that can simply let bubbles emerge or shape them into symbols.

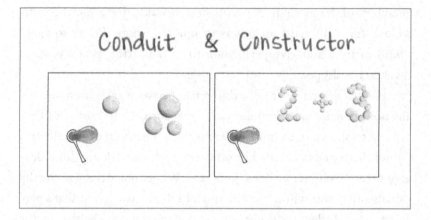

Observation is a gateway to being a witness and then becoming the narrator of an experience. If you like acronyms, as I do, this is how you OWN an experience: observe, witness, and narrate. These are all forms of construction in that there is an observer, a witness, and a narrator, each contributing to the construction of an experience in that moment. This construction can be quite distinct from the sensing flow of being a conduit of experience, of what we can call *conduition*.

The key to starting this reflective breath-awareness practice is to let sensation of the breath be the focus of attention, and let it fill awareness. That is quite different from being invited to observe the breath, or witness it, or narrate the experience of breathing: "I am now breathing." This may perhaps sound like a subtle difference, but as you may come to see, distinguishing the difference between sensing and observing is a fundamental part of integrating your experience and empowering your mind.

A fifth point: Be kind to yourself. These may be simple practices, but that does not make them easy ones. In many ways, reflecting inwardly is one of the biggest challenges we face as human beings. As the French mathematician Blaise Pascal said, "All of humanity's problems stem from man's inability to sit quietly in a room alone." Indeed, our ability to *reflect* lies at the very heart of emotional and social intelligence, skills many people have not learned. These are tools that will empower you to know your inner mind and connect with the inner, mental life of others.

We are so accustomed to focusing outwardly that such reflective practice is often quite new for many people. To sit quietly for any length of time feels unbearable for some. We love to be distracted by external stimuli or to speak and fill the gaps of silence in our lives. And so it is quite important to be gentle with yourself and realize that much of your life may have been focused on the external world and filled with input from your surroundings—from people, gadgets, and other things out in the environment around you. Now you are enriching your life's journey by learning to reflect on your inner life.

It can be frustrating at first to get comfortable with these reflective practices. Again, I invite you to be kind to yourself. This is hard work, and there is no way to do this "perfectly." Remember that your mind has a mind of its own. Part of your task is to realize that energy and information simply flow. Sometimes you can direct them well, guiding attention; sometimes they just take on a life of their own, as attention is pulled this way and that. Being open to whatever happens is the first step. Being kind to yourself as you travel through this guide will assist in that.

At the heart of training the mind is how we learn to focus attention. As William James, the father of modern psychology, once stated, the training of attention allows one to become a master of oneself. As James wrote, "The faculty of voluntarily bringing back a wandering attention, over and over again, is the very root of judgement, character, and will. No one is *compos sui* (master of himself) if he have it not. An education which should improve this faculty would be the education *par excellence*. But it is easier to define this ideal than to give practical instructions for bringing it about."*

---

* William James, *The Principles of Psychology*, Vol. 1 (Cambridge, MA: Harvard University Press, 1890), 463.

James clearly was not familiar with the meditative practice of training focused attention that we'll explore in this next section, a simple practice of mindfulness of the breath that can help you become a master of your own mind. In our research center, a pilot study revealed that such a basic meditation can greatly improve the components of focused attention and help people become more in charge of their lives. Meditation is mind training in action.

A MINDSIGHT LENS

Mindsight is a term both for how we see our own minds and the minds of others, and for our ability to honor our differentiated natures at the same time as we link with one another. This means that mindsight is all about insight, empathy, and integration. To sense the flow of energy and information, we can use a mindsight monitoring skill that is like a perceptual lens focusing that flow into our awareness, enabling us to achieve a clear focus in sensing the mind within and the

mind of others. There is a *tripod* of this mindsight lens that will be helpful to remember here. This is a three-legged set of O's: *openness*, *observation*, and *objectivity*. When you develop these three skills over time, with practice, you stabilize your ability to monitor what is happening in the moment more clearly.

Being *open* to whatever arises means letting go of expectations and being more receptive to and accepting of what is actually occurring at the moment. Since perception is shaped by expectation, being more open and letting go of judgment and anticipation expands our awareness of all the vicissitudes of life.

Observation is the capacity to distance ourselves a bit from an experience, to take note of the contours of all that is unfolding without becoming flooded by it. This is a more constructed form of perception than the conduit function of pure sensation. With observation we can avoid being on automatic pilot when we become lost in a thought or feeling or sensation. Sometimes letting go of observation is important so we can feel the flow of sensation, but other times we gain a broader perspective with the wider view of observation. Both are good; they are simply different from each other. Observation encourages us to become widely aware and active observers of our lives—it enables us to be more centered in our *knowing* in the hub without being swept away by the knowns of the rim that may at times overwhelm our capacity for a more integrated experience of being aware.

Objectivity takes this capacity of observation one step further, as we sense that the knowns of our experience are objects of the mind, not the totality of our identity or equivalent to absolute reality. We maintain an objective stance as we sense and perceive the knowns as simply elements of experience that arise and fall, coming and going in the field of awareness that is our home base. That is objectivity.

Openness, observation, and objectivity stabilize the mindsight lens and enable us to sense energy and information flow with more clarity, depth, and detail. Each of these mind-strengthening legs of the tripod is developed in the practices that we will begin exploring now. Learning how to harness these O's of our mindsight lens in different situations is the skill of learning to live a full and integrated life.

BREATH AWARENESS TO STABILIZE ATTENTION

Let's begin with a basic breath-awareness practice that is found throughout the world.

If possible, find a quiet space free of interruptions. Take a moment to find a comfortable position—you can be seated, lying down, or standing. Turn off any gadgets that might disturb your five-minute practice. If you have a timer, set it to sound a gentle alarm at five minutes. If you are sitting on a chair, uncross your legs, have your back straight but comfortable, and have both feet flat on the floor. If you are sitting on the floor, legs folded underneath you, let your back be straight and your body in a comfortable position that you can maintain for a few minutes. If you sometimes experience back pain, as I do, you might do this practice lying down, but be aware that you may be more likely to take a nap. One technique that helps me avoid falling asleep when lying down is to have one forearm lifted, elbow on the floor, with hand raised up toward the ceiling. If you do fall asleep, you'll know because your arm will likely have fallen down onto your chest (and perhaps even wake you up).

Your eyes can remain open if you like, or you can let them partially close with a soft focus. Some may find it easier to simply let their eyes totally close to remove the sensory distraction of light.

Before closing your eyes, try these four steps:

1. Let your visual attention go to the middle of the room.
2. Now send your attention to the far wall (or ceiling if you are lying down).
3. Next, bring your attention back to the middle of the room.
4. Finally, let your visual attention come to about the distance at which you might hold a book you are reading.

Take a moment to notice how *you* can determine where attention goes. Here with your visual attention you are simply directing the energy of light into awareness.

I invite you to read the following instructions, and as you do, you may use them as a guide to try the practice as you go. Then once you are familiar with the practice, you can go to the Resources tab on my website (DrDanSiegel.com) and listen to my voice as I guide you through this and later practices as well. Once you get familiar with a practice after reading the full instructions first, you can be guided by my voice from the website or try it on your own from memory.

Here are the instructions.

Once you've read through each of these parts of the practice, you can find a quiet place and give this a try. You can also listen to each one at my website under the Resources section: DrDanSiegel.com.

Let attention focus on the breath, beginning with the sensation of air moving in and out of your nostrils. Let the sensations of the in-breath and the out-breath fill awareness. Just ride the wave of the breath, in and out.

Now let your attention focus on your chest, letting the sensation of the rising and falling of your chest fill awareness. In and out, in and out, ride the wave of the breath.

Now let your attention move to your abdomen. If you've never done "belly breathing," you can put a hand on your abdomen and let the sensation of its movement fill awareness. As air fills the lungs, the diaphragm beneath them pulls down and pushes the abdomen outward; as the air escapes the lungs, the diaphragm relaxes and the abdomen moves inward. Continue to let the sensation of the abdomen moving in and out fill awareness. Ride the wave of the breath in and out, letting awareness be filled with the sensation of the abdomen's movement.

Now let attention find the sensation of the breath wherever it feels most natural for you. It may be the sensation of the abdomen moving in and out; it may be the chest rising and falling; it may be the sensation of air moving in and out of the nostrils. Or perhaps it's the whole body just breathing, in and out. Wherever the sensation of the breath is felt most readily for you, let that become the focus of attention.

Now let the sensation of the breath fill awareness. In and out, in and out, ride the wave of the breath, in and out. At some point, awareness may become filled with something other than the breath. When you realize that awareness is no longer with your breath, redirect your attention to the sensation of the breath.

Continue to focus on the breath for a few cycles, refocusing on it whenever a distraction has taken your focus away from the breath, and see how this goes. If you are reading these instructions as you practice, you may like to close your eyes for a few cycles of breath before continuing to read.

In and out, in and out, ride the wave of the breath, in and out.

How was that for you? Take a moment now to reflect on your experience with your breath so far.

Now let's try adding one more component. For some people, finding a general word that represents the distraction that pulled attention away from the breath can be helpful. If a thought took your attention away from streaming the sensation of the breath into awareness, especially if it was a thought that came back repeatedly, you might like to try saying quietly in your inner mind, "Thinking, thinking, thinking." For some, this naming of a distraction helps to let it go and eases the ability to redirect attention to the sensation of the breath. Similarly, if a memory takes over awareness and replaces the breath, then saying internally, "Remembering, remembering, remembering," can be helpful to redirect attention away from the memory and return it to the sensation of the breath. For others, this naming process is itself too distracting and not really helpful. For them, it is more straightforward to simply take note of the distraction without naming it, and then redirect attention to the sensation of the breath.

In addition to labeling or noting distractions—then returning to the breath—remember to try to bring kindness to this experience. It may be helpful to consider this perspective: The breath practice is like contracting and relaxing a muscle during exercise. Focusing on the breath is contracting the muscle; the inevitable distraction is relaxing the muscle. You don't need to create the distractions—they will happen naturally, as the mind has a mind of its own! But you can intentionally create a kind attitude when these distractions come, being *open* to whatever arises, *observing* the distraction, realizing it is an *object* or activity of the mind, and then returning the focus of attention back to the breath—allowing your kindness to frame this process with a gentle, nonjudgmental attitude. This is how you can use kindness with the mindsight tripod of openness, observation, and objectivity.

If you were to only be in the conduit flow of whatever was happening in sensation, then getting lost in a distraction would just be your flowing sensory experience. In this case, you'd only be harnessing the O of openness of your mindsight lens. Instead, stabilizing attention enables us to be in the flow of the sensation of the breath—open to the conduition flow—and then use the construction tools of the mind's capacity for observation and objectivity so we note the new thought or memory as a distraction and do not just flow with it, then construct the redirecting process to get attention back to the sensation of the breath. In broad terms, this simple breath-awareness practice invites us to be open to the flow of the breath, observe when that focus of attention has wandered, and objectively move the object of attention back to the breath. That's the integration of differentiating openness, observation, and objectivity and linking them together as we stabilize attention.

So let's try this basic breath-awareness practice again, this time with the invitation to either label or simply take note of distractions and kindly return, again and again, to the breath. Remember, if you'd like to hear my voice guide you through this breath practice, please go to our website (DrDanSiegel.com/resources/everyday_mindsight_tools).

If you're doing this on your own steam and this is the first time doing this mindfulness of the breath practice, set a timer for three minutes. You may like to consider what type of sound the timer is set to make—one that might be different from what you use to awaken from sleep in the morning. If you've done this before, give five minutes or more a try. Once your timer is set, let yourself sense the breath, refocusing when a distraction has filled awareness with something other than the breath, and then continue to ride the wave of the breath, in and out, until the timer lets you know it is time to stop. Before starting the timer for any reflective practice, find a comfortable position, back straight, in a space in which you will not be interrupted.

Ready? Enjoy the ride!

After the sound signals it is time to stop, you may feel calm or energized, refreshed or tired. If you are having a challenging period in your life, you may even feel more anxious or tense, as spending time dwelling on our interior can also make us more aware of the difficulties we are facing. Recall that this is an exercise. Doing an exercise does not mean we have to feel a certain way afterward, or even that we will feel the same way each time we try it. Why is this considered an exercise? It is an exercise because you are strengthening your capacity to *focus* attention, to *notice* a distraction that is not salient or relevant to the task at hand—a noticing scientists call "salience monitoring"—and then to *redirect* attention intentionally. There are different brain circuits for each of these facets of attention—sustaining focus, noticing, and redirecting—and you are training each of them.

Keep in mind our basic statement: Where attention goes, neural firing flows, and neural connection grows. You've been activating several important parts of your brain in just a few short minutes of practice!

In other reflective exercises that will be part of our Wheel practice, we will explore and expand the capacity for *open awareness*, or *open monitoring*—meaning letting things simply arise, and being in an open, receptive state. This open awareness, along with the fundamental elements of attention practice—sustaining, noticing, and redirecting—will each grow stronger as your practice deepens.

If you've never done reflective practices before, it can be helpful to repeat this breath exercise for a while, on a daily basis if possible, before we begin to try out the Wheel practice in the next sections.

After doing the breath practice for a week or more, some feel ready to try out the basic Wheel practice, while others simply like to dive in right away and see how it goes. You may also like to bring this breath-awareness practice into a number of situations in your life, such as waiting in line, resting at home, or when you wake up. It's simple, but powerful. Over time, you'll not only strengthen attention, but you'll stabilize the mind and create more clarity in the experience of being aware.

There's a certain internal coherence that breath awareness creates, which is likely due to the repeating pattern of the inhalation and the exhalation, the in-breath and the out-breath, as anticipating something and then that something arriving is deeply satisfying and grounding. It can give life a sense of being predictable and reliable. For many, focusing on the breath in this way creates coherence in the physiological balance of the heart as well as the clarity of the mind that can continue long after the practice period itself. Letting this practice of focusing on the breath and returning the focus to it when the mind becomes distracted become part of your daily reflection is a way of giving yourself a gift that keeps on giving.

Before we dive into the Wheel practice in the next section, let's explore some of the aspects of your mind that may have emerged with this empowering breath-awareness practice.

WHAT IS THE MIND?

Let's state from the very beginning that this term does not have a shared definition—in fact, short of saying it is a synonym for *brain activity*, there often is no definition of *mind* at all. Yes, we have descriptions of the activities of the mind, including feelings, thoughts, memories, and attention, but what these mental activities actually are is not clearly defined.

In some settings, the word *mind* is used to indicate thoughts rather than feelings—as in mind versus heart. In my work I don't use it in quite this way. Instead, in my teachings and here on this journey we are using the term *mind* to mean the core of our experience of being alive, from feelings and intuition to thinking, memory, attention, awareness, intention, and the initiation of behavior. Some scientists focus on the neural origins of mind; others focus on the social nature of our mental lives. But what system of the mind might embrace both its embodied and its relational origins?

Broadly speaking, a *relationship can be seen as the sharing of energy and information flow.* For an anthropologist or sociologist or linguist, our mental lives are happening between us. *The brain can be seen as an embodied mechanism of energy and information flow.* And so we have a *within-mind*, within the skin-encased body including the skull-encased brain—what we can simply call our "embodied brain." And we have *between-minds* that happen in our relationships. These can also be called our inner and our inter minds, the within and between origins of our self, of who we are. The mind happens within and between.

I know that this view of mind as being beyond the boundaries of the skull, and even of the skin, may be new for many, and perhaps different from what is often spoken about. But a long line of reason-

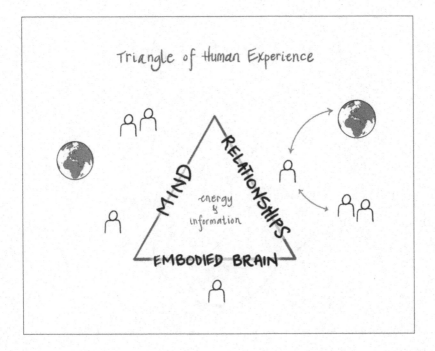

Triangle of Human Experience

MIND

RELATIONSHIPS

energy & information

EMBODIED BRAIN

ing and scientific support underlies this proposal that mind is both embodied *and* relational.

The shared element of the system of your mind is energy and information flow. That flow is not limited by skull or skin.

Mind viewed this way has at least four fundamental facets that we will be harnessing in the Wheel practice to enhance well-being in your life. Each of these four facets of mind will be the building blocks you and I will use throughout our journey to construct a science-based practical path toward cultivating well-being in your life ahead.

1. **Consciousness** is both the subjective experience of being aware *and* all that we are, in the most concrete sense, actually aware of. For instance, in this moment as you read the words on this page you are aware of their existence and particular meaning. In other words, consciousness consists of both the *knowns* and the *knowing*.

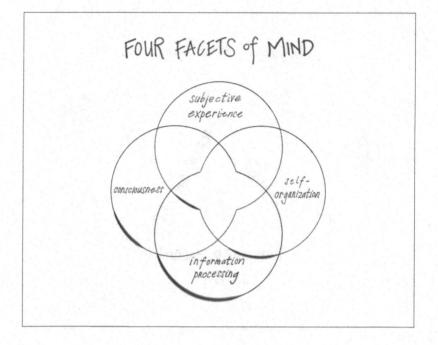

FOUR FACETS of MIND

subjective experience

consciousness

self-organization

information processing

The rim is the metaphoric representation of the knowns; the hub represents the knowing. When we direct energy and information flow, we are using attention, represented by the spoke of the Wheel.

2. **Subjective experience** is the felt texture of life as it is lived. Becoming aware of your subjective experience, and even the act of expressing it to yourself (as in journal writing) and sharing it with others (as in reflective conversations that focus on the inner nature of the mind in dialogue with others), enhances many aspects of well-being. Subjective, or what is sometimes called "first person," experience can be called a *prime* of reality, meaning that it cannot be reduced to anything other than itself. As we'll soon see, a prime may emerge from some mechanism of our reality, and as a prime, this emergent property cannot be reduced to the elements from which it arises. A prime is as basic as we can get in reality. One

notion we are proposing is that our subjective experience of being alive emerges from the flow of energy within and between.

3. **Information processing** is how we take flows of energy—in the brain, in the body, and in our relationships with each other—and make meaning. Information is a pattern of energy with symbolic value; it represents something other than the energy pattern itself. Information processing is sometimes in awareness, but much of the energy and information flow of the mind occurs *without* involving consciousness.

For example, if I write "Golden Gate Bridge," this is a pattern of light (or sound if you and I are connecting via spoken words) that comes to you in a pattern of energy that has symbolic meaning. The term stands for something—it is a symbol of something; the words are not the thing itself. The bridge is not the set of letters or the sound waves forming words—but the words *signify* the bridge. They symbolize or "re-present" the actual bridge as a linguistic representation. We can say that this symbolism is "energy in-formation" because it forms symbolic representations, common elements of our inner and interpersonal lives we are simply going to call *information*. And given that information as a pattern of energy is in a continual state of change, we signify this movement, this transformation, with the terms *processing* and *flow*.

And now, our fourth facet of mind . . .

4. **Self-organization** *regulates* the flow of energy and information. It is an emergent property of complex systems. A brief focus on this regulatory process may help illuminate this important fourth facet of mind. In a very counterintuitive way, this emergent property arises from the flow of a complex system's elements and then turns back onto its origins and shapes that from which it arose. How odd is that? Yet the math of complex systems is quite

clear—in our universe, complex systems have the emergent property of self-organization. This process recursively regulates its own origins, shaping its own becoming, and then further shaping its own emergence. Odd, but a part of our reality.

Self-organization is why clouds don't just line up in a straight, orderly fashion and why they are not random. Self-organization optimizes the system's unfolding by differentiating and linking. The math behind this emergent property of complex systems is, well, complex, but it may be intuitively understood this way. The probability of how the system flows is maximized by differentiating and linking—and this maximizing of complexity actually reinforces its own becoming.

Now, you can block that innate process by shutting down differentiation or linkage, or both, and then the system will not move in harmony but, as we've seen, will go toward chaos or rigidity. But when you release those impediments to self-organization, the natural drive of a complex system is to create the harmony of integration. This may be how the Wheel of Awareness helps us to develop well-being in our lives.

We can propose that beyond consciousness, subjective experience, and information processing, the mind might also include this definition of "the embodied and relational, emergent self-organizing process that regulates the flow of energy and information." As we'll see, this allows us to say what a healthy mind might be, and then shows us steps to cultivate a strong mind that creates integration within and between.

An integrated flow creates harmony. In math terms, we've seen that this flow of optimal self-organization has five features, which spell out the word FACES: Flexibility, Adaptability, Coherence (functioning well over time, or resilience), Energy (a sense of vitality), and Stability.

Studies of well-being have found that the best predictor of health and happiness is having an integrated brain, what the researchers call an "interconnected connectome." This means that having the differentiated areas of the brain linked to each other, a process that enables coordination and balance of the brain as a whole, is likely the mechanism enabling regulation to be optimized—how we regulate attention, emotion, thought, behavior, and our relationships. In meditation studies, too, increases in well-being are associated with the growth of integrative regions of the brain—the prefrontal cortex, corpus callosum, hippocampus, and connectome.

A regulatory process, as we've seen, both monitors what it regulates and modifies what it is regulating—like when you ride a bike or drive a car. By offering this fourth facet of mind as the self-organizing regulatory process, we can see how a natural implication is to stabilize monitoring and then learn to modify toward integration. What is being monitored and then modified? Energy and information flow. Where is this? Within the body, and between the body and other people and the world around, the planet.

The Wheel of Awareness as idea and practice was inspired by this view of mind. To cultivate a healthy mind, stabilize the capacity to monitor energy and information flow within and between. And then once monitoring is strengthened, learn to modulate energy and information flow toward integration by differentiating and linking that now clearly sensed flow.

In summary, our fourth facet of mind defines the mind as, in part, a regulatory process. And so strengthening the mind is simply building these two steps of regulation.

1. *Stabilize monitoring* so you can sense with more depth, clarity, and detail.
2. *Modulate toward integration* so you can shape with differentiation and linkage.

From this perspective, we can see what the fundamental elements of training a stronger mind might actually be.

THREE PILLARS OF MIND TRAINING

Reviews of research on mind training suggest that the three factors we discussed—focused attention, open awareness, and the training of compassion, or what we are calling *kind intention*—are three of the core ingredients of how we create well-being and happiness in our lives. In the future, other core elements may be discovered for how we can also support the training of our minds to move our lives toward well-being.

Three aspects of research-proven elements of mind training include:

1. **Focused attention:** the capacity to sustain one's concentration, ignore distractions or let go of them when they arise, and refocus attention on the intended object of attention

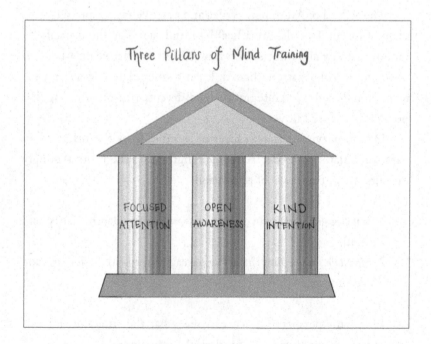

2. **Open awareness:** the experience of presence of mind in which a state of being receptive to objects within awareness but not getting attached to them or lost in them is sustained

3. **Kind intention:** the ability to have a state of mind with positive regard, compassion, and love internally (what is sometimes called "self" compassion, which we are calling "inner compassion") and interpersonally (what is sometimes termed "other"-directed compassion, which we are calling "inter compassion")

Research on focused attention, open awareness, and kind intention trainings suggests they each complement each other and support the movement toward well-being in the body and its brain, our relationships with self and other, and our mental life of attention, feelings, thoughts, and memory.

Taken as a whole, these mind training results may reveal the mechanism we've described earlier—that where attention goes, neural firing flows, and neural connection grows.

One way that we can develop more presence in our lives, how we can become more mindful in our day-to-day living so that we are aware of what is happening as it is happening, as well as cultivating kind regard within that open awareness, is to do a regular practice that trains the mind in these three interrelated ways. That training of the mind is sometimes called meditation. When we learn to strengthen focused attention, we are essentially harnessing the power of our spoke to direct attention toward different points along our rim. We learn to direct, sustain, and detect deviations in our focus, and then to redirect attention. With open awareness we learn to strengthen our access to the hub, distinguishing the knowing of awareness from the knowns on the rim. With this open monitoring we can achieve emotional equilibrium by knowing when we get swept up into the rim, and then harness the ability to return to the equanimity of the hub. And with the training of kind intention, we develop the foundations of empathy and compassion, the caring for and about others and our-selves.

The term *mindfulness* that is often used with the term *mindfulness meditation* actually does not have a singular, fixed definition shared by all practitioners and researchers. The gist of this term, however, can be summarized with the following notions. Being aware of what is happening as it happens without being swept up by preestablished mental activities like judgments or ideas, memories or emotions, is one way of describing mindful awareness. In our research center at UCLA, we offer trainings in MAPs, or mindful awareness practices, which science has revealed promote well-being in body, mind, and relationships. MAPs include sitting meditation, walking meditation, yoga, tai chi chuan, qigong, and centering prayer. These are all ways we can strengthen the mind and bring health to our lives.

For me, these MAPs can be seen as sharing the following set of common features. Naturally, they all involve awareness. But more than being aware, they include paying attention to one's intention and becoming aware of the experience of awareness itself. In many but not all of these practices, there is a kind regard, a sense of care and compassion toward oneself and others in what my psychologist colleagues Trudy Goodman Kornfield and Jack Kornfield, along with Ram Dass, have called loving awareness, and Shauna Shapiro and her colleagues have called kind attention. Shelly Herrell uses the term *soulfulness* to reach out to individuals from a range of cultural backgrounds who resonate more with the notion of being soulful than being mindful. Other psychologists, such as Paul Gilbert, have focused more on compassion, while still others, like Kristin Neff and Christopher Germer, have distinguished this compassion component from mindfulness itself, and specifically have been naming and studying self-compassion.

A general term, *presence*, is sometimes also used for the notion of showing up in awareness and being receptive to what is happening. Presence embraces the sensibility that we can vary in our state of mind even if our physical body is there in an experience. We can have receptive awareness of what is happening as it is happening, and then we would say we are "being mindful." Or we can be distracted as our mind wanders to other concerns no matter what we had been trying to focus on or what activity we are physically involved in. When our minds wander *unintentionally*, we are not present, we are not receptively aware, we are not mindful, and, studies suggest, we inhibit being happy—even if we are daydreaming about exciting things. Mental presence is a state of being wide awake and receptive to what is happening, as it is happening in the moment, within us and between the world and us. Presence cultivates happiness.

I have used the acronym COAL to remind myself of the features of this state of presence that is, I believe, at the heart of what receptive awareness and being in what may be called a mindful, or what others might call a heartful, soulful, or kindful state is all about: Curiosity, Openness, Acceptance, and Love. In a COAL state of mind, we are present for life.

While the common term *mindful* involves a wide set of variables used by a range of clinicians and researchers, the popular interest in "being mindful" has exploded in recent years despite a lack of knowing exactly what this means. For me, the exciting part of this expanded curiosity is that people seem interested in exploring how they might cultivate more presence in their lives so they can be healthier, happier, and kinder to themselves and to others. Each of these can be seen as a way of sensing the mind itself, a process with various names that I call mindsight. Mindsight enables us to have insight, empathy, and integration.

Amazingly, we develop these important skills of the mind by the focus of attention. You may have noticed in our first practice on breath awareness that your mind's focus would regularly wander from its intended focus. Let's explore what these different features of attention may be at the heart of a practice as simple as focusing on the sensation of the breath.

FOCAL AND NON-FOCAL ATTENTION

One important way to distinguish different forms of attention is to determine whether the stream of energy that is the focus of our attention enters awareness. If the focus of attention involves consciousness, it is called *focal attention*; if it does not, it is *non-focal attention*. In order to better understand this difference, take a moment to try the following short activity: Simply move around the room you are presently in. As you do so, notice what you are aware of as you sense and observe what is in front of your eyes, what you feel with your feet, or hands if you are moving in a wheelchair, or, if you are blind, what you feel with your cane or your hands as you move around. Take in as many of the signals from the outside world as you can and bring them into the awareness of your consciousness. This is the knowing of being aware, and the knowns are what you are aware of. In other words, be as *aware* as you possibly can of your surroundings. Place the

"spotlight of attention," like the beam of a flashlight along a dark pathway, on whatever you can as you move around the room.

The spotlight of focal attention aims your mental ability to focus energy flow into awareness. That is *focal* attention filling consciousness with certain aspects of your moving-around-the-room experience. At the very same time, studies reveal, your mind is also focusing a perhaps broader spotlight of attention on many aspects of your experience that never enter awareness. We call this *non-focal* attention. For example, on this journey you were attending non-focally to your balance so you would not fall over, and you were attending to the space around you so you wouldn't bump into something as you moved around the room. You may have found that during this exercise you became absorbed in some thought or memory. At this moment, your focal attention was on these mental processes and no longer on your surroundings. But you didn't fall down or bump into something because your non-focal attention was taking care of attending to those potentially hazardous obstacles and keeping you safe—even without your awareness. Our nonconscious mind has profound impacts on what we do with our behavior, and on how we feel and think even when we are not aware of these influences of non-focal attention on our mental lives.

Reflecting on this exercise, think about other scenarios in which you are both aware and not aware of your surroundings. For example, if you are walking along a hiking trail, you may pay attention to the rocks on the path ahead, disregarding the stones you've already passed by. Attention helps you survive; it helps you navigate the world in which you live. If you didn't pay attention, focal or non-focal, you could trip and fall. If you do pay attention, you're more likely to survive and thrive.

Attention, whether focal or non-focal—with or without awareness—helps you navigate through a world of energy.

By bringing important energy patterns into awareness, we can discern what meaning they have; we can create and interpret "energy in-formation," so that we unravel the information in front of us and determine its significance for our journey ahead. As we've seen, information is simply a pattern of energy with symbolic value. When that information is in awareness, we can then reflect on its meaning and choose how to respond to it. That's one way consciousness gives us choice and enables us to create change. With this consciousness, we can make choices about how to proceed, where to step, what to avoid, which direction to take—both physically and emotionally. We can pause and reflect on various choices and then select which ones best suit our situation and preferences.

Consciousness gives us the opportunity for choice and change.

With such focal attention, with attention streaming energy and information flow into awareness, we can reflect and make intentional, thoughtful decisions as we monitor with more focus and clarity, so we can make modifications with more intention and efficacy.

This is why attention within awareness—focal attention—is so important. Focused attention, recall, is one of the three major pillars of the research-proven ways to create more well-being in our lives—along with open awareness and kind intention, practices we'll be developing and discussing more in later chapters.

With non-focal attention, our minds are also attending to what is going on, directing energy and information flow in a manner that does not enter consciousness. In this way, you can be on automatic pilot and have a conversation with a friend or lose yourself in your imagination while walking down a hiking trail and yet not trip or fall. Because tripping is not so helpful, your nonconscious mind places importance on avoiding obstacles like rocks, or dangerous animals, to help you survive your stroll. That nonconscious mind is monitoring the pathway even if your conscious mind, your awareness in that moment, is not filled with visual images of the trail. You might miss your turning point on the path because you were not paying (focal) attention, but it's unlikely you'll trip over a stone or a branch in your way, because you were in fact paying non-focal attention to the trail. Your nonconscious mind is minding your journey. Non-focal attention can shape our behavior so we don't stumble, and it even influences what enters our awareness as a distraction during an attempt to stay focused, as with the breath-awareness practice.

And so both focal attention with consciousness and non-focal attention without consciousness involve an evaluative process that places meaning and significance on energy patterns and their informational value as they arise moment by moment. Paying attention to branches and snakes is important to our survival, and we register that salience in both our conscious and nonconscious forms of attention. In the brain the regions that focus our attention and evaluate or appraise the significance of events as they unfold are interconnected in their structure and their function. Attention is directly shaped by this evaluation, by the salience or relevance of unfolding events in our lives.

MONITORING ATTENTION AND AWARENESS

Our days are filled with a combination of both guided and pulled attention. Sometimes we choose what to pay attention to, and sometimes the world's circumstances pull our attention, directing where the flashlight of attention is aimed. Interestingly, we need both guided and pulled attention and we need both focal and non-focal attention. Imagine again our rocky hiking trail. We need to intentionally guide our attention to the path itself so that we do not trip over a rock and fall. But if a bear suddenly decides to cross our path, we need to be able to have our attention pulled to this new fact of our experience (and quickly!). As we navigate this world, we must be nimble in terms of guided or pulled attention. And yet when it comes to the more day-to-day experience of living our lives—in other words, when there is no bear appearing on our path—our salience monitoring automatically evaluates what is significant enough for us to focus our attention on moment by moment, and this is usually happening

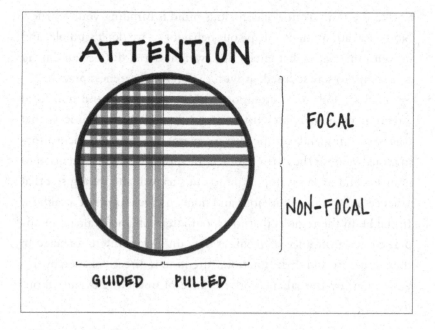

without our even being conscious that these appraisals are being made by our nonconscious mind.

Here's an example to illustrate this important distinction. Imagine that you find yourself preoccupied with a challenging conversation you had with a friend last week. Without your even realizing it, feelings of sadness or anger that may have arisen at that time can be easily triggered now because salience has encouraged you to place significance on any scenario that feels intuitively related to the upsetting conversation you had with your friend. These emotions are now more relevant, more activated or "primed," because of the quarrel—even if they are not in your awareness at the moment.

This illustrative case of the disagreement helps illuminate the distinctions between awareness and attention. We engage in nonfocal attention all the time. This is how our mind processes and keeps track of important things without using up the relatively limited mental space of awareness. This mental space of knowing, the subjective experience of being aware, can only work on a few items of information at a time—like a chalkboard of the mind, sometimes called working memory, that allows us to manipulate information and create new combinations consciously. Yet information processing does not require consciousness, and so we can imagine and calculate and come up with solutions to problems without using up this limited working memory space. To avoid flooding that space, we have non-focal attention direct energy and information flow without awareness. The direction of that information processing is still being shaped by the mind; it simply is not a part of our conscious subjective experience of knowing, of being aware.

The great news is that you can learn to sense these various aspects of attention, whether they are guided by you or pulled by things not directed by you, or whether they involve awareness and are focal or do not and are non-focal. This directing of energy and information flow is attention. Awareness is the subjective experience of knowing within consciousness. We "know" what is going on around and within us, with the term *know* here meaning not factual knowledge, but rather a subjectively felt texture of the present moment's unfolding. We can cultivate access to a more open experience of being aware, and this capacity for conscious choice and change empowers our lives to move with flexibility and intention toward a more integrated way of living. Training the mind is all about building these skills of attention, awareness, and intention.

The key to a reflective practice that can strengthen your brain, your mind, and your relationships and improve the health of your body in all the ways we've discussed (reducing inflammation and optimizing cardiovascular, immune, epigenetic, and telomerase functions) is to cultivate your intentionally created guided and focal attention as you stream energy and information flow into awareness. In many ways this exercise to strengthen the monitoring capacity of the mind is the first step toward strengthening your capacity for presence. And mental presence is the gateway to releasing the mind's ability to naturally create integration.

Yes, there will always be moments of pulled attention, but the act of bringing attention back to a guided experience is what the practice is all about. And yes, you'll have non-focal attention processes happening, too, but your focal attention—how you stream things into awareness—will be where our work will be taking place. The great news is that you don't need to worry about these pulled and non-focal attentional moments; your goal will be to harness and strengthen guided and focal attention. How? With intention and awareness.

We now have some clarifications to enjoy and deepen our experience as we move forward on our journey. Attention is the process that directs energy and information flow. Awareness is our subjective experience of receptive knowing. What, then, is intention?

Intention is the way you set your motivation to engage in a certain activity in a certain way. Having the intention to be aware of what is going on, for example, can make guided focal attention more likely to be engaged. Similarly, you can have the intention to be kind to yourself when attention becomes pulled, not guided, and with this intention you can now realize that wandering is just what the mind does—no need to judge or be angry at the wandering, or at yourself. If your mind wanders and attention strays, it means one thing: You are human. With kindness you can simply recognize you've become distracted as something pulled your attention elsewhere, and now you can intentionally guide your attention back to the intended focus. Likewise, if some distraction repeatedly takes over awareness, you can notice this pattern as simply revealing where your non-focal attention has been placing its spotlight, making it more likely to intrude on consciousness. When you are open to whatever arises, such intrusions in a mental practice simply become glimpses into your nonconscious mind. You merely notice the distraction and then redirect to the breath, for example, if that is the exercise you are intentionally engaged in at that moment.

The great news is that as you do this you will be strengthening both your guided and your focal attention. These skills will also cultivate a stronger and wider capacity to become aware of what is going on as it is going on. Stronger capacity means you can maintain attention, monitor awareness, notice salience breaks, and redirect focal attention to fill awareness with the intended focus. Wider means you can hold items within awareness for a longer period of time, and also sense the various dimensions of what you are aware of with more richness, breadth, focus, depth, and detail. You'll be building those three legs of the mindsight lens tripod of openness, observation, and objectivity. Rather than being swept up into what you think should be happening, you can learn the skill of being present for what is. Cultivating consciousness in this way will be the beginning of enhancing your life, creating a vitality and fullness to your conscious experience of being alive that can be quite exhilarating.

A simple way to envision this is with a concept we've mentioned briefly: presence. When you are open to what is happening as it is happening, you are present for an experience. A wide range of research reveals that presence is the best predictor of a number of indicators of well-being, including physiological measures, relational satisfaction, and happiness.

Some people naturally have a kind of presence in what are called *mindfulness traits*, which has been studied by researchers. Others acquire these traits through intentional mind-training practice that strengthens focal attention, opens awareness, and cultivates kind intention. Either way, we can all benefit from doing some regular focused attention practice, just like we can keep our body healthy with physical activity and keep our teeth and gums healthy with proper dental hygiene. Some people may have stronger bodies or teeth than others, but most of us can benefit from exercising or brushing—and the benefit requires us to do these things on a regular basis, not just once a year, or even once a month. How would you feel if you only brushed your teeth once a month? Daily may be the frequency as an ideal to aim for, but instead, thinking of a *regular* practice may work better for you. If you can't do this every day, fine—but find a way to make this mind-hygiene a regular routine. We can practice good mental hygiene. For many people, making a practice daily makes it easier to create a regular habit. With these practices you will be cultivating a habit of health. When you make that practice the Wheel of Awareness we'll dive into next, you bring the three pillars of cultivating focused attention, open awareness, and kind intention into your daily routine.

THE BASIC WHEEL
OF AWARENESS

MAPS, METAPHORS, AND MECHANISMS

As we prepare for any journey, we orient ourselves for the trip ahead by getting an overall picture of where we are going and the path to getting there. A map is a useful tool that visually displays the terrain awaiting us—the mountains and valleys, rivers and lakes, highways and roads that we may encounter on our journey. Maps serve as visual depictions of geographical space. The Wheel of Awareness offers the common notion of a wheel to depict aspects of mental life, processes of the mind that do not necessarily correspond with specific spatial locations within our brains or other physical structures. It is a visual metaphor that attempts to offer a map of the terrain of our mental lives. Our mind may be more like a verb—a process—than a nounlike location somewhere in space.

Yet visualizing a spatial mapping, such as the wheel, can be of great benefit in guiding us on our journey into the mind. For these reasons, it is important to remember that the Wheel—and maps in general—is only a symbolic representation; it is not the actual territory. If a map is taken as the terrain itself, there may be much confusion and frustration ahead. For example, if you are traveling from

California to Arizona's Grand Canyon and, as you make your way, you visualize the lovely springtime photographs on the colorful map you are using as your guide, you may well be dismayed when you arrive and instead discover only snow-covered cliffs because it is, in fact, December in the Grand Canyon. In this scenario, it is possible that by becoming attached to the images of the map, you might lose sight of the magnificence of the actual canyon.

Another potential risk of using maps is that you might set out focused only on the final destination and miss out on the opportunity to experience the reality of the riches that the journey itself offers.

Using the Wheel as a visual metaphor—a map—for the mind has these same potential downsides. Gaining the benefits of the map as a guide will depend upon how it is used. As we go forward in exploring the Wheel of Awareness as a tool for personal transformation, rather than focusing only on an imagined endpoint or idealized destination, let us enjoy and experience the journey. This will be essential in utilizing the Wheel in a constructive and liberating way. That said, let's take a look at the map's parts and see what they may mean in our lives.

As we've discussed, the central hub of our Wheel depicts the experience of being aware, of knowing. The rim represents what we are aware of, the knowns of consciousness. The Wheel image depicts a linkage of the knowing of the hub to the knowns of the rim by way of a spoke of attention. The Wheel's lone spoke (versus the many spokes on an actual wheel) is a symbol for focal attention, the precise streaming of energy and information flow we are directing into awareness in any given moment.

The whole idea is to integrate consciousness and strengthen the mind by differentiating and then linking energy and information flow within awareness. As regulation involves monitoring and modifying, the Wheel is strengthening the mind by stabilizing how we track energy and information flow and then how we transform that flow in an integrated manner. That's how we use the Wheel to integrate our lives.

As you explore the Wheel as idea and practice, it may be useful to remember that this metaphoric visual depiction of the mind can be a powerful aid to exploring your mental life. But once you set off on your journey to the Grand Canyon, and especially once you get there, keep the map in your pocket and enjoy the experience of the journey itself. Let the map be your aid, not your prison. Explore and enjoy your mind.

THE BASIC AND THE FULL WHEEL OF AWARENESS

Before we begin our practice of the Basic Wheel of Awareness, I'd like to take this opportunity to lay out the entire journey ahead. More detailed instructions for each part of the practice will be offered in the sections that follow, but here you'll find the overall steps. The Basic Wheel of Awareness guides you through the essential experience of the metaphor of the wheel to illuminate the nature of consciousness and its differentiated parts, including the hub of knowing, the rim of the knowns, and the spoke of attention (numbers 1 through 4 and then 6 in the Full Wheel Practice). The Full Wheel Practice then expands upon this to cultivate awareness of awareness with the bending of the spoke of attention back toward the hub of knowing (number 5), and then a focus within the fourth segment of the rim with the addition of statements of positive intentions and kindness offered to promote within-, between-, and "MWe"-directed caring and concern (number 7).

To review, if you are just starting with the Wheel as a practice, I recommend you begin with the Basic steps, numbers 1 through 6, leaving out step 5. If you are experienced with other reflective practices, or are simply feeling ready to dive into the Full Wheel, then try out all of these steps, 1 through 7. As with the breath practice, recall that you can read these steps and then try them out by memory, have a friend read them to you, or go to my website and listen to my voice walk you through the Basic or Full Wheel of Awareness practice.

Each of these seven steps, all of which taken together comprise the Full Wheel of Awareness, is summarized in the following outline of the Wheel practice.

THE FULL WHEEL PRACTICE

The Full Wheel of Awareness practice can be outlined this way:

1. **BREATH:** Start with the breath to anchor attention and get grounded for the Wheel practice.

2. **FIRST FIVE SENSES ON THE FIRST RIM SEGMENT:** Let go of the breath as a focus of attention and begin the focus on the first segment of the rim—the first five senses, attending to one sense at a time: hearing, sight, smell, taste, touch.

3. **INTEROCEPTION ON THE SECOND RIM SEGMENT:** Take a deep breath and move the spoke over to the second segment of the rim, which represents the internal signals of the body. Systematically move the spoke of attention around the body, beginning with the sensations of the muscles and bones of the facial region, then moving on, one at a time, to the sensations of the head, neck, shoulders, arms, upper back and chest, lower back and muscles of the abdomen, hips, legs, pelvic region. Now move to the sensations of the genitals, intestines, respiratory system, heart, and whole body.

4. **MENTAL ACTIVITIES ON THE THIRD RIM SEGMENT:** Take a deep breath and move the spoke over to the third segment of the rim, which represents mental activities. First part: Invite any mental activity—feeling, thought, memory, whatever—into awareness. Many things may arise or nothing may arise; whatever happens is fine. Second part: Again, invite anything into awareness, but this time pay special attention to the way mental activities first arise, stay present,

and then leave awareness. If a mental activity is not immediately re-placed by another activity, what does the gap feel like before a new one arises?

5. HUB-IN-HUB WITH AWARENESS OF AWARENESS: Before we move the spoke of attention over to the fourth and final segment of the rim, we will explore the hub itself. In other words, we will strengthen our ability to be aware of awareness. This can be accomplished by imagining the bending of the spoke of attention around so it aims it-self back into the hub; some prefer the image of retracting the spoke or simply leaving the spoke of attention in the hub of awareness. Whichever notion or visual image works best for you, the idea of this part of the practice is the same: awareness of awareness itself (let a minute or more pass). Finding the breath again and riding its wave, in and out. . . . You can now get ready to straighten and extend the spoke to the fourth and final segment of the rim, our relational sense.

6. RELATIONAL SENSE OF OUR FOURTH RIM SEGMENT: In this final segment of the rim review, we'll explore our connections with other people and things outside of these bodies we were born into. Let's begin with a sense of connection to those physically closest to you right now. Open to the connection to friends and family . . . to a connection to people you work with . . . to people who live in your neighborhood, who share your community . . . who live in your city. . . . Open to a sense of connection to those who share your state or region . . . to people who live in your country. . . . Now open to a sense of connection to all people who live on earth . . . and now see if you can open that sense of connection to all living beings on earth. . . .

7. STATEMENTS OF KIND INTENTION: Now, knowing that science has recently revealed what wisdom traditions have known for many years—that cultivating intentions of kindness, care, empathy, and compassion can bring positive changes into our inner and interper-sonal worlds—I invite you to repeat the following phrases silently, in

your inner mind. We'll begin with short, basic statements of kindness, and then move on to these same intentions stated in a more elaborate way.

May *all living beings* . . . be happy.

May all living beings . . . be healthy.

May all living beings . . . be safe.

May all living beings . . . flourish and thrive.

Now, taking a deeper breath, we send those same wishes, now more elaborate, to an inner sense of who we are, to a Me or I:

May *I* . . . be happy and live with meaning, connection, and equanimity, and a playful, grateful, and joyful heart.

May I . . . be healthy and have a body that gives energy and flexibility, strength and stability.

May I . . . be safe and protected from all sorts of inner and outer harm.

May I . . . flourish and thrive and live with the ease of well-being.

Now, again taking a bit of a deeper breath, we will send those same elaborated wishes to an integrated sense of who we are. Combining our inner Me with our interconnected We, we continue with statements of kind intention for MWe:

May *MWe* . . . be happy and live with meaning, connection, and equanimity, and a playful, grateful, and joyful heart.

May MWe . . . be healthy and have a body that gives energy and flexibility, strength and stability.

May MWe . . . be safe and protected from all sorts of inner and outer harm.

May MWe . . . flourish and thrive and live with the ease of well-being.

I invite you to once again find the breath and ride the wave of the breath, in and out. . . . And now, letting your eyes come open if they are closed, we'll bring this Wheel of Awareness practice to a close for now.

A MAP OF THE BASIC WHEEL OF AWARENESS

You'll be given an opportunity in just a moment to dive into the Wheel as a practice, but first let's review our map. You will recall that the rim can be divided into four segments. The first segment includes our *first five senses*: hearing, sight, smell, taste, and touch. The second segment of the rim includes the sensations of the interior of the body—the signals of our muscles and bones, and the sensations arising from our internal organs, such as our intestines, lungs, and heart. In science we call this *interoception*, for the perception (-ception) of the interior (intero-), and we also call this the *sixth sense*. The third seg-

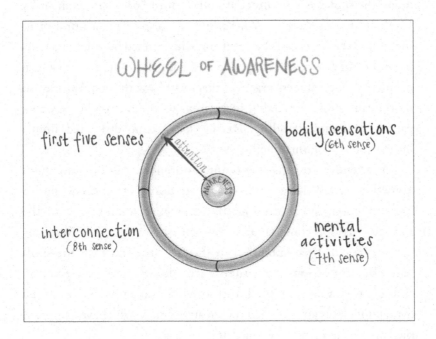

ment of the rim represents our mental activities, such as our emotions, thoughts, and memories. To keep the numbers for these senses going in sequence, we can call this our *seventh sense*—our ability to be aware of such mental activities. On the fourth segment of the rim is our sense of connection to things outside the body—our relationships with other people, pets, the planet, nature, God, and anything else outside or extending beyond the body. This we can call our relational sense, our *eighth sense*.

Each of these senses is a form of energy and information flow, a particular aspect of energy that varies along what we can call its CLIFF features of contour, location, intensity, frequency, and form. To "sense energy flow" simply means to be open to these variables and how they form various patterns of energy and transform in your experience.

The spoke of attention can systematically direct these patterns of energy into the hub of awareness, the *knowing* experience. You can guide the spoke as you direct attention in the practice, segment by segment around the rim. Your mind can also "have a mind of its own," and attention can change from being guided by you to becoming pulled in directions independent of your choosing. As we've seen in the breath-awareness practice, that's just how the mind works, so if you can, please remember to be kind to yourself by being open, patient, and understanding. Recall that getting distracted simply means you are a human being.

As attention streams energy into awareness, it is focal attention. Sometimes you'll have guided focal attention; other times, pulled focal attention. At certain times in the practice you'll be honing the focused attention component, as in the first two segments. With intention, you'll direct attention to the first five and then the sixth sense. But distractions can naturally arise during the Wheel practice, and just as you do with the breath exercise, simply take note of the distraction, let it go, and then return attention to whichever aspect of the rim we are focusing on at that moment.

Throughout the practice you will be guided to shift attention to take in new aspects of the flow of energy and information, rim segment by rim segment, and in doing so you will strengthen your ability to guide attention, to shift the focus of attention with intention.

When we get to the third segment of the rim, we'll be dipping into another aspect of strengthening the mind, a process called *open awareness*. In contrast to the intentional focus on a rim point with focused attention in the first two segments, now you'll be trying out a different process, open monitoring. Here, let awareness become filled with whatever is streaming in. Nothing may come, or many things may come. Whatever arises is simply whatever emerges into consciousness. As we will discuss more at length later on, strengthening our open-awareness ability is just as important as strengthening our focused attention because it enables us to distinguish the experience of being aware (the knowing of the hub) from that which we are aware of (the points on the rim). This capacity to differentiate knowing from known, hub from rim, offers a profound source of mental freedom in our lives. This integration of consciousness allows us to avoid identifying ourselves as only the ever-changing rim contents of our mind, mental activities that we may often get swept up in as we get "lost on our rim." Open awareness permits the hub of the Wheel to become a sanctuary of clarity amid the sometimes-incessant chatter of mental activities on the rim. This is the clarity that integrating consciousness—differentiating and linking hub and rim—can empower us to achieve as a state of mind in the practice, and then enjoy as a trait of equanimity and resilience in our day-to-day experiences of life.

We'll then move from this open awareness of the third segment to explore the fourth segment of the rim, the sense of connection to people or other entities outside of the body. This relational sense will involve focusing attention on particular sensations, and as such, we are continuing to strengthen the monitoring aspect of the mind. This segment also brings up a sense of interconnectedness and kind regard, enabling us to experience an extension of who we are—even before we add, in the Full Wheel practice version, kindness statements— and in these ways the relational segment of the rim review helps develop the third research-based pillar of mind-training practice, the cultivation of kind intention, developing our sense of compassion and connection with the world.

The Wheel practice also gives us the opportunity, in one sitting, to systematically tour the vast array of experiences that occur within our mental lives on a daily basis, and in this manner, it can help us to hone our ability to approach our often more fragmented and hectic lives outside the reflective practice in a now more focused, calm, and compassionate manner.

Ready to begin?

PRACTICING THE BASIC WHEEL OF AWARENESS

Find a quiet place where you'll be able to sit, lie down, or stand for about half an hour, uninterrupted. Turn off your gadgets. Take another look at the diagram of the Wheel (see the figure in the prior section). Just knowing the Wheel's structure is all you need; it's not necessary to be able to visualize the Wheel as a map. Recall that the hub represents the knowing of awareness; the rim, the knowns; and the spoke, the focus of attention. (Again, you may find it useful to read through the entire exercise before trying out the practice, and then guide yourself from memory. Alternatively, you can go to the Resources section on my website, DrDanSiegel.com, if you are interested in being guided by my voice through the practice.) Start with the Basic Wheel; we'll explore the more advanced Full Wheel as we go along.

Let's begin by focusing on the breath as a way to become centered. Just let the sensation of the breath fill awareness. Now shift your attention away from your breath. Imagine yourself in the center of the Wheel, in the hub of knowing, of being aware. Imagine sending a spoke of attention out from the hub of knowing to the first segment of the rim. Let's begin with focusing attention on the sensation of hearing, letting awareness become filled with sound. . . . (Staying with each sensation for fifteen to thirty seconds can be a helpful duration.)

Now letting hearing go, imagine moving the spoke of attention over a bit on this first segment to the sense of sight, letting awareness become filled with light. . . .

Now move the spoke of attention over, letting light go and moving to the sense of smell, letting aromas fill awareness. . . .

Now move the spoke of attention over, opening to the sense of taste, letting tastes fill awareness. . . .

Now let the spoke of attention move over to the sense of touch, letting awareness become filled with the sensation of skin touching skin (hand in hand), skin touching clothing, touching the floor. . . .

Taking a deeper breath, imagine moving the spoke of attention over to the next segment of the rim, which represents the interior of the body—the sensations of the muscles and bones, and of the internal organs. (Here the timing for each part of the body mentioned will vary, anywhere from a few seconds to fifteen seconds or so.) Let's begin with the facial region, letting the sensations of the muscles and bones of the face fill awareness . . . moving attention up to the forehead and top of the scalp, now down the sides of the scalp passing by the ears, and now to the muscles and bones of the throat and neck. Now moving attention to the shoulders, and then streaming attention down both arms to the ends of the fingers . . . now bringing attention to the upper back and chest . . . now the lower back and the muscles of the abdomen . . . and now focusing attention on the sensations of the hips . . . and now streaming attention down both legs, to the ends of the toes.

And now focusing attention on the pelvic region. Opening awareness to the sensations of the genitals . . . and now focusing attention on the sensations of the intestines, beginning deep in the abdomen with the lower intestines . . . and now moving upward toward the stomach region at the top of the abdomen . . . and now following those gut sensations up from the stomach through the center of the chest, opening to the sensations of the esophagus connecting the stomach to the throat and the interior of the mouth. Now moving to the respiratory system, beginning behind the cheekbones with the sensations of the sinuses . . . then to the nose . . . and to the mouth . . . and then down the front of the throat to the trachea, the tube that brings life-giving air down into the center of the lungs, into the interior of the chest . . . the lungs on both sides expanding and contracting . . . Now let the focus of attention move to the heart region, opening awareness to the sensations of the heart.

Now let the sensations of the whole of the interior of the body fill awareness, from head to toe. Knowing that science has now shown what wisdom traditions have known for a long time, that opening awareness to the sensations of the body is a powerful source of wisdom and intuition, I invite you to take a deeper breath, knowing you can always return to exploring this sixth sense of the sensations of the body, and now move the spoke of attention over to the next segment of the rim.

We will now direct the spoke of attention to focus on the third segment of the rim, the segment that represents the mental activities of emotions, thoughts, memories, beliefs, intentions, hopes, and dreams. I encourage you to invite any mental activities—thoughts, feelings, memories—to come into the hub of knowing. Just be open to whatever arises from the rim—or doesn't arise. There is no right or wrong. Many things may come or nothing may come. Simply open the hub to whatever might arise from the rim of mental activities. Let's begin that practice right now. . . . (Continue for about a minute and a half.)

Next, again inviting anything from mental activities into the hub of knowing, I invite you to pay special attention to how a mental activity, such as a thought, first arises in awareness. Does it arise suddenly or gradually? Once it has presented itself to awareness, how does it stay present? Is it solid? Vibrating? And how does the mental activity, the thought, memory, or emotion, leave awareness? Does it leave from one "place" or another? Gradually or suddenly? Does it just get replaced by one mental activity or another, like a thought, a feeling, or a memory? And if it doesn't immediately get replaced by another mental activity, what does the gap feel like between one mental activity and the next? Here, I invite you to become a student of the architecture of mental life, studying how mental activities first present to awareness, stay present, and then leave awareness. Let's begin that practice, right now. . . . (Continue for a minute and a half.)

(Note: If you were doing the Full Wheel practice, this is when you would do the hub-in-hub bending or retracting of the spoke portion of the practice which we will dive into in a later chapter.)

I invite you now to take a deeper breath. And now imagine moving the spoke of attention over to the fourth and final segment of the rim. This is the part of the rim that represents our relational sense, our connections to people and things outside these bodies we were born into.

With the spoke of attention on this fourth segment of the rim, the relational segment, let awareness become filled with the sense of connection to people physically closest to you, right now. Now open to the sense of connection to family and friends not immediately next to you. Now let awareness become filled with a sense of connection to people with whom you work—in school, at work, in your community. Now open to the sense of connection to people who live in your neighborhood . . . to a sense of connection to people who share your community . . . to people who live in your town or city . . . and now opening to a sense of connection to people who live in your region or state . . . and to people who live in your country . . . to people with whom you share your continent. And now see if you can open your sense of connection to all people who live on this precious planet, this place we've named Earth.

And now see if you can expand that sense of connection to all living beings on earth. . . .

(In the Full Wheel practice, this is when you would add the statements of kind intention.)

I invite you now to find the breath again and ride the wave of the breath, in and out. . . . Now, taking a more intentional and perhaps deeper breath, I invite you to let your eyes get ready to open if they've been closed, and we'll let this Wheel of Awareness practice come to a close for now.

REFLECTING ON MIND: YOUR EXPERIENCE OF THE BASIC WHEEL

You've just completed the basic Wheel of Awareness practice. How was that for you? Did you find it challenging to hold your attention on the various segments of the rim? What was it like to return attention once a distraction took over awareness? How did the various aspects of the practice feel for you? Let's review them, segment by segment. In this and future sections, you may find it helpful to write down your reflections in a special journal, a place you can return to as we proceed on our journey into these explorations and cultivations of your mind.

In the first segment, the five senses, what did sound feel like? Did you notice any shift in the quality of hearing when sound was selected as the singular focus in that moment? What did light feel like as you focused on visual sensations? How did color and contrast seem to you as vision was differentiated from other senses? With olfaction as the focus, what did aromas feel like in awareness? Were they more difficult or easier to sense than the other sensations so far? How did it feel to then move to taste? Did you notice your mouth or tongue moving to increase the sensations of taste? And what was it like to scan the body's skin in becoming aware of the sensation of touch? Did certain areas feel more sensitive than others?

For many people, taking this time to differentiate the first five senses from each other enables a heightened experience of being aware of each sensory stream. With practice, this capacity to sense with more clarity and detail will begin to enhance your enjoyment of daily life, bringing more intensity and pleasure, more vitality to your everyday experiences.

Focusing on the second segment of the rim, what did turning attention inward feel like? How did being invited to focus on the sensations of the muscles and bones feel? Did you become aware of sensations that perhaps were new to your awareness? Sensations exist even outside awareness, but they only become a part of our subjective experience when we bring them into consciousness with focal attention, guided or pulled. How did it feel to move throughout the body's muscles and bones? What was it like to guide attention to these sensations? Were any areas more challenging than others?

When we moved to the body's organs, beginning with the sensations of the genitals, what did that feel like? Various sensations may evoke different feelings, including memories of the past as well as bodily signals happening right now. Becoming open to these signals, especially of the genitals if growing up in certain communities where that is uncomfortable to discuss, or if there has been an experience of sexual trauma, can make this segment of the Wheel practice quite challenging. If you found those signals didn't come easily or they flooded you, this may be a way that rigidity or chaos are a part of that bodily region's history for you. If that is your experience, consider taking time for a special focus on that area in future practices, and if the experience becomes overwhelming, then writing in your journal or seeking professional support can be quite helpful.

If some part of the Wheel practice evokes an overwhelming

sensation, you can always modify the practice to let yourself monitor
what is going on and then modify what you do to accommodate any
discomfort that feels intolerable in the moment. Recall Teresa's experience of the Wheel that we discussed in the second section of the
book, and how moving through aspects of the practice helped her
transform unresolved traumatic issues. Returning to an aspect of the
rim that may have been particularly troubling is something you may
choose to do to help integrate that experience into your overall life.
What may feel uncomfortable on a first pass can, with practice, become more deeply understood as you make sense of what those
sensations mean in your life—now and in the past. We are unique
individuals, and honoring your particular experience is important as
you set out on this journey.

When we moved to the focus on the intestines, what was that
like for you? The intestines have a wide array of neural networks and
neurotransmitters, and becoming open to their signals within awareness may be an important window into the wisdom of "gut feelings."
Not every intuition of the gut or body in general is accurate, but
being open to what these signals hold for us can be a useful way of
being in touch with nonlogical processing.

As you moved attention up from the lower intestines to the stomach region, what was that like for you? How was it to open to the
sensations of the esophagus? For many, that's quite new. And within
the oral cavity, inside the mouth, there are many signals that may be
connected to all sorts of prior experiences. You may discover that
when you expand your awareness of these different bodily sensations,
often what arises is a blend of what is happening right in the given
moment and elements of the past.

As we moved the focus to the respiratory system, how did it feel
to guide focal attention to the sinuses and then down the front of the
throat? Sometimes we hold anxiety in this region, and that can be felt
as we move down the trachea and into the lungs and find it hard to

catch our breath. Befriending the sensations of the body, in whatever areas that might be sending prominent signals at that moment, is an important part of interoceptive or internal bodily awareness.

As we moved to the heart region, what did that feel like? Focusing attention on the heart area—even if you aren't actually aware of the sensations of your heart beating—has been shown in some studies to help calm the mind, as it coordinates our brain's control of what is called the autonomic nervous system. This can be true, too, for becoming aware of the cycles of the breath. With these aspects of bodily awareness, research reveals we are able to balance the equivalent of the brain's accelerator and brakes so that we learn to "drive the car" of the body in a smoother, more coordinated manner. Would you want to press on the brakes and accelerator at the same time? No—you'd want to coordinate these two slowing-down and speeding-up control functions. Focusing on the heart region or the breath gives us coordination and balance of the body and helps stabilize the mind.

When we take in the interior of the body as a whole, it can sometimes feel overwhelming after having taken each system, part by part. What did it feel like to be invited to become so receptive? The notion behind that whole-body awareness is simply to set the stage for your everyday life. For example, if I'm having a difficult interaction with someone, I'll remind myself to check in with my body before I respond. My heart may send prominent signals at that moment, or my intestines may be calling out for attention. I might feel tension in the muscles of my arms, or I might feel a tightening of my jaws. Being able to simply ask the whole body to bring sensations into awareness is finding a way to invite any especially relevant signals to arise into consciousness so they can be respected, inspected, and integrated into my awareness of the meaning of what is happening at that moment. Studies suggest that people who have more interoceptive abilities have more capacity for insight and empathy, as well as emotional balance and intuition. And so building these body-awareness skills is a direct route to a deeper connection to our inner and interpersonal lives.

As we moved to the third segment, mental activities—our seventh sense—what did it feel like to shift focus from the outer senses and the interior of the body's signals to the mental activities of feelings, thoughts, memories, and intentions? What was it like to simply be "open" to whatever was arising, or didn't arise, within awareness? This shift from the *focused attention* on a very particular point on the first two segments of the rim (sound, sight, a sensation of a particular body part) to an *open awareness* that invites into awareness whatever comes up is perhaps similar, in a way, to the whole-body moment of the second-segment part of the Wheel practice—just being open to whatever broad set of sensations might arise. What came up as you invited anything in? Some get flooded with feelings or images. That's a natural way that the mind can become receptive to the many things on our mind.

In contrast, for others, this experience brings a peaceful openness, a clarity and calm that feels ironic given they've invited anything to come into awareness, but nothing comes. Individuals with this response often state they've never experienced such stillness before, being more familiar with a monkey-mind chatter of everyday worries, the busy, often incessant feeling of being overwhelmed by emotions, memories, and thoughts to sort through. Giving the mind permission to be open to whatever arises can enable it to become clear and receptive.

When we then came to the next aspect of the seventh sense review, what was it like for you to pay special attention to the dynamics of mental activities—how they first arose, stayed present, and then left consciousness? This can be especially challenging for many, as it seems to involve both an openness to whatever arises (as in the first part of this segment review), but then also a special focus on the nature of comings and goings. For some, the gap between mental activities is especially intriguing, as this space between, say, two thoughts, or memories or emotions, has a very unusual quality that is new for many people to suddenly become aware of. For many of us who have not yet experienced a meditation or reflective practice such as the Wheel, it can be quite revelatory to be aware of the more subtle details of mental activity. Often, our previous experience may have been that one mental activity or another has dominated our awareness as chattering of the mind's activities, the ever-present streams of thoughts, and we haven't had the opportunity to experience that we in fact are more than our mind's chatter. With this third segment review, a new experience of open awareness—the hub—distinguishes itself even more from the elements of the rim. For many, this new awareness can be life changing and, literally, mind altering—even mind-boggling. This is the beginning of more fully distinguishing the knowing from the knowns.

As a mother once said to me as I taught this practice to her and her adolescent son, "I never knew I was more than my thoughts or feelings." For her, distinguishing hub from rim was a revolutionary experience that empowered her to engage with life in a much more rich and nuanced way.

When we turned attention to the fourth segment of the rim, what did that relational sense, our eighth sense, feel like for you? What was it like to let attention to mental activities go and shift to a focus on connections with others? This eighth relational sense can be experienced by some as confusing, as they are not sure what exactly they are focusing on. For others, a deep sense of love, of peace, of kindness and connection arises and they become filled with tears of joy and gratitude. Whatever your experience is, that is your experience. The next time you do this practice, you may have a different experience. In the next section, we'll add direct statements of kindness and care that build on these connecting experiences and that research has shown bring positive changes into our inner and interpersonal lives.

KIND INTENTION

I n this section we will build on the training of focused attention and open awareness during the first three segments of the rim to now deepen and expand a focus on the cultivation of kind intention within the fourth segment. Why is this expanding and not introducing this state of kindness? Since you have been invited to be kind to yourself as your mind becomes distracted, you've already been practicing a way of being gentle with your experience, being open to the inevitable distractions that pull your attention away from its intended focus and having an inner sense of compassion. With the fourth-segment portion of the overall Wheel practice, you will be cultivating the integration of these aspects of attention, awareness, and intention as they mutually reinforce one another with repeated practice in your life, and now with the specific focusing directly on our state of interconnectedness and kind regard toward others, and your inner self.

WEAVING KINDNESS, EMPATHY, AND COMPASSION INTO YOUR LIFE

The Wheel of Awareness is a tool for helping us to differentiate and link energy and information in our lives. With the immersion in the first segment of the rim, we open to the energy flow from the outside world through our five senses. With the second segment review of the wheel, we focus attention on the reality that we live in a body and that our bodily self can be differentiated from other people and other living beings. This is a part of our inner experience of self—the flow of energy and information within these bodies in which we were born, the inner source of our embodied mind that is one source shaping how we live. Our immersion in the third segment of the rim, our mental activities, reveals another source of our inner self, one filled with the subjective experience of feelings and thoughts, memories and beliefs, each of which shapes the story of our lives. With this third segment review we invite anything into awareness, moving from the training of focused attention in the first two segments to open awareness in this segment.

With the fourth segment of the wheel, we build upon these skills of focused attention and open awareness and this knowledge of our inner lives of sensation and mental activities by focusing more closely on the ways we are differentiated, embodied living beings who are in fact interconnected. Each of us has an inner sense of self emerging from the inner aspect of the mind. We can learn to be more aware of this inner sense of self, and we can also cultivate the capacity to sense our inter self—a connection we have with other people and the larger planet on which we live. This is our inter mind, the extension of our subjective experience—the feelings and awareness of who we are emerging in the betweenness of our relationships with people and the planet. We become aware of this mind between by opening to these interconnections with our relational eighth sense.

What are these relational interconnections actually made of? We can propose that we are connected to one another—to other people and our natural world—by way of linkages of some sort. But what are these linkages that interconnect us? In the broadest sense, we can propose from a science perspective that we are a part of an interconnected system, and the fundamental element of that system is energy and information. We've discussed how complex systems function with emergent properties that arise from the interactions of the elements, be they water and salt for the sea, or energy and information flow for our interconnections and the nature of mind. Relationships and our "relational self" can be envisioned as how we *share* energy and information flow. An array of scientists—from physicists and biologists to sociologists, linguists, and anthropologists—describe these linkages in various ways. Some might call this our interconnectedness; others, our interdependence; others, our shared cultural meaning; and still others, simply a web of life. We can view each of these ways of studying our connections as revealing fields of energy and information flow, sometimes invisible to the eye or so subtle that these patterns of flow are not detected in awareness, but they nevertheless can be scientifically established as real aspects of our relational reality—our interconnectedness. Not everything that is real can be picked up readily by our first five senses—hence what we are naming our eighth, relational sense may be drawing on another way of monitoring this sharing or linking of energy and information flow.

Beyond merely imagining these connections, it may be that we are literally sensing in some yet-to-be-determined manner these energy fields we cannot usually detect. One possibility, then, is that we sense these energy linkages; another possibility is that we simply imagine them from what we observe with our five senses—so we create, or construct, a view and a story that we are connected. This constructed relational sense is built from experience, not imagined out of thin air. For now, let's leave this as an open question: Is our relational self and its connectivity something we construct or something we perceive as a sensory conduit? Our relational sense may actually comprise both construction and conduition. Bringing a sense of connection into awareness—whether constructed or felt directly in the moment—strengthens our sense of interconnection within the world.

But what does "connection" really mean? On one level, it is possible to experience life in an isolated way. We are born into a body, we will live in this body, and we will die in this body. That's it. We are born alone and we die alone. And in modern society, such an isolated self is often reinforced by a sense of separateness with a focus on the independent individual who is encouraged, in so many ways, to go it alone. Even more, as we've seen since the time of Hippocrates, twenty-five hundred years ago, and reaffirmed in modern times, a medical view has often stated that the mind—and the self emerging from it—was *only* something that came from the head, from the skull-encased brain. With this contemporary scientific perspective, the self is a solo entity, surrounded by skin and skull, and the mind from which it comes is simply brain activity. In this way, the skin becomes an impermeable boundary defining the "self."

Perhaps this is all there is.

Yet we do know that subjective experience is simply not the same as brain activity, even if it is dependent on this neural functioning of the body. When we have a gut feeling or a heartfelt sense, aren't we becoming aware of the role of the whole body in our mental lives? Surely the mind is at least fully embodied, not just enskulled. And we also know that relationships with others have profound effects on our mental lives. What we feel in the depths of our subjective lives is profoundly shaped by our sense of belonging, by our connections in the world. Feelings are at the core of our subjective lives, and they are extended directly into our relational worlds. These embodied and relational sources of our mental subjective lives have powerful effects on our well-being. For example, one of the most robust predictors of our mental health—as well as our medical health, our happiness, and how long we live—is our network of social support. Why would these social connections be so profoundly important to our well-being? Research findings point out that these connections we have with one another are real, and really important.

My suggestion to you is that the reason these robust research findings are empirically found, over and over, is that the mind is *not* the same as brain activity alone. The mind, as we've discussed, can instead be seen as fully *embodied*, involving all the physiological processes throughout the body, not just enskulled and emerging from the brain in the head. And we can also propose that the mind can additionally be seen as *relational*, involving our interconnections with other people and our natural world, the planet. A review of how people shift toward well-being when given the opportunity to be out in nature, or to become connected to a social network in which they can belong, to have what is called "social integration," reveals two lines of empirical research pointing to the health-promoting power of our relationships—with people and the planet.

Who we are is bigger than the body and broader than the brain.

We are more than our inner, mental lives—we have an interconnected reality to our identity. When we realize the self comes from the mind, and that the mind has both an inner and inter aspect to it, then the self is an aspect of both our body *and* our relationships.

But what, really, is a relationship? A relationship is how we share energy and information with one another. The *embodied brain* is a term we have been using for the internal mechanism of energy and information flow; relationships are how we share energy and information flow with people and other entities outside the bodies we're born into.

By "sensing the connection" on this fourth segment of the rim, we're referring to our relationships with people, pets, and the planet— with all sorts of entities, even ones that don't begin with the letter *p*—outside the body. "Connection" refers to how energy and information are flowing between our bodily selves and "others." As we'll see, we need to use quotation marks around that term, "others," in order to remind our "selves" that the self may actually not be limited to the skin-encased body, but may, in some very real ways, involve our interconnections beyond the body. Simply put, we are connected to people and the planet, and these connections deeply, meaningfully, and medically define and shape who we are. The self is more than the common image of a solo self isolated in the head or the body alone.

These connections can be simply viewed as energy and information sharing. We share the planet, and science affirms this reality that we are all deeply connected with one another. Within our experience of consciousness, we may not be aware of these interconnections. We may have the illusion of separateness; we may believe that we are isolated. In fact, we may have been inadvertently taught, by our parents, peers, teachers, and society, that the consensus view is of a separate self—who I am is my body alone. But for many, this contemporary construction of a solo self may have a sad sense of meaninglessness and disconnection. Cultivating the eighth sense may open the doorway to dissolving a shared myth of our separateness and opening us to the awareness of our meaningful connections in life, ones we may not have even known were actually there. In this way, the fourth segment of the rim is an opportunity to open to what is, and not to fabricate something imagined from thin air. We in fact breathe the same air, share the same water, live in the same ecosphere, and inhabit the same planet as it spins through space. Opening to our connectedness by exploring the eighth sense is not about what you think or what you believe or what you've been told from your earliest days; it's opening to what *is*. These relational connections exist whether you are aware of them or not.

The basic Wheel practice invites us to open awareness to the reality of our connections to other people, to other living beings, to the web of life on the planet. With the suggestion from neuroscientist Richie Davidson's research group that specific compassion training components, established to be helpful, might be added to enhance the Wheel's positive impact on integration, I decided to incorporate specific statements of kind intention, wishes of happiness, health, safety, and well-being, directed to all living beings, to an inner "I," and to an integrated self, a "MWe," that combines the differentiated inner "me" within the body with the inter "we" in our connections with people and the planet. These statements fit well in the fourth segment review, after becoming aware of our interconnectedness, and so you'll find them naturally at the conclusion of the Full Wheel practice.

In the various wisdom traditions throughout the world, including a number of religious practices, compassion is considered one of the highest values that enhance well-being in both the individual and the community. Compassion can be defined as the way we sense the suffering of another, imagine ways of decreasing that suffering, and then make attempts to help another reduce their suffering. Perception, imagination, and action are each a part of what compassion entails.

The perception of suffering in another usually requires a process called empathy. Empathy can be viewed as having at least five aspects, including emotional resonance (feeling another's feelings), perspective taking (seeing through the eyes of another), cognitive understanding (imagining the mental experiences of another and their meaning), empathic concern (caring about the well-being of others), and sympathetic or empathic joy (feeling happy about another's happiness and success). For many, the Wheel cultivates each of these aspects of being empathic. Empathic concern—sensing another's subjective experience and caring about their welfare—can be seen as the motivation and gateway for compassion.

There are some confusing views sometimes expressed by a range of writers that suggest something like "empathy is bad; compassion is good" or that there is a downside to emotional intelligence and being emotionally tuned in to other people. The reality is that compassion may not be possible in most people without empathy that enables us to tune in to the inner life, the emotions and subjective experience, of others. This is how mindsight's insight, empathy, and integration have been suggested as the foundations of emotional and social intelligence. What's the downside to having mindsight in our lives? When we see that empathy includes empathic concern, which essentially is the portal for compassion, we realize that "empathy is bad and compassion is good" is a misleading and confusing statement.

I once taught a workshop in Berlin, and during the evening part of the event, the social neuroscientist Tania Singer gave a lecture about her studies revealing how the training of empathic resonance alone can lead to emotional distress, whereas teaching compassion activates the deep circuits of caring, concern, and affiliation. This afforded us the opportunity to teach together after her talk. I mentioned to professor Singer that some recent reviewers of a book manuscript I had submitted had said that I shouldn't be encouraging empathy as I was in that book, and then quoted her work as support for their perspective that "empathy was bad, compassion was good." She said that the reviewers had misinterpreted her work. Too much identification with the emotional state of another can lead to empathic distress, yes, but when that emotional resonance is coupled with compassion, the individual retains a sense of balance, of equanimity. In fact, virtually all people need to have empathy in order to generate compassion. The key is that empathy alone can sometimes lead to distress.

Matthieu Ricard, a science-trained Buddhist monk and frequent collaborator with the Mind and Life Institute scientists who have been studying contemplative practices like meditation for decades, addressed this important issue at a scientific meeting following Tania Singer's presentation to His Holiness the Dalai Lama: "The point is not to get rid of empathy, of course. We want to continue to be aware of others' feelings. But we need to place empathy in the larger space of altruistic love and compassion. This space will act like a buffer for empathic distress. Since altruism and compassion are positive mental states, they reinforce our courage and give us the resources to deal with the suffering of others in a constructive way. Empathy without compassion is like an electric water pump without water: it quickly overheats and shuts down. So we need the water of love and compassion to continuously cool down empathic distress and counteract emotional exhaustion."*

Arthur Zajonc, a quantum physicist who was also the president of Mind and Life at the time, focusing on professional empathy and compassion in clinicians, noted at their meeting that, "On the one hand, we have coldness, cynicism, distancing oneself from patients and those suffering in order to maintain our own equilibrium and dispassionate professional judgment. On the other hand, we can become so involved that it leads to burnout, self-destruction, and so forth. We tend to move between these two extremes. . . . There must be a middle way, where empathic concern connects one to the feelings of others, but in a way that allows for an intelligent response as a physician, as a caring and concerned person, as a mother or a father, or as a companion or friend in life."†

In response to a question from Richie Davidson about the Buddhist perspective on training compassion, here is how the Dalai Lama responded: "I think it's not only within the Buddhist tradition. All major religious traditions stress the importance of the practice of love and compassion. It's really more in the form of a potential. For example, a basic capacity for awareness exists. But we have to cultivate it and improve it through developing knowledge and education."‡

Our term *kind intention* is a phrase attempting to embrace these ways we can cultivate both a caring motivation as well as a concep-

---

* Wendy Hasenkamp and Janna White, eds., *The Monastery and the Microscope* (New Haven, CT: Yale University Press, 2017), 253.

† Ibid., 252.

‡ Ibid., 254.

tual stance, a state of mind of kind intention, that sets the emotional and intellectual stage for us being empathic and compassionate in life—not only with those whom we may know directly or are similar to us, but also for a wider circle of care and concern including other people and living beings.

These active debates point out an important issue: Empathic resonance alone—feeling the suffering of another without empathic concern and compassion, and without the ability to skillfully differentiate oneself from the suffering of others—can lead to burnout. That is a potential downside to being tuned in to others without proper training in resilience—without the ability to be both linked *and* differentiated. In other words, we risk overidentifying and shutting down if integration is not maintained. I deal with this a lot when I work with clinicians and other care providers who have not been given the tools of integration to help prevent burnout. And from these debates, a suggestion has arisen to replace the term *compassion fatigue* with *empathy fatigue*, which, as you can see, may be made even more specific with the terms *empathic resonance fatigue* and *empathic distress*. This is a crucial distinction to make in order to remind ourselves of the way integration creates resilience. Integration is the process underlying compassion and kindness. But let's not throw out the wide and wonderful skills of the fullness of empathy, and how this full spectrum of empathy is essential in life, essential even for compassion itself!

As individuals would practice the Wheel at home with a recording we'd make in the office or from our website, they'd begin to experience a reduction in anxiety and fear and improve their mild to moderate degrees of dysthymia—of feeling down in the dumps. People with trauma histories would find a new strength in approaching past events from what some would come to call the "sanctuary" of the hub. In many ways, people would become kinder and more compassionate toward their inner distress and suffering, even without the specific statements of kind intention that would be added later on.

Intention is a mental process that sets the tone or direction of the unfolding of energy and information within the mind. Kind intention facilitates the arising of integrative mental processes—like empathic concern and compassion—and makes them more likely to be enacted within us and in our behavior interacting with the world, in our inner and inter mind. When we train a state of kind intention, we harness particular patterns in the brain that research reveals are integrative—they link widely separated regions to each other, enabling the coordination and balance of neural firing. When we exercise those neural networks of kindness, we strengthen their connections and make those trained states become traits of kind intention in our lives.

As we've seen, regular practice supports the movement from a state created during a practice to a trait that becomes a learned skill or way of being. A trait essentially is a baseline propensity or way of behaving that happens without effort or conscious planning in a person's life. In my own personal experience, clinical work with patients, and educational interactions with workshop participants, and also found in the research on numerous subjects from a broad set of carefully conducted studies, the following has been observed: *What you create in the moment can become strengthened in the long run with practice.* This is how a state becomes a trait.

If the trait you seek is being kinder and more compassionate with your inner self or your inter self—your connections with others—then the state you can practice is integration. Research supports this fundamental statement: Being kind and compassionate in our inner and interconnections creates more integration in the brain and more well-being in our lives.

Put simply, *integrative states become healthy traits.*

The Wheel of Awareness has its origins and its fundamental structure steeped in integration, as we've seen. The Wheel in idea and practice cultivates integration in our inner and interconnected lives. If health is what you are striving for, then I invite you to consider making the Wheel practice something you do every day, if possible, or on some kind of regular basis, meaning several times a week at a minimum. Your brain needs repeated and regular practice to reinforce integrative growth. Repeated practice will enhance the positive outcomes for your life as you create intentional though brief states of mind during a practice session that will become traits of resilience and well-being in your day-to-day life.

A repeated state of integration can become an enduring trait of health.

When I presented the Wheel practice to Richie Davidson's research group studying the brain and meditation, they were intrigued by the approach and asked me why I hadn't included even more specific aspects of compassion training as part of the Wheel steps. I told them that the Wheel was simply constructed from the science-inspired notion of differentiating the knowns from the knowing, rim from hub, and that it needed to stay based in science. They then told me of a study they had just completed, the first of many that would be conducted and published, demonstrating that training the intention of compassion actually improves mental functioning, enhances relationships, and is even associated with more integrated brain functioning.

With compassion practice, for example, the electrical signals of the brain, measured with an electroencephalogram, reveal high degrees of gamma waves that emerge from the coordination of widely separated brain regions. And even functional and structural linkages in the brain could be seen in other studies to be enhanced with compassion training, revealing a more integrated brain with practice. In the Human Connectome Project, independent from these studies of meditation, overall well-being was found to be associated with a more "interconnected connectome," meaning how the differentiated regions of the brain were linked to each other. Meditation research also reveals how such practices increase the interconnections of the connectome. The gist of these findings for formal compassion training and for overall health is that they involve integration in the brain.

In the field I work in, interpersonal neurobiology, we see compassion and kindness as the outcomes of integration. For example, when we honor differences between ourselves and others, we are differentiating interpersonally. When we then feel the suffering of another person, imagine how to help them, and then take action to reduce that suffering—when we are compassionate—we are linking to the differentiated person who is suffering. When we feel the joy and achievement of another and feel happy with their success, when we wish them well, we have empathic joy, another aspect of integration. Kindness, too, can be seen as an outcome of integration. Kindness can be defined as how we honor and support one another's vulnerability. Kindness in this way involves respecting the risks and wounds that arise with unfulfilled needs—with being vulnerable. While the connotation of kindness for some may have a sense of it being a weakness rather than a strength, kind intention actually creates the mental stance reinforcing prosocial relationships and inner sources of well-being. Kindness and love are deep sources of resilience and courage, of strength both within and between. Kind actions can also be seen as ones that are offered without expectation of anything in return. One understanding of this way of being kind is that another person is seen as a differentiated aspect of who we are, and so connecting with kindness can be seen as emerging when we sense "our self" as simply one part of a larger whole—we are an inner self, yes, but we also are an inter self.

In these ways, we can see the scientific grounding for the statement: Kindness and compassion are integration made visible.

Focusing on the fourth segment of the rim, bringing attention to the various differentiated individuals and sensing our connection to them can be seen as a form of interpersonal integration. When we expand that sense of connection, opening awareness to our interconnections with all living beings, we extend that differentiation and linkage to a larger sphere of what comprises our inter self. Though the specific words used in this aspect of the practice are simply about connection, the subjective reports of those doing the Basic Wheel practice—even without the kindness statements—support the notion that this fourth segment review, this focus on our eighth, relational sense of our interconnectedness, is filled with a feeling of kindness, compassion, and being a part of a larger whole than what before may have felt like an isolated, private self doing a meditation. When we then add specific aspirational statements of kindness toward all living beings, to our inner sense of "I," and to our integrated self of "MWe," we broaden and deepen that awareness of our integrated way of living in the world.

Those studies of longevity, happiness, and our medical and mental health that reveal that one of the best predictors of these positive factors in life is our connection within a network of social support illuminate the importance of these interpersonal connections. Relationships are not icing on the cake; they *are* the cake. In fact, they are the main course, as well as the dessert.

INTEGRATION, SPIRITUALITY, HEALTH

A human experience related to having a sense of being connected to a larger whole is sometimes called "spirituality." Informal interviews of people interested in what they term "spiritual growth" identify two facets of their journey that define being spiritual for them: connection to something larger than a private self and meaning beyond their individual survival. Fascinating. If being spiritual means experiencing our connections beyond the skin and meaning beyond survival, then could this compelling part of our human experience be related to integration? In other words, if the linking of a differentiated inner self with a larger inter self emerges as the interconnected aspect of our reality, and if this differentiated and linked identity gives rise to a vibrant sense of meaning in life, might this sense of the spiritual be fundamentally related to the process of integration in our lives? Many individuals have described that a sense of meaning and connection emerge for them as they experience the Wheel practice, as we've seen in the case of Zachary, who felt this larger sense of connection and purpose after doing the practice that led to transformations in his personal and work lives.

Integration is a powerful, scientifically grounded conceptual framework enabling us to understand a number of human experiences, from spirituality to health. Insight into the impediments to integration even help illuminate the nature of human suffering and what we might do to alleviate it. A wide range of studies of individuals with challenges to mental well-being reveal impaired integration in the brain, along with a sense of personal isolation and meaninglessness in their lives. For those who are in the helping professions, too, the experience of burnout, the opposite of feeling spiritually enriched, may be seen when the vitality of meaning and connection in work and in life become lost. This loss of meaning and connection can be seen as coming from impediments to integration. If we don't distinguish our inner experience of self from another's experience of pain, but instead overidentify with the suffering person as simply being the same as our inner self, we are at risk of empathic distress and burnout. Such emotional resonance—one aspect of empathy, as we've discussed—which arises without the differentiation necessary for integration to unfold, can lead to excessive brain firing, exhaustion, and withdrawal. Human suffering can be seen as chaotic or rigid states that arise from impaired differentiation and linkage, from blockages to integration. Empathy by itself, even emotional resonance as part of empathy, needs to be made a part of integration, not excessive differentiation with aloofness or excessive linkage with overidentification. Resonating with another *without* differentiating is not integration—it is one aspect of empathy without the equanimity that integration makes available. Integration enables us to be emotionally nimble, feeling the experience of others fully while not losing the capacity to care and live with equanimity. Life is full of challenges and suffering; the impact of integration at the heart of spiritual growth may be to enable us to experience joy and gratitude not only despite the pain of the world, but as a responsibility to keep those positive states and a sense of hope and possibility alive for all of us in our deeply interconnected lives.

OUR INNER AND INTER SELVES

If we sense that we as individuals do have an inner self as well as a shared, relational inter self, then we can see how fusing two inner selves—ours and another person's—would mean a lack of differentiation. Our inner life is real in each of us, and it is important to identify so that we can fully connect with one another via our inter self and what is often called "another" but is actually a part of who we really are. I am not offering this view to you to be poetic, but rather as a scientific statement about the nature of an integrated identity. Too much isolation, too much focus on the inner self as the sole source of our identity without acknowledging our inter self, and we have excessive differentiation without linkage. The result of such isolation can be despair and a sense of meaninglessness. Living a life "all about me" has been shown to be unhealthy. This is an unintegrated way of living in our world.

On the other side of the integration spectrum, too much connection without necessary differentiation also creates impaired integration. This is the case when we become burned out in our caregiving work or are in enmeshed relationships, becoming fused and lost in the confusion, as a differentiated inner life is not recognized and respected by others or even cultivated by ourselves.

Honoring both the inner and the inter, we can become fully present for both aspects of our sense of self. That term, *self*, can be quite challenging, as we live in a modern culture that equates the self with the skin-encased body, or even in a more constrained anatomy, with the skull-encased brain in the head. As we'll see, this linguistic association of the term *self* with *skin* or *skull* creates a sense of who we are that may unfortunately impede living an integrated life. Research is quite clear: Being connected to others, finding ways of being of service to support well-being in the world beyond your private skull- or skin-defined self, is a time-tested path toward a life well lived. Compassion, kindness, and empathy are fundamental to living an integrated life.

The "self-transcendent" emotions of awe, gratitude, and com-passion studied by University of California, Berkeley, psychology researcher Dacher Keltner and his colleagues at the Greater Good Science Center may arise from this integrated state of energy and information flow. When we experience *awe* we have a sense of being faced with something beyond what we can initially understand, and what emerges is a feeling of being a part of a larger whole, a part of something bigger than the body in which we reside. With *gratitude*, we feel a deep sense of appreciation. As Emiliana Simon-Thomas, Keltner's colleague at the GGSC, says, "Experiences that heighten meaningful connections with others—like noticing how another person has helped you, acknowledging the effort it took, and savor-ing how you benefited from it—engage biological systems for trust and affection, alongside circuits for pleasure and reward. This pro-vides a synergistic and enduring boost to the positive experience. Saying 'thank you' to a person, your brain registers that something good has happened and that you are more richly enmeshed in a meaningful social community."* At the University of Southern Cal-ifornia, Mary Helen Immordino-Yang has found that similar emo-tional states actually activate deep regions in the brain stem that are associated with our basic life-giving bodily processes. She suggests that part of the feeling of being alive, of being filled with vitality, comes from these ways that social emotions activate our most funda-

---

* Jeremy Adam Smith, "Six Habits of Highly Grateful People," Greater Good Science Center, November 20, 2013, https://greatergood.berkeley.edu/article/item/six_habits_of_ highly_grateful_people.

mental neural circuits of life. Gratitude is awesome. And *compassion* is also considered a moral sentiment, or self-transcendent social emotion, in that it meaningfully connects us to this larger whole. We become more alive when we embrace the reality of our interconnectedness.

Compassion builds on empathy and kindness, supporting our ability to maintain health and reach out and support the well-being of what we usually simply call "others." As we've discussed, what is sometimes termed "self-compassion" might be better named "inner compassion," so that compassion directed toward "others" might then be called "inter compassion." When we support this view of who we really are, who we are truly capable of being when we live fully, and that *our self is in fact both inner and inter,* we can then cultivate a more integrated and vital way of being in the world. Compassion training is a way to cultivate such integration, both in our inter relationships and in our inner skin-encased bodies and their skull-encased brains.

Inspired by the neuroscience researchers' suggestions to add specific empirically supported compassion training elements as the Wheel practice was developing, I decided to include a more in-depth component of the fourth rim segment of our relational connections to elaborate this aspect of building kind intention. Because compassion and kindness arise from and reinforce integration, it seemed both appropriate and helpful to incorporate this addition into the Wheel, which has been, from the beginning, all about integration.

BUILDING COMPASSION WITH STATEMENTS OF INTENTION

You may be wondering how research can demonstrate the impact of compassion on our lives, including the ways the brain works. Recall that meditation simply means a practice that trains the mind. What research has shown is that when an inner intention is created that is imbued with a positive stance toward the well-being of others and ourselves—wishing wellness to arise and desiring that suffering be alleviated—the brain becomes integrated in its functioning. As mentioned earlier, various ways of measuring brain activity have been used to demonstrate that wide regions of the brain become coordinated and balanced with the generation of such inner states of compassion. The brain seems to thrive on this state of care and concern, what I simply call kind intention, whether it's directed toward particular individuals or is a nondirected broad and generalized sense of compassion and love. Kindness includes compassion and empathic joy—feeling good about others' thriving. Intention is simply setting a mental state that shapes the direction and quality of the patterns of energy and information that are most likely to arise. Kind intention primes the mind in pro-social and interconnecting ways.

In addition to increased functional and structural integration in the brain, other studies have shown decreases in markers of inflammation, decreases in stress, and improvements in how our heart functions, so our whole body is soothed with compassion. I even did a mini-study with family members, in which we measured the balance of the acceleration and braking functions of their autonomic nervous system by measuring heart rate variability. When they wished others harm—the opposite of kind intention—the system became dysregulated; when they wished for the well-being of others, the system became balanced as it differentiated and then linked these activating and deactivating aspects of our physiological regulation. These findings suggest that when we intentionally and meaningfully, with authenticity and honesty, generate kind thoughts, we create integration in our bodies and our brains.

As we've seen again and again, what you do with your mind changes your body, including the brain. It's as if your body is listening to the feelings, thoughts, and intentions your mind creates—and empirical evidence supports that notion that the body's cells, epigenetic regulators, and physiological systems respond. Intention primes the mind for maliciousness or for kindness, and shapes the inner life of our body and the inter life of our relationships.

If kind intention, empathic joy, and a compassionate state of mind are so helpful in our inner lives of the body, and it helps in our approach to others in making us more open and caring, how can we develop such states in our lives?

The answer is simple: with the cultivation of intention. Intention acts like a mental vector, a kind of funnel, as it sets a particular direction for energy and information to flow. Recall our simple equation: Where attention goes, neural firing flows, and neural connection grows. We can now expand that a few steps further:

How intention glows determines where attention goes, neural firing flows, and neural and interpersonal connection grow.

Your intention sets the direction of attention and connection.

When we set intention in awareness with initial purposeful effort, we influence what will also become intention even outside awareness. This creates a state of mind that can be present without our conscious effort. This is how a repeated, purposefully created state of mind during a practice becomes an automatic trait in our lives.

When that state is one of kindness and compassion, that trait is one of connection.

Frame of mind, mental state, mindset, and mental stance all refer to a state of mind that can be viewed as a collection of features of the mind including intention, attention, awareness, emotion, memory, and patterns of behaving. These behavioral aspects of mind would involve *priming*—or getting one ready to act in a certain manner—and then enacting those behaviors themselves.

Ancient practices and modern scientific studies have demonstrated this state of compassionate intention can be created with *internal statements*, experienced as an inner voice of the individual. Studies of the brain reveal that when we use linguistic symbols during these inner articulations, we do far more than simply activate linguistic centers mediating the definition of those terms. With words, we also activate brain regions that represent the fuller concepts, not just the word itself that symbolizes the concept. This is how new brain-imaging technologies can "read minds," in that they can take complex sentences built from words and predict the brain activation regions based on the meaning of the words themselves. Imagine how word-based statements of kind intention will then activate circuitry of caring, empathy, compassion, and love. *Kindness* is the simple word we will use to represent this broad range of positive feelings that involve integrative inner global brain states and interpersonal attitudes and behavior. In the brain, we'd see the activation of aspects of our social circuitry, including regions in the front and back of our cortical areas that are involved in empathy and compassion and a process called theory of mind. These social circuits enable us to make a neural map of the minds of others, and of ourselves, and then get ready to act on behalf of the well-being of others.

These statements of kind intention are filled with positivity, caring, and compassion. You could call them statements of love, respect, and concern. The key point is that a verbal phrase, such as inner wishes for the well-being of oneself or others, activates the mind states the simple words symbolize. Statements are more than just a bunch of words strung together when stated with authenticity, intention, and care.

The internal statements I'll be inviting you to make are made with words we'll review soon. As you state these phrases in your inner voice, you may find that various feelings or images arise. You can stay with the statements as they unfold, and simply be present for whatever arises as it emerges. Later on, creating kind intention may also be experienced as a feeling of positive regard, a feeling of love, a compassionate stance toward others—and even toward one's inner self. What research has shown is that such compassion training, the practice of kind intention, actually can lead not only to positive internal sensations but also to a likelihood of reaching out to help others as well.

I've modified the various versions available in a number of practices that have been studied in a wide array of research projects to fit in with the flow of the Wheel practice. These can be elaborated to include processes of forgiveness for a given relationship or tailored to address specific individuals. In those modifications, one *offers* forgiveness for whatever pain or harm someone else may have caused to the practitioner; and then one *asks* for forgiveness for whatever may have been done by the practitioner to cause pain or harm to someone else. Forgiveness is not stating that what happened was right or good; forgiveness, as my colleague and friend Jack Kornfield suggests, is giving up all hope for a better past.

For the Wheel practice, keeping the statements as broad and open as possible seemed to fit best, and it was consistent with the research on what is called "non-referential compassion," in which the general states of positive regard and love are created in the practice, revealing some of the highest degrees of brain integration ever seen. It seemed, too, that the most suitable placement of these statements is following the eighth sense review of our interconnections, furthering the process in that segment of focusing on our relationships—inter and even inner.

If you'd like to try this now as part of the whole Wheel practice, please go to my website and follow the "Full Wheel," or go to the previous chapter of this book, begin with the Basic Wheel, and then add this section. Because some people feel uncomfortable wishing others or themselves well, I begin this part of the Wheel practice, in the fourth segment of the rim and after our focus on interconnectivity, with a reminder that goes like this and then continues on to the kind intention statements:

"Recent scientific research has revealed what many ancient wisdom traditions have taught for a long time—that the creation of a state of kindness and compassion is not only good for others, but it is helpful for our own individual well-being. With this finding in mind, I invite you to repeat these phrases in your inner voice. I'll state a phrase or part of a phrase and pause, and then you can silently repeat these words of kind regard and compassionate intention in your inner mind. Then I'll move on to the next part of the phrase. We'll begin with very basic phrases, and then move to more elaborate ones. Ready? Let's begin."

Here are the phrases:

>May all living beings be happy. . .

>May all living beings be healthy . . .

>May all living beings be safe . . .

>And may all living beings flourish and thrive.

First taking a deeper breath, we will now focus these same statements of kind intention, in a bit more elaborate form, toward our inner selves by using the word *I*.

May I be happy . . .

>And live with meaning, connection, and equanimity . . .

>And a playful, grateful, and joyful heart.

May I be healthy . . .

>And have a body that gives me energy and flexibility . . .

>Strength and stability.

May I be safe . . .

>And protected from all sorts of inner and outer harm.

And may I flourish and thrive . . .

>And live with the ease of well-being.

Now taking a bit of a deeper breath, our self is not only what exists in the inner life of the body—the "I" of who we are. We are also part of an interconnected whole, part of a "we." But how can we integrate this differentiated bodily me or I with a relational us or we? Integration is the honoring of differences and then their compassionate, respectful linkage. If we integrate "me" and "we," we come up with an integrated identity, one that we can name with a new term: "MWe."

Let's send these same aspirational statements of kind and compassionate intention toward MWe.

May MWe be happy . . .

And live with meaning, connection, and equanimity . . .

And a playful, grateful, and joyful heart.

May MWe be healthy . . .

And have a body that gives energy and flexibility . . .

Strength and stability.

May MWe be safe . . .

And protected from all sorts of inner and outer harm.

And may MWe flourish and thrive . . .

And live with the ease of well-being.

And now I invite you once again to find the breath, and ride the wave of the breath, in and out. . . .

And now, if your eyes are closed, you can get ready to let them come open. Taking a more intentional and perhaps deeper breath, we will let this Wheel of Awareness practice come to a close for now.

REFLECTING ON KIND AND COMPASSIONATE INTENTION

Seems simple, doesn't it? Beginning with an intention to care for the well-being of others, you make internal statements of kindness and compassion. How did that feel for you? Some find making these statements a bit awkward, something they've never done before. Others find the moment of turning these positive wishes of care and concern to the inner self somewhat anxiety provoking. "Do I really deserve such kindness?" is a question some people ask. For many people, especially after the newness of these phrases wears off, the practice of offering positive statements for the well-being of others and the inner self is actually quite invigorating. When we add the part about the integrated self, about the MWe, we then get the extra boost of realizing how interconnected we all are. In many ways, adding these positive statements of compassionate intention is a natural way to extend the eighth relational sense of our interconnectivity and to conclude the Wheel practice.

What these studies and practices suggest is that setting an intention within awareness has powerful effects on creating positive states in our lives. Our physiology responds with more balanced and healthy functioning. Our interactions with others, including diminishing implicit racial biases, improve. Even our connection to our inner self is enhanced with kindness emerging toward our inner experience.

Kristin Neff's research on self-compassion includes the notions of being mindful, of being kind to the self, and of realizing we are part of a larger humanity. As we've explored, this term might be phrased as "inner compassion" to reduce our focus on self versus other, acknowledging in the words we choose the deeply interconnected nature of who we are, of who the self is, of where the mind emerges—from within and between.

Inner compassion is an important part of kind intention. If I stub my toe, I can be aware of the pain and yell at myself for being so

clumsy. In this case, I would not be exhibiting self-compassion. Instead, I can be aware of the pain and treat myself as if I were approaching my best friend. I'd be gentle. I'd be kind. I'd be caring. Instead of
resisting the pain and creating suffering, I'd be embracing it and letting it become simply a sensation and a part of life's inevitable colli-
sions we don't anticipate. And I would realize that it's just human to
become distracted and stub your toe. It's just what we occasionally do.

Kindness has a sense of something being done with care and
concern. Some definitions of kindness, as we've seen, state that it is a
way of interacting with others without expecting anything in return.
I like the notion of kindness as a way of honoring and supporting one
another's vulnerabilities, acknowledging our need for others and our
human frailties. We each carry potential wounds and ways we've
become brokenhearted. Being kind to ourselves and others means
caring for each other's most vulnerable ways of being.

We can have an act of kindness, and we can have kind intention
that sets the mental state for such actions. With compassion, too, we
can have a state of compassionate intention in addition to compassionate action. As we've discussed, *empathic concern* is a gateway for
this compassionate stance that readies us to feel another's suffering
and then think through how to effectively help them reduce that
suffering, helping them to feel better. *Kindness, compassion,* and *empathy* are three terms reflecting how we are all deeply interconnected.
When we focus on empathic joy, on how we can share the thrill of
another's achievements and happiness, we can see how there are elements of empathy, kindness, and compassion that are each unique,
and each important.

When we set an internal intention toward these three—to be
kind, compassionate, and empathic—we are really creating a mindset
of integration. Why? Because with these three integrative intentional
states, we can respect and even enjoy differences while also creating
meaningful connections with others. Kindness sets the mind for being open and caring; empathy sets the mind for deep feeling, sharing,

and understanding; compassion primes the mind for connecting in feeling, thought, and action around suffering and its alleviation. Kindness, empathy, and compassion are three fundamental ingredients of an integrating mind.

Psychologist and researcher Barbara Fredrickson has written about love as "positivity resonance," a way in which we connect with one another and reinforce positive emotions of joy, respect, and connection. She and I have written together, too, about the notion that love may be a state in which integration is increased—not only around sharing positive states but also when we connect with others who are suffering. When we join with others even around painful states, two previously separate individuals become part of a larger whole. This bearing witness to the pain of another is a form of increasing the state of integration for each person, the sufferer and the witness. Love connects us and expands who we are.

Scientists in the past rarely wrote about love, so naturally I feel the echoes of that professional discomfort in speaking directly about this essential aspect of our lives. Trained as an attachment researcher, though, I know that the health of our lives depends on the love in our relationships. And as a scientist familiar with the brain, I know, too, that love in a relationship supports the optimal growth of the brain's integration, enabling it to function in a coordinated and balanced way as widely separated regions become linked to one another. When we love someone, we differentiate and link in an integrative relationship. Love is interpersonal integration that stimulates the growth of inner neural integration, each reinforcing the other, each creating well-being in our lives.

If you put together all that we've been exploring to this point about the Wheel of Awareness, focusing on our interconnections, honoring our vulnerabilities, respecting the deep ways we are both differentiated and linked, embracing how we need one another, it is scientifically reasonable to state that empathy, compassion, and kindness are certainly fundamental aspects of a loving state of mind. Kind intention training creates an integrating state that, with practice, can reinforce the trait of love in our life. Integrative states become healthy traits. Kindness and compassion are integration made visible; love is a trait of a healthy life.

DEEPENING THE WHEEL PRACTICE

May I suggest that you try out the Wheel practice that now includes these kind intention statements for the next few days? With this fourth segment of our relational sense expanded to include this way of cultivating kindness, empathy, and compassion, the Wheel can now become a reinforcing practice that continues to build on these positive internal states.

You may find that as the days of doing this practice unfold, your inner experience of interpersonal events will take on a new hue. For example, a few days before writing this chapter, I was driving through a small town along a coastal highway. It had been raining a lot, and there were very few cars on the road. As I approached a small town, I saw that the speed limit had suddenly changed, and as I was reducing my car's speed, a police officer appeared in my rearview mirror. His red and blue lights came on, and he pulled me over to issue a speeding violation. I knew that no amount of arguing with him would get him to change his mind. I waited for him to appear at my door, and as I handed him my driver's license I felt this calm, clear sensation as I looked into his eyes. I realized he probably had some kind of quota for tickets he needed to issue. I also realized that it was a speed trap—that there was no way to slow down quickly enough without slamming on the brakes once that sign appeared. And there he was, waiting for the next victim.

While I was frustrated with the unfolding of these events, knowing I'd have to pay a fine and attend traffic school, somehow I felt deeply caring for this officer. I imagined the small town needed the funds it would soon receive from my account, I felt that he was treating me with respect, and I felt that fighting back would offer nothing positive to the experience. Waiting to get irritated with him, or with myself, I was pleasantly surprised to find myself almost imagining being in his boots. I looked out at the sea, and felt that this ticket was a small price to pay compared to the larger issues that faced our planet. I smiled at the officer and actually thanked him for the ticket. He looked at me, puzzled, and I felt this kindness, this love, this caring well up inside me. Perhaps he would treat the next person well because of the kindness I showed him. Who knows? But as he drove off, I felt strong in the whole experience. If there was some injustice that needed correcting, something worth putting energy and time into, I felt this inner state of clarity and calm would be the better place from which to begin, rather than being filled with anxiety, fear, or irritation. That morning, as usual, I had done the Wheel, and I could feel its capacity to create and sustain this sense of interconnection and caring.

It was a great drive up the coast, and now, as I write to you look-ing over the Pacific's wild waves, it feels like that intention of kind-ness, empathy, and compassion is a way of setting our lives in context. We attain resilience with this broader perspective, seeing that waves of energy and information flow toward us and through us, and we are more than just the waves. We are perhaps more like the ocean, and the waves are simply the expression of the sea's passion, moment by moment, wave by wave.

What is this larger sea who MWe are?

When I first started exploring the Wheel with my patients, there'd be this experience of the gap between mental activities on the third segment review that filled their sense of life with a new vision into the nature of reality. That space between thoughts, the mental pause be-tween feelings or memories, felt like the experience of awareness itself.

And with the inspiration of their reflections, joined by our mu-tual curiosity about what that space between mental activities might actually *be*, I elected to add one more step to complete the Wheel of Awareness practice. Let's dive into this Full Wheel practice in the next section.

OPEN AWARENESS

EXPLORING THE HUB

The Wheel of Awareness helps us distinguish the knowns of thoughts, feelings, sensations, and perceptions on the rim from the knowing of the hub. Once we have gained this experiential knowledge, we can then move to experiencing the knowing in and of itself. In this section we will explore the hub specifically, focusing on the knowing as distinct from the knowns. In other words, we will explore what being aware might actually *be*.

As we turn our attention to the hub itself, we will also dive more deeply into some of the fundamental questions about the nature of the mind, and then perhaps understand more fully how we can integrate and strengthen the mind to create more health and well-being in our lives.

How can we explore the knowing of awareness directly? In the old story of Willie the jailed bank robber, when the police detectives asked Willie why he robbed the bank, he replied, "That's where the money was." In the same way, to explore the knowing of consciousness, why not explore the hub itself? At the point in the Wheel practice in which I invite my patients or workshop participants to turn

their attention to the hub, I often suggest that they bend the spoke of attention around 180 degrees to focus on it.

For some, bending the spoke seemed odd, and instead, they suggested that they could just retract the spoke into the hub. Others felt that they could best explore the hub directly by not sending out any spoke at all, just letting attention rest in the hub. Bent spoke, retracted spoke, staying-put spoke—all roads lead to experiencing the hub directly. Some feel a distinction between focusing attention on awareness with a bent or retracted spoke and simply resting in pure awareness. Whichever ways you conceptualize and utilize the Wheel metaphor, the intention is the same: to get direct access to the knowing of consciousness itself—to become aware of awareness.

At first I would offer this new hub-exploration part of the practice at the end of the whole experience, after the kindness statements. The thinking at that time was that awareness embraces it all, so why not end with a deep dive into the knowing of awareness itself? But

that approach didn't work so well, as people in shorter workshops would feel they were left hanging, and they didn't want to leave in that wide-open state. I moved the timing of this hub exploration to just after the seventh-sense review of mental activities, between the third and fourth segments of the rim; it felt like a natural place to position this new step, and people responded well. You can try it between these two rim segments in the practice, too, but feel free to move these steps around to suit your own needs and disposition.

5. (This step is often done after the Wheel Practice reaches the completion of the third segment review of mental activities, and before moving on to the fourth segment review of relational connections and statements of kind intention.)

Take a deep breath. *Here is the new part*: Before we move the spoke of attention over to the fourth and final segment of our relational sense, we'll explore the hub itself. Some find it helpful to imagine bending the metaphoric spoke of attention around 180 degrees, aiming attention right into the hub itself. Others find it more useful to imagine sending the spoke of attention out a bit and then retracting it into the hub. Still others prefer to simply leave the spoke of attention inside the hub, or to have no spoke at all, and rest in the knowing of the hub of the Wheel. Whatever way works best for you, the idea is the same: Open the hub of the Wheel to the experience of becoming aware of awareness. Let's begin that practice right now. (I often let two to three minutes pass for this experience. When that time has gone by, continue with the following.) Now I invite you to find the breath and ride the wave of the breath, in and out. . . . Now, taking a deeper breath, straighten out the spoke and send it out to the fourth and final segment of the rim, our relational sense of connection.

REFLECTING ON KNOWING

What was this hub-in-hub experience like for you? Many of my patients and workshop participants have found that it felt odd, at least at first. Did it feel disorienting or confusing for you? For some, there is simply a sense of becoming lost, of spacing out, of not knowing what to do. No need to worry. In many ways, this step of resting awareness in awareness, of being aware of awareness, is quite advanced. I once taught this to someone who ran a meditation center; he said that in his forty years of teaching, this was, for him, the most advanced stage of his practice.

Yet after teaching the Wheel of Awareness in person to well over thirty thousand people, and systematically recording the responses of about ten thousand individuals who attended small workshops or seminars, it's become clear that while the responses differ among individuals, there is a remarkable consistency to the experiences that people describe. No matter the educational background, history with meditation (be it a long history or none at all), religious affiliation, age, gender, nationality, or other demographic features, the responses are quite unique yet quite similar.

Whatever *your* experience is, that is what you are experiencing. In reviewing the findings of the ten-thousand-person study, it has become clear that a common experience is shared across the globe. With this finding, we can then put together some relevant views from science about what the Wheel practice may be revealing about the nature of the mind itself, a journey we'll dive deeply into as we move into part II soon.

ENERGY AROUND THE WHEEL

On the first segment of the rim, we've seen that you may heighten your awareness of the first five senses, hearing with more acuity, seeing with more vividness, smelling with more sensitivity, tasting with more intensity, touching with more tactile discernment. What might be going on here is that the differentiation of the five senses from other energy streams allows the limited mental space of focal attention to become clearer. One sense at a time makes less become more—more vivid in focus, depth, and detail. That's a great skill to now have, as you can use this technique of differentiating sensory input to heighten your experience of being alive in this sensory-rich world.

Next time you have a meal, try just tasting, smelling, touching, and seeing your food, one sensory stream at a time. I've even tried to listen to my food! Why we have our social time over meals and communicate using words with one another instead of immersing ourselves in the shared sensory flow of the eating, at least for part of the time, I've never understood. On the other hand, being together in a safe and supportive way with the social connection and joining around mealtimes is itself a sensory experience of being interconnected, and in this way there is a balance between the opportunities to connect with the inner mind and sensations as well as with the inter mind and our relational connections. An integrated approach would invite us to find some natural way to bring both inner and inter experiences into the process synergistically, with a manner that mutually respects and reinforces the importance and differentiated nature of each. When we sense our food, we are in conduit mode; when we use words to communicate, we are in construction mode. Finding a way to honor our experience as both conduit and constructor would be one way to envision becoming more integrative in our mealtime experience. Try that out sometime and see how distinguishing the sensory conduition and social construction feel, and what it's like to link them in one mealtime gathering.

On the second segment of the rim, people often experience a range of responses, from numbness and confusion to a rich sense of inner connection and fullness as they open to the sensations of the body. If there are leftover issues from past difficult experiences, certain areas of the body may become filled with emotional or sensory reactions or memories, such as fear, panic, sadness, or even pain and challenging images from the past. As with the whole Wheel practice, being open to what is happening as it happens can give you the strength to simply be with what is, exploring bodily sensations that may hold an invitation for you to explore even further what their meaning in your past or current life experiences might be.

Recall that the Wheel reinforces what we learned in the breath-awareness practice, to cultivate the mindsight tripod of openness, observation, and objectivity (please see the figure on page 32). Letting things simply arise is being *open* to what is. Letting yourself have the spaciousness of *observing* at times, not just sensing, can give you the freedom to not become lost in thought or memory, and even to redirect attention using that observational stance. Recall that observing is not the same as sensing; both are good, but each is different. *Objectivity* gives you the capacity to be aware that whatever arises is a transient emergence of an object of attention—it's not the whole of your identity or necessarily a true reality. It's a mental process, an object of the mind. In these ways, being open, observant, and objective stabilizes the mind's ability to take in the wide swath of experience, inside and out.

On the third segment of the rim, people in the study frequently described a strange and surprising finding. When inviting anything to enter awareness from this seventh sense of mental activities, often nothing came. That clarity, as we've discussed, was not only surprising, it often was calming. While we said that mind-training practice is not the same as relaxation training, having access to this calming and clarifying mind, to this spaciousness of awareness without mental activities, can create a sense of peace.

One way people often describe mental activities is as if they are "bubbling up out of nowhere." In fact, at a recent meditation retreat I asked a science-trained meditation teacher what the mind is. He said, "The mind is experience." And when I asked him what experience is, he said, "Experience is simply experience." So I tried to push him a little further, and asked him what experience feels like. This is what he said: "The mind is the bubbling up of experience; it bubbles up, and then vanishes away."

For many people, exploring the dynamics of how mental activities come and go is quite challenging. You may have found this to be true, too, and when people are able to articulate it, they often state that they were surprised to find that each mental activity—each thought, feeling, memory, or belief—had a labile and transient quality to it that they had not been aware of before. Nothing could be grasped. Everything seemed to come and go, often without a clear connection to things that had come before, or things that came next. It was, in fact, like bubbles just emerging from some carbonated drink, bubbling up, and bursting as they disappeared at the surface of awareness.

And then there is the step of turning the spoke of attention back into the hub, our hub-in-hub section of the practice. Whether the spoke is bent around, retracted, or simply not extended toward the rim, the results are similar. Some find that being aware of awareness is quite new. Some find it confusing, disorienting, difficult to hold on to. Some find it bizarre.

In one workshop, for example, a participant called this awareness of awareness experience "really odd." When I asked what "odd" felt like, he said, "I mean, it was really weird." So I asked him what "weird" felt like, and he said, "Just really strange." Then I felt a need to say something like this: "The words we use are linguistic symbols that don't often capture exactly what we mean, or what we experienced. And sometimes those words reflect our comparing what we have experienced in the past and what we expect now with what is happening in the present moment. If you let the comparisons and the symbols of *odd, weird,* and *strange* go, and just let yourself sit for a moment with what the experience was like, just see if you can feel what it feels like, what it felt like, to be aware of awareness." He was silent as the group waited for his response. Then he smiled, and actually had a glow to his expression, and he said, "It was incredibly peaceful. It was so clear, so empty, yet so full. It was amazing."

He was not alone. Others in that same group have come to say similar things, as has happened in workshops around the world. Here are some of the phrases that have been used to try to express what awareness of awareness feels like for them: "As wide as the sky." "As deep as the ocean." "Complete peace." "Joy." "Tranquility." "Safety." "Connection to the world." "God." "Love." "At home in the universe." "Timeless." "Expansive." "Infinity."

What is going on here? Why would these statements, though not expressed by all, be offered from such a disparate group of people from around the world? To be clear, some participants have great difficulty with this step and don't offer any descriptions, or simply say that their minds wandered or that they felt confused or simply focused on the breath. But many others, in every workshop I've offered, no matter their meditation history, have come up with these common statements. Recently I offered the Wheel practice to three thousand people in one room, and hundreds raised their hands when asked if they felt a sense of expansiveness or of a loss of time. Students traveling with me to various teaching events have commented, "No one will believe that these statements happen over and over." Fortunately, I've recorded the statements in the ten-thousand-person systematic survey so we have the data. And the pattern keeps on emerging as people dive into the practice. One participant even handed me a note after the sharing part of the workshop; it said she couldn't openly state what happened in that step, which she experienced as "an amazing sense of expansiveness and peace, a feeling of wholeness I've never had before," because she thought others would think she was bragging. One person even said he felt so much love that he couldn't share that experience for fear his professional colleagues in the seminar would consider him weak. While each of these descriptions is unique, they share very similar senses of love, joy, and a wide-open, timeless expanse. I know for me, each time I do my regular Wheel practice, the hub-in-hub step feels subtly different. Sometimes a shift doesn't even seem to happen and I am stuck on the rim, thinking of things I hope would happen, or being swept up by memories of past hub-in-hub practices and wishing those would occur again. If I expect things to go a certain way, they usually don't. Part of the challenge of a repeated practice is to let go of prior experiences and simply drop into the flow—in this case, of resting in the hub of awareness.

To address these inquiries about what this may all mean more fully, we'll need to ask some fundamental questions about the Wheel practice and what awareness might involve in part II, as we dive into the implications regarding mechanisms of the mind that extend our understanding of how to apply the Wheel of Awareness as idea and as practice. Exploring these experiences opens a window into the nature of the mind and how you might come to use the Wheel practice in a deeper way in your life. Here as we conclude our first part of the book, let's try out the Wheel practice once again, this time as a consolidated practice of the Full Wheel, set to your own rhythm of the breath.

CONSOLIDATED WHEEL PRACTICE

To integrate the Wheel in idea and practice into your life, it is helpful to reflect on these concepts and experiential immersions. Sometimes we are just too busy to engage in the practice, which, when done at leisure or to my voice recording, usually takes a little less than half an hour. Even if you are strapped for time in your life, finding space to focus on the breath is a good way to be sure you are doing some basic focused attention practice, doable even as you are waiting in line at the store. Another way to be sure to get some reflection practice into each day is to do segments of the rim in any given five-minute interval that might be available to you throughout the day. So there are many ways to keep the practice going—and it may even be that dividing a daily twenty-minute reflective practice into four five-minute sections is just as beneficial as one continuous twenty-minute session, though it has yet to be definitively researched. Some is better than none; regular is better than random. You may find that a daily reflective practice is a helpful way to make this health-promoting integrative mind training a regular part of your life.

The Wheel as a whole has a certain rhythm and fullness to it that many have wanted to preserve and yet find a way to do the Full Wheel practice within shorter session times. So I invited myself, and then others, to try the following practice, which I simply call the Consolidated Wheel, as it is done at a different pace but also helps incorporate the whole Wheel, in idea and practice, into your life. In this way we integrate the ideas and practice of the Wheel as a whole entity. The one you will find on my website is seven minutes long!

The basic idea is this: With each movement of the spoke of attention, we are harnessing focused attention skills to focus the spoke, take in the rim elements, and then move the spoke as we redirect attention. In the first segment, the first five senses—hearing, sight, smell, taste, and touch—are taken in with each in-breath and out-breath cycle. Naturally, the timing of this movement is coordinated with your specific breathing rhythm, so though we have this consolidated version available to you on our website, it may work better for you to time this to your own breathing, not mine or my voice determining the transitions. What this may entail, then, is you learning by heart, encoding in memory the different steps. They are outlined in a previous section for an ease of reference (see page 62), and the key approach here is to move the spoke at the timing of your in-breath, soaking in the rim point with the in- and out-breaths, and then shifting focus on the next in-breath.

For the second segment of the rim, it can be an added feature to imagine the sensation of the breath coming in from that part of the body and in addition or instead going out to that part of the body. Try either way and see what works best for you. As we begin, say, with the sensations of the muscles and bones of the face, on the in-breath you can imagine the air coming in through the face, or on the out-breath the air being breathed out through the face. Then imagining the breath in through the scalp, or out through the scalp. For me, the shift to the sensations of the new part of the body with the in-breath feels right, and then sending the breath out to that part of the body before shifting on the next in-breath. The shift for you feels best there or during the out-breath. And if there is a part of the body that needs a little extra breath, go for it. Take whatever time you need, and whatever time you have.

On the third segment of the rim, cultivating open awareness, I find a few cycles of the breath seem to work well for the two parts of that rim review of mental activities. And then for the bending or retracting of the spoke, for the hub-in-hub step, I give myself whatever number of breaths I need. Sometimes for this hub-in-hub part of the practice, I lose track of the breath altogether, so it's helpful to set a timer if I am on a schedule, so I'm not late for my next appointment. I may set a three-minute interval bell to ring before the ending tone so I can get the fourth segment review in without rushing through the end of this consolidated Wheel practice.

On the fourth segment, it becomes very natural again to time the shift of focus from those closest to us outward to all living beings with each breath cycle, in and out. And then when it comes to the statements of kind intention, you can try out many ways to fit each set of phrases into the breath. One way I find very soothing is to make the initial statement with the in-breath and then the details on the out-breath. Then I repeat the basic phrase—for example, "May all living beings be happy"—at the end of the out-breath. Here it might be something like this:

(in-breath): May MWe be happy
(out-breath): and live with meaning, connection, and equanimity
(in-breath): and a playful, grateful, and joyful heart.
(out-breath): May MWe be happy.

In this way, you can play with the timing of these statements to find something that suits both you and the particular phrasing.

Breathing into the Consolidated Wheel of Awareness practice is a wonderful way to take these few minutes to do a complete Wheel and coordinate it with the natural rhythm of your breath.

Take your time, feel your life, and breathe into the Wheel. As we explore the implications and more applications of these ideas and practices in the chapters ahead, I invite you to continue to immerse yourself in regular practice, letting the integration of the Wheel become a part of your life in whatever ways that arise for you. This continued practice as we move forward can empower you to expand your experience and integrate these upcoming concepts with the opportunity to further strengthen your mind and enhance well-being in your life.

PART II

THE WHEEL OF AWARENESS AND MECHANISMS OF MIND

MIND AND THE ENERGY
FLOW OF THE BODY

As we engage in the Wheel of Awareness practice, we have the subjective experience of the rim, spoke, and hub. This visual image of the Wheel is a metaphor helping us distinguish knowing from known and linking them with attention. Here in part II of our journey, we will build on your direct immersion in the Wheel practice and explore more fully some of the potential mechanisms of the mind that are the essence of these experiences.

Here we'll explore the highlights of these mechanisms—in the body and its brain, as well as other notions of the connection of mind to energy flow itself—so that we can have a deeper and more accessible understanding of the Wheel of Awareness. Why do we need to build a framework of potential mechanisms beneath the metaphor of the Wheel? By deepening our understanding of the processes that might actually be unfolding, we will be better able to harness the power of awareness in daily life. Louis Pasteur once said, "Chance favors the prepared mind." Experiencing the Wheel of Awareness and understanding its possible mechanisms will prepare your mind for the chance encounters that life inevitably brings your way.

In the first segment of the rim, we focus on the flow of energy into the body in the form of sound, light, chemical interactions as smell and taste, and kinetic pressure with touch. We are born with receptors to detect these forms of energy in our world, and our first five senses are how we take this energy flow into our bodies. This input of energy can influence the body without our knowing it, and it can also be sensed as subjective experience within awareness. Energy impacting our body's receptors is transduced into energy flow within our body itself, shaping how neural firing unfolds and our physiology shifts in ways that enable us to sense, perceive, and interact with the outer world—the world outside the body.

For many scientists, the exact way these bodily states are felt as subjective experience within awareness remains a challenging puzzle to solve. Yes, body processes may be essential for mind's awareness, as many scientists propose. But *how* that happens—moving from molecules and energy flow to conscious experience—no one has the final word. We have many questions about this step, many processes that have been proposed from matter to mind, and many theories that are debated in the academic world, but the bottom line is that we simply don't know how we become aware.

Twenty-five hundred years ago, Hippocrates proclaimed the brain to be the unique origin of our joys and sorrows, the sole source of mind. That traditional medical view, while still commonly held, may not actually be the full story. While moving beyond the brain to the whole body is not very common in neuroscience, let's see what the physician and neuroscientist Antonio Damasio has to say about this view in the following transcript of a public lecture he delivered to twelve hundred professionals in London, which summarizes some important arguments in his book, *The Strange Order of Things: Life, Feeling, and the Making of Cultures.*

"Most of life on earth has been lived without nervous systems. Nervous systems are recent evolutionary developments. Once nervous systems began, they gave rise, eventually, to the appearance of minds with faculties on which our cultures are based. But until that point life proceeded very well without nervous systems."

Here Damasio reminds us to consider the body proper as something that preceded the existence of brains.

"Another interesting point is that very often when people think of minds they only think about the brain. . . . They have the idea that minds come out of brains *only* as if the brain were the *sole* generator of minds. This is false. Minds are made by nervous systems in cooperation with the body."

Here we have an important moment in mainstream neuroscience in which an accomplished researcher in the field is suggesting we look beyond the common statement that "mind is what brain does." And Damasio continues to expand on why this view is false: "For the basic reason that before there were brains, before there were nervous systems, there were bodies that were doing extremely complex things, and that nervous systems are sub-products of bodies that need to have a regulator for their complexity."

We will follow this notion of the need for regulating complexity and track that idea when we consider the mechanisms beneath the aspect of mind that we mentioned earlier, that of a self-organizing emergent property of a complex system. Damasio goes on:

So contrary to the usual idea in which you think of the brain as being the royal organ system that is running things and producing minds, think instead of bodies, with all of their complex biology, rising up to the point where they're so complex that they require coordinators. Those coordinators are in fact nervous systems. We need to realize that we do not have brains served by the body; it's the other way around. We have bodies that are served by the nervous system. Once you see nervous systems as the servants of life and not the other way around, things begin to make a bit more sense.

Making sense of the mind, we can propose, means moving beyond the traditional view that mind is merely an outcome of the brain-in-the-head's activity. With Damasio's perspective, we can see that our mental lives at least are something fully embodied. Focusing for now within the skin-encased body, what actually is being regulated? What is this system of complexity all about, really?

Let's use as an example the nature of feelings as they connect our mental, subjective experience with our body's physiology. In the Wheel practice, during the second segment of the rim review, you were invited to become aware of the body's state. This sixth-sense rim activity is a visual notion of the energy flow of the body—the body's current state. These body states are the basis for our feelings.

Then, on the third segment of the rim, you were invited to be open to whatever emotions, thoughts, memories, intentions, beliefs, or other mental activities might arise. You then could explore how the subjective experience of knowing, of being aware, could enable you to know the arising, staying present, and leaving of these activities of mental life. It is possible that these more constructed mental activities are also embodied patterns of energy flow, ones that might be shaped primarily by complex neural firing in the brain's various regions. This suggests that while the second segment of the rim might be bodily states, the third segment might predominantly be arising from neural firing in the head.

But what might these mental activities actually *be*? What might these bodily sensations actually be? Could these second and third rim elements share something with each other, and possibly with the first segment of the sensations of the outer world of sight, hearing, smell, taste, and touch? And what about the fourth segment, our relationships to things outside these bodies we inhabit? Could these also share some fundamental element, a common mechanism underneath the metaphor and experience of the Wheel?

In other words, what are those rim points really made of? What are these *knowns* of the mind?

Let's return for a moment to Damasio's ideas focusing on the centrality of feelings in our lives. Many feelings may have arisen during the Wheel practice, and from the hub you became aware of them. But what *is* a feeling, really?

Damasio suggests that signals from the body are the means by which an emotional state enters consciousness as what is called a "feeling." In this way, a feeling is our conscious experience of emotion. Okay, fine. But what are emotions? These body states are signals passed to the central nervous system in many ways, including the bloodstream, peripheral branches of our nervous system, and the system within the intestines called the "enteric nervous system." As Damasio states, "The intestinal nervous system is actually the first brain . . . it's where nervous systems began."

Within the head brain itself, as opposed to the gut brain or the heart brain—the interconnected neural systems around these organs—the deepest and most evolutionarily oldest part, the brain stem, receives the first input from these bodily signals. As Damasio notes, clusters of neurons in the brain stem, called nuclei, "provide the first full organism integration of body states available" to the central nervous system. These brain stem nuclei exist even in insects—meaning feelings have been a part of the life of living organisms for hundreds of millions of years. A feeling, then, is essentially some kind of representation of the state of the body.

As mammals, we have an extensively developed set of regions above the brain stem, giving us a more complex neural passage of signals than an insect. That doesn't make it better, only different in many ways, including its complexity.

We can build on this sense of an embodied mind that is beyond the brain in the head as being made up of patterns of embodied energy flow. What our first three rim segments represent are various forms of energy flow—from the outside world, from the body, and from the complex neural constructions that create mental activities. Our fourth segment of relational connections, as we've discussed, might be a form of the sharing of energy flow, a pattern of interactions between our inner, embodied self and the inter or relational connections we have with other selves and the world in which we live.

In sum, the Wheel's rim points may be a visual metaphor for various forms and locations of energy flow—the first segment's conduit of the outside world, the conduit of somatic senses of the second segment, neural constructions of the third segment's mental activities, and the interconnection, as conduition and construction, of our relational lives. Our basic proposal is that the rim's knowns represent patterns of energy flow and the spoke signifies the directing of that flow with attention. The question remains, then, what might the hub of knowing be? To address that fundamental question about the origin of awareness, we'll need to explore some of the basic ideas of the mind and research strategies to study consciousness.

MINDING YOUR BRAIN

Recall that we discussed in part I how the mind has four facets: subjective experience, consciousness, information processing, and self-organization. We are exploring how the Wheel practice may involve each of these facets—and the potential mechanism they each share. That essential mechanism may be energy flow.

Your mind is able to sense and direct the flow of energy. Subjective experience may simply be sensing the feeling of that flow—whether it is coming from inside or outside the body.

Your mind directs the flow of energy down the physical substance of interconnected neurons as ions move in and out of their membranes and release neurotransmitters, that neural flow in turn activating DNA, leading to protein synthesis and the modification or new development of connections called synapses, sculpting circuits and enabling signals to be passed among linked neurons, and even stimulating the growth of the myelin sheath that strengthens functional connections and enhances neural communication. Myelin, when laid down among synaptically interconnected neurons, makes the action potential—the flow of ions—stream one hundred times faster and the resting period, or the refractory period between firings, thirty times briefer. One hundred times thirty equals three thousand. So with the focus of attention, with what you can do with your *mind*, you can make new or modify existing synaptic connections and lay down myelin to make the energy flow happen three thousand times faster, as well as in a more coordinated way to make more complex neural firing patterns possible, forming the maps of information in the body and its brain in the head.

Add to this the fact that the activation of neural patterns by the mind or other experiences can change the chemical regulators sitting on top of genes, the epigenetic regulators, which include histones and methyl groups as the non-DNA molecules that shape how genes will be expressed and proteins produced, and you have a third way the mind can change the brain. Epigenetic modifications alter the way the brain will grow in response to future experience.

Amazingly, as we can see, your mind can influence neural firing, shaping synaptic growth, myelin formation, and epigenetic modification. Each of these scientifically documented findings means that your mind shapes experience—energy and information flow—which changes brain function and structure. How does the mind do this? By *directing* the flow of energy and information. Go, mind, go!

This sequence is one reason why at our Mindsight Institute, we have the fun phrases *mind your brain* and *inspire to rewire*, meaning your mind can be used to integrate your brain and reconfigure your life to be fuller, freer, and filled with more meaning and well-being. At the core of this view is that mind and brain are not the same—sometimes brain pulls the experience of mind in certain directions and we are on automatic pilot; other times we can use our mind to harness the power of attention, directing energy and information flow with intention and awareness, to have the brain become active in ways it might not naturally. This is how doing the Wheel practice can change your brain. When you repeatedly engage in the Wheel's training of focused attention, open awareness, and kind intention, you promote a certain pattern of firing or of neural state—an integrated state— that research suggests will enable an integrated set of traits, from integrative brain growth, to become a part of your life.

In this manner, we can inspire each other to rewire the brain in particular ways. When we are caring for our well-being, we can mind the brain to create more neural integration as we rewire toward health.

YOUR HEAD BRAIN IN A HAND MODEL

To envision how your Wheel practice may help cultivate a more integrated brain, it can be useful to have a handy model of the brain available at a moment's notice. If you take your hand, put your thumb in the middle of your palm, and fold your fingers over your thumb, you'll have a useful hand model of the human brain, which I often

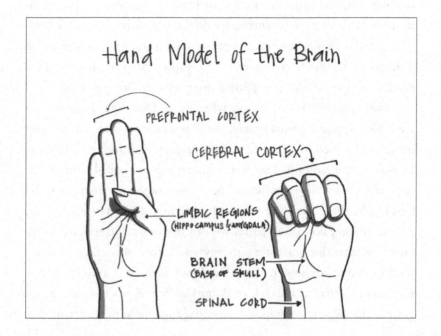

Hand Model of the Brain

PREFRONTAL CORTEX

CEREBRAL CORTEX

LIMBIC REGIONS
(HIPPOCAMPUS & AMYGDALA)

BRAIN STEM
(BASE OF SKULL)

SPINAL CORD

use to help visualize in an accessible way this complex organ and how it becomes integrated.

In the orientation of this brain in your hand, the eyes and face would be in front of the knuckles, with your wrist representing your spinal cord in your neck. If you lift up your fingers and then your thumb, you'll see your palm, which represents the brain stem region. This is the part of the head brain, deep in your skull and deep in your ancestors' history, that first makes an integrated set of neural firing patterns that symbolize, or re-present, what Antonio Damasio refers to as "full organism integration."

Next we add what traditionally has been termed the limbic region, represented by your thumb, which in reality is a set of areas also interconnected widely to other regions of the whole brain. This region will be connected with the brain stem below it, and the cortex above it, a large area represented by your fingers folded over that limbic thumb area. While the boundaries of these areas may be less distinct than their separate names imply, seeing how they are spatially arranged in your hand model of the brain can be quite, well, handy to have at your disposal. We'll explore some aspects of each of these areas soon in order to understand possible inner mechanisms of mind, but here let's simply examine one area that links body, limbic region, and cortex, an important interconnecting circuit we've discussed that grows with meditation practice, the anterior *insular cortex*, or simply the insula.

Damasio has studied this complex neural circuit and has found that "Insular cortices provide (a) a more explicit map of feeling states than the brain stem can provide; and (b) a map suitable for interconnecting to other cortical maps related to memory, reasoning, and language (socio-cultural homeostasis)."

Here we see a link between something happening in the body proper and the passage of that bodily state into the head's brain stem and insula. That "something" is conveyed as a signal and then re-presented inside the head brain as what is commonly called a "map" by scientists. This neural representation, or the brain's map, is thought to be a pattern of neural firing, a set of neurons that are activated in a certain manner or pattern that stands for, or maps out, neural information. Neural activation is an energy pattern of neural firing. In this case, the insula activation is representing the state of the body. And unlike the brain stem's mappings, the insula reaches up into the other head-brain regions, which can then make far more complex map-linked associations that shape our imagination, our self-awareness, our language, and our sociocultural ways of balancing our functioning. Each of these processes contributes to our homeostasis—the ways we survive and thrive.

Regulation of our system, according to Damasio, involves the nervous system and how it creates what he calls "action programs" that enable the organism to survive and the species to thrive—for us to achieve homeostasis. These programs involve neural "commands" that lead to action: "The command can result from *internal* conditions of the organism or from events in the *external* world. . . . The brain's sensory systems continuously survey the internal state of the organism, the environment that surrounds it, and the imaginative process. *The mental experience of the action programs and of their results is known as feelings.* Feelings are conscious and valenced. . . . Feelings are natural reports on the state of life within the organism."

The state of life is the state of our body. This supports the notion that we, our minds, are fully embodied. The body is not simply a transport vehicle carrying the head around—it is an important internal source of the essence of who we are. So while we are exploring a hand model of the head brain, this map is but one aspect of a fuller bodily self that shapes who we are.

As Damasio elaborates further "the making of minds—and of feelings in particular—is grounded on *interactions* of the nervous system and its organism. *Nervous systems make minds not by themselves but in cooperation with the rest of their own organisms.* This is a departure from the traditional view of brains as the sole source of minds."* This supports our basic proposal that the mind is both fully embodied and relational.

In addressing the question of why we have feelings in the first place, this is Damasio's response: "This is the crux of it: Once you have feelings you can guide your life, your mental life, and what you plan to do, from the feelings you have. . . . The feeling system is a way of having your body, your physiology, your homeostatic state, influence your behavior."

For Damasio, feelings are crucial in organizing behavior; they evoke motion as what we call "e-motions." And as a predictive machine, he suggests, too, we need our feelings to guide behavior in an organized manner. We learn from the past and anticipate the future all embedded in the feelings in the present. Feelings are not a side component of a life well lived; they are essential ways we live as a whole, embodied being.

One part of our body, the brain in the head, plays a particularly prominent role in shaping who we think we are, and how we think in the first place. Arising from the brain stem's first mapping of the body's signals, and then the limbic region's weaving together of a sense of emotion, motivation, evaluation, memory, and attachment, we then come upward to the cortex. The new cortex, or neomammalian or neocortex, grew in our mammalian evolution. This region became quite enlarged in primates, and then in our human emergence the front-most part, the prefrontal region, became more intricately interconnected with other regions. This prefrontal cortex is a major integrative hub of the brain, linking cortex, limbic, brain stem, somatic, and even social flows of energy and information to each other.

Is it fair to say that we are certain that consciousness arises solely

---

* Antonio Damasio, *The Strange Order of Things* (New York: Pantheon, 2018), 28.

from the cortex? The answer is no. Here is Damasio's take on consciousness and the brain: "There is no specific region or system of the brain that satisfies all the requirements of consciousness, the perspective and feeling components of subjectivity, and the integrating of experiences. Not surprisingly, the attempts to find one brain locus for consciousness have not been successful." In looking at the range of areas that contribute to these aspects of consciousness, he states further, "These regions and systems participate in the process as an ensemble, entering and departing the assembly line in orderly fashion. Once again, those brain regions are not doing it alone; they work in intense cooperation with the body proper."* In this way, consciousness is fully embodied.

The neural representations or maps generated by the cortical regions clearly contribute to the images and ideas we experience in consciousness. One area of this mapmaking, reasoning, reflecting cortex enables us to have a sense of the minds of others—and of ourselves. The capacity for this mind-mindedness—or what has also been called theory of mind, mentalization, or reflective functioning—involves a number of areas, including the prefrontal cortex. When the midline aspect of this prefrontal area links with a posterior midline area, the posterior cingulate cortex, they form two nodes in a system that, along with other cortical areas, is active even when we are at rest. Because of this background activity, this default way of being even when we are not assigned a task to perform, scientists have labeled this set of interconnected, mostly midline structures, front to back, the *default mode network*—the DMN.

"The process related to the integration of experiences requires the narrative-like ordering of images and the coordination of those images with the subjectivity process. This is achieved by association cortices of both cerebral hemispheres arranged in large-scale networks, of which the default mode network is the best known exam-

---

* Damasio, *The Strange Order of Things*, 154.

ple. Large scale networks manage to interconnect noncontinuous brain regions by fairly long bidirectional pathways."*

Let's see how this interlinking DMN may relate to your experiences with the Wheel of Awareness practice.

THE DEFAULT MODE NETWORK

Exciting new insights from brain research raise some fascinating questions about who we are, how we got to be this way, and what mind-training practices such as the Wheel might be doing to shape our sense of self in the world. Explorations into mind and brain naturally give rise to questions about the self and consciousness—inquiries that help us focus our exploration of the potential mechanisms of the Wheel.

Take a look at your hand model of the brain, with your cortical fingers now folded over your limbic thumb sitting atop your brain stem palm. The frontal lobe of the cortex, which sits just behind the forehead, is represented by the fingers from the second knuckles forward to the fingernails. From the middle of the frontal lobe, extending down the middle of the brain in this midline axis, back toward the posterior regions, are the interconnected areas forming the midline nodes of the default mode network.

The DMN's circuits can be visualized as a series of interconnected mostly midline areas that run through the center of the brain, front to back. Here we'll focus only on the midline areas for ease of reference.

Here is one way to consider how the DMN plays a role in our lives. In many people, these midline areas are very tightly linked to each other in a way that creates a highly differentiated circuit that can dominate the activity of other areas of the brain. Imagine a tight clique of friends at school who are not open to including others in

---

* Damasio, *The Strange Order of Things*, 155.

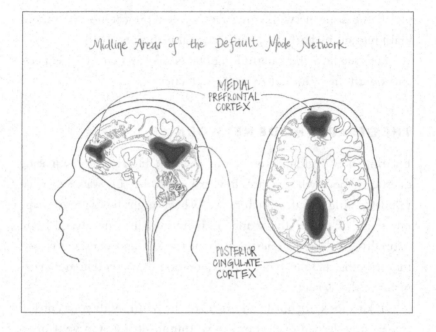

Midline Areas of the Default Mode Network

MEDIAL
PREFRONTAL
CORTEX

POSTERIOR
CINGULATE
CORTEX

their group. That's the sense of the various regions interconnected as their baseline state, their default mode. This tight bonding of the friends can lead to the exclusion of other kids in the classroom; the tight binding of these midline front-to-back areas can exclude involvement of other regions of the brain and body.

One of the key components of this midline network is an area called the *posterior cingulate cortex*, or PCC. The PCC, in anatomic and functional terms, can be considered a coordinating node of the DMN, a kind of ringleader of the clique of kids at school. Working closely with the PCC is a frontal midline area called the *ventral medial prefrontal cortex*, which plays a crucial role in social cognition and theory of mind—thinking about the mind in others and in oneself (along with other non-midline DMN areas we'll discuss later). When the PCC is activated along with other areas of the default mode circuitry, we tend to have the subjective experience of thinking about ourselves, or thinking about what others are thinking about us.

Sound familiar? It's like the refrain of many a love song: "Will you still love me tomorrow?" That's a crooning DMN. This region plays an important role in situating ourselves mentally in the social world, and even the world of defining our inner sense of self.

The DMN can facilitate a sense of our inner, mental lives, and also focuses on others' mental states. As social creatures, understanding the focus of attention, the intentions, and the awareness of another person—understanding their mental state—can be essential to our surviving and thriving. In this way, social awareness and self-awareness may be woven from the same cloth. And each of these ways in which we are aware of the mind itself, aware of the subjective experience of self and other, helps us achieve homeostasis.

If the DMN becomes isolated, the sense of self may feel isolated as well. In this case when the DMN is not integrated with the rest of the brain and body, we can propose, its capacity for focusing on mental states may construct a sense of a solo self, and become especially concerned about the mental states of others and how those states refer to us. In Hollywood the joke is often stated this way: "Enough about me. Now, what do *you* think about me?" This self-preoccupation is naturally a part of our social brain's concern about how we fit in, but it can go beyond that, sometimes defining a private self that may become obsessed with the status of the self, preoccupied with where a self-concerned self fits into the world. There's potentially lots of solo-selfing here, and less about interconnection and a broader sense of who we are. This self-obsession, we can imagine, may come from a DMN excessively linked within its own circuitry, and not connecting to the wider neural systems in the brain, the body as a whole, or even the flow from others and the larger world. This is what we mean by suggesting that an excessively differentiated DMN is like a clique that excludes the other kids at school. A more integrated DMN would instead involve processes of empathy and compassion, as well as a flexible form of self-awareness, harnessing the power of our social brains to focus beyond solo-self preoccupation. Because the DMN is about the minds of ourselves and others, my acronym-addicted mind has nicknamed this network the OATS circuitry, as it focuses our mind's attention on concerns about the status of others and the self.

Others
And
The
Self
= OATS

If this DMN is well integrated with other neural areas and the social world, it can mean empathy and insight emerge as these default mode areas facilitate our social cognition and self-awareness, the way we see the mind of others and the self. But if the DMN is too differentiated and not linked well with the other regions, then this OATS activity may create distress about exclusion, obsession with others' responses, and preoccupation that becomes associated with anxiety and depression. The DMN is not good or bad by itself; it is simply that without integration, as we've pointed out, it can lead to states of rigid or chaotic internal mental activities and external behaviors. We are proposing that, with a more integrated DMN, we can make sense of life and relax these preoccupations with feeling left out and inadequate as was perseverate on excessive issues of self-concern.

HOW TO INTEGRATE THE DMN

When we get to the third segment of the rim, there may be a lot of solo OATS activity from the default mode, a kind of monkey mind chatter filled with discursive internal dialogues, the thinking and preoccupation with the status of the self and its relation to others. Research from psychologists Zindel Segal, Norman Farb, and their colleagues reveals that without mindfulness training, many subjects have very robust PCC and related DMN activity that is hard to quiet down, even if they're given a task to simply be aware of sensations. Instead of going with the conduit flow of sensory input from the outside world or the body—our Wheel's first and second segments— many untrained subjects respond with preoccupation about the self and the constructed responses of the self-concerned meaning of experience. If this were with our Wheel practice, we'd see a lot of third segment constructed mental activities instead of the flow of conduit streams of sensation of the first and second rim segments of the Wheel.

This research has powerfully demonstrated a simple finding that has a visually concrete way of being remembered. The DMN is mostly midline, and when not integrated well, it mediates a lot of worries and self-referential thinking. The side areas, what are called *lateralized circuits*, including the anterior insula mediating our perception of the body's state, enable our sensory processing to flow and enter awareness. This is how we sense the rim elements of our first two segments of the Wheel. When we are aware of the first five senses or the interior of the body, the sixth sense of interoception, we are activating our lateral circuitry.

These lateral circuits are the neural correlates of the mechanism for the sensory conduit function of the mind—the energy flow patterns from the outside world and the somatic world of our first two rim segments. In contrast, we can build complex energy patterns into information that represents intricate ideas, including constructed views of the self and concerns about our place in the world. Construction in the mind has the neural correlate of activity in the limbic and cortical areas, including but certainly not limited to the mostly midline DMN. Our sense of self in the social world may arise as energy patterns from the cortical constructions of the DMN. How tightly linked together these differentiated nodes are within the DMN to the exclusion of other areas, such as the lateralized sensory circuitry, will shape the nature and intensity of the construction of the self we experience in awareness. This sense of self is a construction of mind shaped, in part, by the experientially molded circuits of the brain.

Construction does not have to be self-preoccupied, but with excessive differentiation of the network and its underdeveloped linkage to other areas, such an unintegrated DMN may be the mechanism underlying a solo-self OATS dominant preoccupation in our default constructions, our baseline mental chatter. During the Wheel practice, you may get a sense of this as distractions that pull your attention away from the focus on sensation; or you may experience this default mode of information processing during the open awareness of the third segment review. These circuits are formed in the crucible of our experiences—with parents, peers, teachers, and the larger culture in which we live. And as we'll see, they can be shaped directly by meditative practice, mind training that research suggests creates a more integrated DMN. This means a DMN that is less isolated and more linked to other functions of the brain itself in ways that would create a less solo-self OATS preoccupation.

The side sensory circuits mediating conduition and the midline DMN construction circuits of our OATS preoccupation are mutually inhibitory. In other words, conduition slows down construction; likewise, construction slows down conduition. Get in a jag of midline DMN self-preoccupation and lateralized sensory flow is minimized. Focus on the sensory flow of the first two segments of the rim and the midline DMN will be temporarily quieted. Train that distinction between conduit sensation and constructive thought over time and you'll be likely to alter your default mode way of being in the world.

Here is the powerful finding from this research, which you may find consistent with your own subjective experience: When you get in the conduit flow of sensation, the constructed discursive thunder of the storms of thought quiet down. Sensation from the side regions and midline mental chatter inhibit each other.

Lost in thought, low in sensation; flow in sensation, quiet in thought.

With mind training, the lateralized sensory circuits of the brain become more differentiated and able to hold their own, so when tasked with sensing experience, awareness can be more readily filled with sensation rather than constructed thought. Once this differentiation is established, the conduition of sensation can become linked to the overall functioning of the brain. With this differentiation and then linkage of sensation, the individual achieves higher states of whole-brain integration. This is how the side sensory regions mediating sensation are strengthened during practice in contrast to the rumination of the excessively differentiated midline default areas that, for most of us, dominate in the "chatter" of the mind. Just being with sensation quiets self-preoccupation. This is a powerfully helpful finding from rigorous research illuminating a useful mechanism of the mind.

As Nobel Laureate Elizabeth Blackburn and her research colleague and coauthor Elissa Epel suggest:

> We are largely unaware of the mental chatter in our minds, and how it affects us. Certain thought patterns appear to be unhealthy for telomeres. These include thought suppression and rumination as well as the negative thinking that characterizes hostility and pessimism. We can't totally change our automatic thought response—some of us are born ruminators or pessimists—but we can learn how to keep these automatic patterns from hurting us and even find humor in them. Here we invite you to become more aware of your habits of mind. Learning about your styles of thinking can be surprising and empowering.*

---

* Elizabeth Blackburn and Elissa Epel, *The Telomere Effect* (New York: Grand Central Publishing, 2017), 100.

They go on to state, "Self-awareness of tendencies that make us more vulnerable to stress reactivity (and possibly telomere shortening, in several studies) is valuable! Awareness can help us notice unhealthy thought patterns and choose different responses. It can also help us know and accept our tendencies. As Aristotle said, 'Knowing yourself is the beginning of all wisdom.'"*

An excessively active default mode network is considered by some scientists to be a neural correlate of excessive preoccupation with the self, one possible mechanism for negative ruminations. For some individuals, this isolated DMN activity may reveal ways that experience within families and the larger culture have reinforced a sense of a separate, solo self. Ideally, in connection we would grow toward a more integrated self that has differentiation and autonomy as well as linkage and belonging—a way of being a member of a group without losing individual identity. This would be an integrated experience of self in the world, one that would likely be associated with a deeper sense of connection and meaning in life. Living a life with a sense of purpose can even improve your body's state by optimizing telomeres, as Blackburn and Epel suggest: "The more that the meditators improved on scores of purpose in life, the higher their telomerase. Meditation, if it is of interest to you, is, obviously, one important way to enhance your own purpose in life. There are innumerable ways, and it depends on what is meaningful to you."†

Ironically, without an integrated sense of self—one with differentiation and linkage—constructing a separate self-identity may be an attempt to avoid the experience of obliteration feared by joining a larger whole. For a number of reasons, we might see the construction of a rigid definition of the self to avoid the chaos of merging and

---

* Blackburn and Epel, *The Telomere Effect*, 133.
† Ibid., 116.

losing any sense of self at all. The outcome of such rigid and chaotic manifestations of these nonintegrated senses of self may be in an excessively autonomous and differentiated DMN, making it more activated and less integrated, and giving the individual a feeling of disconnection and potential sense of lack of meaning or purpose in life.

Consider this notion: Our sense of self in the world may feel so fragile that we construct a nounlike fixed notion of who we are. This rigid sense of identity is understandably attempting to help us create homeostasis, but its inflexibility simply reinforces its own excessively differentiated nature. Without embracing the more fluid, verblike nature of self as an unfolding, emergent process, we are left with the differentiation without linkage as a solo self. This stance, when taken to an extreme, may make the individual prone to a number of problems that researchers and clinicians call difficulties with self-regulation, conditions that range from anxiety and depression to addiction and social isolation.

LOOSENING THE GRIP OF A SEPARATE SELF

Research has revealed that with mind training, the excessively differentiated and tight binding of the PCC with other nodes of the default mode such as the medial prefrontal cortex actually becomes less dominant in its isolated activity and more an integrated part of the now more accessible full spectrum of the brain's activity. What this finding may reveal is how a more integrated sense of self emerges as the brain's activity itself becomes more integrated as a result of mind training, an experience you may be having now, as others have reported, with continuation of the Wheel practice.

Construction in the mind by itself is not a problem. A balance of the construction of thought with sensory conduition may be the integration of the mind we can seek. Excessive and isolated forms of construction that emerge as self-preoccupation may reveal block-ages to a more integrative way the mind could function. Neuro-science and clinical researcher Judson Brewer has demonstrated the power of mind training to fight off addiction and anxiety by making a previously PCC-dominant mode more a part of an inte-grated whole. In other words, this research supports the view that too much differentiation of the default mode without linkage to other regions can be seen as a neural sign of impediments to integra-tion and health. The result of this impaired integration is the chaos and rigidity of depression, anxiety, and addiction as sources of human suffering.

Put simply, many people may live with excessively differentiated DMN circuitry whose activation makes them prone to the rumina-tions of self-preoccupation, comparing themselves with others, feel-ing inadequate, and becoming filled with a number of other causes of emotional distress.

Imagine the self-reinforcing loop that can be created with such a situation. It's like overworking one set of muscles to the exclusion of others in your body, leading to physical imbalance. Recall the axiom that where attention goes, neural firing flows, and neural connection grows. Repeated preoccupation mediated by an overactive and iso-lated DMN can increase the strength of these internal DMN connec-tions with each other, linking the nodes of the network in a tightly bound and now more isolated way.

It's helpful to keep in mind that attention does not have to be guided by you or even need to involve consciousness for it to strengthen neural connections. Attention merely directs the flow of energy and information. When that attention is within us, the neural firing patterns are repeatedly activated. Cultural messages of sep-arateness can also direct our attention, even without our awareness, and these messages of a separate and inadequate self can become em-bedded in the brain. How? Our limbic appraisal systems and other aspects of our social brain closely monitor our place in the world and make an association between social inclusion and the evaluation of meaning. It matters to be a member. If we get messages from social media or other aspects of our society that we are not good enough, that there is something wrong with our gender, our race, our sexual orientation, or even more generally that who we are is separate and insufficient, these packets of information can enter the nervous system and shape where attention goes, whether we are aware of them or not.

Unfortunately, a life reinforced in our modern society that may tend to isolate and dehumanize people, making them feel disrespected, disempowered, and discarded from the larger community, can repeatedly send our non-focal as well as focal attention into a neuroplastic loop that continuously emphasizes a sense of our selves as being separate and inadequate. We walk through life unaccompanied, without a sense of belonging or support. In turn, this repeated experience of isolation reinforces the neural connections that affirm this status of the separateness of the self.

Finding a way to make communities more welcoming and inclusive naturally is an important step to take in helping change this societal focus on a separate self. Belonging is a basic human need. In addition, meditative practice—the three pillars of focused attention, open awareness, and kind intention—has been shown in research studies to loosen this tightly bound DMN activity and may help with the cultivation of a more integrated sense of self and a more receptive way of finding connection in community. In this way, reflective practices like the Wheel of Awareness, which includes these three pillars, may lead to changing this baseline trait by creating a more integrative state that, with repetition during practice, becomes a new baseline, with the integrative traits of a kinder, more compassionate individual. Mind training can change our default mode and make it more integrated in our lives.

CLINGING VERSUS ATTACHMENT

As we have discussed, mind-training practices have been found to loosen the tightly bound neural functioning of the DMN. Other studies have suggested that meditative practices may also diminish the intensity of our vertically distributed reward system—extending from the brain stem (your palm), up through the limbic area (your thumb), and into the cortex (your folded fingers). This shift in the reward system can diminish the hold of cravings on our behavior, a change that most certainly can improve our chances for health and happiness in our lives. These neural regions share the neurotransmitter called dopamine. When dopamine is released by and into this system, we feel rewarded. The things that reward us are shaped by this dopamine-mediated reward system, so an activity leading to a squirt of the neurotransmitter makes us feel, "That was rewarding—let me do that again to have more of that." I get a big dopamine hit with dark chocolate, for sure. If we can do something to lower the intensity of that release—not to remove dopamine from our lives entirely but to decrease, for example, the rapid speed of its discharge in our brain—we can become less invested in and less compulsively driven toward things, whether they are substances or activities, that we may otherwise become addicted to. This change in the dopamine release can free us from being so intensely invested in things that in fact may not be good for us.

In important ways, the shift in the reward system's functioning, along with an expanded sense of awareness in the hub, may allow us the mental space and neural functions to differentiate the feeling of *liking* something and being able to choose it, or not, from that of *wanting* or *needing* something that may get us to crave and cling to that thing. Even in the reward system regions, these two processes of *like* versus *want* appear to be mediated in slightly distinct regions. When I see the chocolate and feel aware that I like it, I can take it or leave it. I am complete knowing I like something even if I don't have that thing. I can choose my behavior. If instead I don't distinguish liking from wanting, if these become mixed up in my mind with an intensely activated reward system and limited access to my hub of being aware, then the object I like—a bar of chocolate—becomes something I want and my behavior is no longer under my conscious control.

In some circles the phrase used for such craving is "becoming attached to" something; however, I tend not to use it because the word *attached* in my field of attachment research refers to the love between a parent and a child. So let's use the term *clinging* for that sense of being drawn to something and unable to let it go, even if it isn't good for you. When we do not distinguish the sense of liking something and the gratitude we may have for that enjoyment from the feeling of wanting something and its sense of craving and clinging, we are vulnerable to addiction and a sense of inadequacy. Without the thing, we are incomplete. With diminished intensity of the reward circuitry's release of dopamine following mind training, as revealed in preliminary studies, we can see that a sense of *a more open mind comes along with an ease of well-being as clinging is naturally diminished.* You can take it or leave it; the decision is up to you, not your reward circuit. Imagine walking the earth with a feeling of wholeness and completion rather than insufficiency and clinging. You can be grateful for what you enjoy, not longing for what you are missing. That's a difference that makes a difference.

I think it is important to point out here that the things we can find ourselves clinging to—from me with my chocolate to a person in an unhealthy relationship clinging to someone who is ultimately not good for them—may include our ways of thinking and relating to our inner sense of self. There might actually be a clinging to a separate self with self-preoccupation that can become a form of addiction. Like all such ways of becoming consumed with something and unable to shift gears away from our preoccupation with it, craving and addiction seem to be mediated by the dopamine reward circuitry of the brain. Put in simple terms, research shows that obsessing about the self can be just as addicting as any addictive substance—it actually activates our reward system. A look at our current obsession with social media can provide a helpful window into understanding this. We can wonder about some aspects of social media and the intense amount of time and energy being put into presenting images of the self to others, so much so that it could in fact be renamed a DMN media platform. Our OATS baseline circuitry becomes activated with social media, even as we may find ourselves becoming unsettled and feeling incomplete, as if something is missing if we cannot document ourselves as whole and good and acknowledged on a social media platform. Fear of missing out actually has its own acronym, FOMO. Sadly, so much of the time the images presented on these sites depict a positive spin on life that is rarely a reality. The audience for these images is often unaware of this mirage, feeling inadequate in their relentless comparison to the reality of their own lives.

OATS circuitries have gone wild in our digital world. Within this framework our reward systems give us the setup in which the dopamine release with solo-self-preoccupation gets us a temporary hit of "That felt rewarding" each time we post a fantasy image of ourselves, and the addiction to self-preoccupation is reinforced. No wonder people check their smartphones when driving. We can only imagine how a sense of never being quite done, never complete, never enough is massively amplifying the intensity of a DMN-mediated preoccupation with the inadequacy of the self in comparison to others. These feelings, as Antonio Damasio broadly suggests, are about homeostasis—about surviving and thriving. Pulling on the most basic aspects of our existence as social beings, a default mode network's concerns with others and the self is right at home, with a sense of vital urgency, in the social media world. This may be the OATS process gone digitally wild as it is put into hyperdrive. If only in response to the way social media has changed our lives—although there are many more reasons, to be sure—we need now more than ever practices for cultivating a more integrative way of being, of walking in the world with a sense of wholeness and true, meaningful connection.

If a sense of self is defined as a solo player, a mind in isolation, then the sad reality is that this nonintegrated way of living, with only an inner mind and not the fullness of the inter mind as well, makes the individual prone to feeling unsettled, incomplete, that something is missing in their life even before the lure of the positive spin of social media.

Part of the neural processes of loosening the tightly bound default mode would be to loosen the grip of solo-self-preoccupation, which would involve diminishing the reward system's response as well as lessening the tightly interconnected DMN components. These may be the mechanisms of changing the baseline default mode trait for an individual often described with meditative practice, a loosening of a separate self and a feeling of a more connected way of being in the world—of becoming more at ease in your own skin.

As you experience the third and fourth segments of the rim, you may find over time that this loosening of a separate self may begin to unfold. This is not something you need to make happen or worry about if it does not appear to be happening. It's not that the self disappears; the descriptions from many people I have heard who have practiced the Wheel are more that the sense of self becomes connected, extended, expanded, a part of something beyond the interiority of the skin-encased inner mind.

Here we are reminded of a powerful interface of the subjective and the objective. Subjectively, individuals repeatedly describe an expanded sense of their belonging to a larger whole, of becoming aware of their membership in an interconnected way of being. This broader sense of who the self is has a deep feeling of meaning and connection. Observing this pattern of an expanded subjective sense of self is an important empirical finding that is correlated with the objective findings of changes in the brain with mind-training practice.

The mechanism beneath this subjective mental experience of an expanded and connected sense of self may be the loosening of the previously tight connections of the DMN, which could be the neural mechanism of an excessively differentiated sense of a solo self. The good news about such loosening of the solo self is that depression and anxiety, as we've seen, seem to correlate with excessive default mode isolation. Even studies of rats being offered dopamine-releasing substances such as cocaine reveal that when they are living in isolation, they choose the cocaine over water or food—and then they die. But socially connected rats choose the water and food and avoid the cocaine. Amazing. Recall that we mammals are profoundly social creatures. So for a complex social being such as us humans to have a brain circuit—the DMN—that can, in contemporary culture, at least, become excessively differentiated within our skulls and create a sense of not belonging is a big deal. Our human brain's vulnerability to create a mental experience of identity as a solo self, one that lives in a mentally constructed and neurally mediated isolation from others, may be a huge source of suffering in our contemporary lives.

We are social beings. As we shall soon see, even our experience of being conscious may have its origins in our focusing attention on the inner, mental states of others. In this way, awareness of others' minds may be the precursor for awareness of our own inner, mental states. When our brains pick up the message of our separation from the larger social world, the very roots of identity and of being aware become constricted. This condition would be the opposite of what research on the electrical energy patterns during compassion practice reveals as the high degree of gamma waves activated when engaging our minds to focus on care for and connection with others. This neural electrical pattern of gamma waves occurs when broadly distributed areas of the brain balance and coordinate their functioning with one another—when the brain is in a state of integration. Those gamma waves were found to be highest with the non-referential sense of compassion, kindness, and love. This may be one aspect of the mechanism by which developing kind intention, along with focused attention and open awareness, supports the ways we can create more integration and cultivate more meaning and connection in our lives. As such, the Wheel practice may widen our sense of self as it makes our head brains—and our social selves—more integrated.

THE FOURTH SEGMENT OF THE RIM AND THE RELATIONAL MIND

As we turn toward the fourth segment of the rim, we can again ask what the mechanism of feeling connected to others versus feeling separate and alone really might be. What does a loosening of a separate self really mean? What does the experience, so often described as "being a part of a larger whole," as a subjective sense mean in terms of the actual workings of the mind, the brain, and our relational worlds? And what do the invitations to become aware of connection and have kind intention of compassionate concern imply in terms of fundamental mechanisms of the mind?

As we've discussed, when we invite ourselves to sense the connection to family and friends on the fourth segment of the rim, we may become aware of a sensory flow of energy, or we may be activating a constructed memory or imagined relational connection.

British scientist Michael Faraday proposed in the nineteenth century that electromagnetic fields, though not visible to the eye, existed in reality. My old dear friend John O'Donohue used to call himself a mystic, which he defined as someone who believes in the reality of the invisible. John, as a former Irish Catholic priest, philosopher, and poet, felt that the world was filled with interconnections we simply could not perceive directly with our eyes, but that were quite real. The book he released, just before his sudden death, is called *To Bless the Space Between Us*. That space between may be the inter aspect of mind we've been exploring.

If I feel a connection to John now, is that merely a memory of our relationship and our experiences together—something I am constructing, through the mechanisms of my brain's neural firing patterns? Or might it be something more—something I am sensing now, not constructed, but a form of sensory conduition? When I feel my connections now to people I know and love, or even to people I have never met, or to all living beings on this planet we share, is this just some construction of my head brain, or my body, something built by my inner mind? Or am I feeling some kind of field, as Faraday proposed, that I can't see with my eyes but that is quite real? Is this sense of connection stemming from my conduit intake of stimuli that is occurring in the here and now, a conduition of the flow of something happening now, or is it a construction being put together perhaps from neural firings of memory and imagination?

Though many disbelieved Michael Faraday back then, now most of our electronic gadgets are built upon these fields that he affirmed were real, even though so many at the time doubted their existence. Energy can be studied as waves, and these manifestations of energy can be transmitted across long distances. I once marveled with my farmer father-in-law, Neil Welch, his body now years gone, as he spoke with his grandson, Alex, via a visual image on my smartphone. How could he possibly be talking and seeing his grandson in a little box? Whether he was in the next room or all the way around the world (where he was at the time), it was a marvel to behold for me, and for Neil. If this were four hundred years ago, Neil and I would be burned at the stake for bringing dangerous magic into the world. Now we are just charged a monthly fee for the phone service.

Energy comes in many forms and from locations that are quite close to us or at a long distance, transforming in its CLIFF features. And energy can flow from far, far away. Sunlight is one example, and starlight another. When we sense light with the photoreceptors of our eyes, we don't get agitated and say, "Oh, that energy you are feeling as light is just your imagination; it's coming from a memory in your head!" We've come to accept that the sensory organs we have are a reliable measure of reality. But Neil and I could speak with Alex, see him, and connect with him using our sensory systems of sight and hearing, and yet the deeper mechanisms with which this smartphone gadget could translate invisible electromagnetic waves into accessible forms of light and sound remained in the background. Could this be the same with our minds? Is there some kind of conduition that allows something to flow and we simply become aware of this something as a sense of connection to a larger world beyond the boundaries of our skin?

When I was watching the live video of the proceedings of the United Nations on the 2030 strategic planning to promote well-being across the planet, I could feel the connection of many of the speakers to each other and to the future health of the world. My daughter was an intern in one of those rooms at the meeting, and I could imagine what she might be feeling working in such a global setting. Was this imagination, or might I have also been feeling something of her experience as she was there? We'll explore later the ways in which energy can flow across space as a force, whether it is light or sound or electricity. We also now know that regardless of location, energy can also be coupled in a way quantum physicists call *entanglement*. Spatial separation does not diminish the interconnectivity of coupled forms of energy. This coupling of energy, or entanglement, is now a proven aspect of the universe we live in. It's not a force flowing; it's a relationship between energy states that is not changed with spatial distance. I'm not suggesting that this is a proven way we are connected to one another, or that our minds are detecting this nonlocal impact of one mind to another, as we simply don't know this yet from scientifically established views of the nature of our mental lives. However we come to feel that interconnectivity, I am inviting you to think about ways you may have sensed something in your relationships with others, or with nature, that may reflect how you are receiving the input from feeling distant waves of energy, or perhaps—just perhaps—even your own entanglements with others or the world at large.

At a quantum physics think tank I once attended, the first speaker had on the initial slide of his presentation the following statement: "We've established through science that the world is deeply interconnected; the question is, what is wrong with the human brain that people think it is not?" To this I say indeed. Why do our brains tell us that we are not profoundly interconnected when in fact we are?

As physicist Carlo Rovelli suggests, "Physics opens windows through which we see far into the distance. What we see does not cease to astonish us. We realize that we are full of prejudices and that our intuitive image of the world is partial, parochial, inadequate. Earth is not flat; it is not stationary. The world continues to change before our eyes as we gradually see it more extensively and more clearly."*

Perhaps the mind, existing within the same world that physics studies, also has many characteristics that we do not consider in our current frameworks of understanding. If we open our minds to new possibilities, ones we may not even presently be able to imagine, we might be well suited to consider more fully the mechanisms of mind beneath our subjective experiences of life, our interconnectedness, and even the nature of how we become aware.

Rovelli continues, "Here, in the vanguard, beyond the borders of knowledge, science becomes even more beautiful—incandescent in the forge of nascent ideas, of intuitions, of attempts. Of roads not

---

* Carlo Rovelli, *Seven Brief Lessons on Physics* (New York: Riverhead Books, 2014), 49.

taken and then abandoned, of enthusiasms. In the effort to imagine what has not yet been imagined."*

We can sense connection, the fourth segment's focus, likely with a variety of mechanisms underneath that subjective sensation. Let's keep an open mind as to the ways in which the science of energy might or might not apply to our view of the mind as an emergent property of energy and the mechanisms underlying our capacity to sense our interconnections. The answer at this moment, from a scientific viewpoint, is that we don't know exactly what those mechanisms may in fact be for our fourth segment of the rim, our sense of interconnectedness.

A scientific stance reminds us that we live in a body, and this body we inhabit has a limited set of neural patterns with which to sense reality, be aware of those sensations, and even conceive of the nature of reality itself. What this means is that what we sense and what we think are, by the very nature of their arising from our bodies, quite limited. Reality doesn't really care if we can understand its fundamental mechanisms or not—those mechanisms exist independent of our awareness of them. But with a scientific stance, if we assume that there is a reality beyond our initial sensing or comprehending, then we can stay open to realizing aspects of that reality that, with an open and receptive mind, we can then come to appreciate more fully. Being scientific doesn't mean knowing everything; it means being humble and acknowledging our limitations while following our curiosity so that we can learn more as we grow, deepen, and broaden our skills of perceiving and knowing.

For years my colleagues Peter Senge and Otto Scharmer, working in the field of systems science at the Massachusetts Institute of Technology, have been exploring the nature of *relational fields* and how these social systems influence the ways we interact with one

---

* Rovelli, *Seven Brief Lessons on Physics*, 41–42.

another. When relational fields support compassionate connections and inspire collaboration and creativity, they're called *generative social fields*. In the work we are doing together, our hope is that we can study these ways our interconnections support a healthier, more integrated world. What the mechanisms are beneath these relational fields, we just don't know at this time. If our explorations of the inner and inter nature of the mind with the Wheel practice are relevant, there may be a useful application of the notion of energy, including its non-visible fields, as well as the fundamental process of integration in illuminating a path to cultivating more generative social fields in our world.

GROWING AN INTEGRATED BRAIN WITH MIND TRAINING

With the focused attention training all along the Wheel's first and second segments of the rim, we'd be activating the energy of regions of the body and its brains within the head, gut, and heart that are involved in streaming energy and information flow into awareness. Neural correlates of this attentional practice within the head brain involve prefrontal regions just behind the forehead; in your hand model these are the parts near the fingernails up to the first knuckles. These prefrontal regions work in concert with the anterior cingulate—in your limbic thumb region—and with practice are likely growing connections as we develop the ability to sustain attention; note distractions with our salience circuitry, which also includes the insula; and then redirect attention.

Several areas of neural change with overall mind-training practice have been revealed. One is that aspects of this prefrontal cortex grow, supporting the finding that energy and information regulation is enhanced in terms of strengthened attention and emotion regulation. The prefrontal region broadly links cortex, limbic area, brain stem, body proper, and the social world into one interconnected whole. The regulation that arises from this neural integration helps shape emotion and mood, attention and thought, relationships and morality. These are all part of what are termed executive functions, and they arise from integration.

Another region that changes with mind-training practice is the limbic area. The hippocampus grows with practice and serves as a neural node linking widely separated areas and supporting memory processing; it is also related to emotion regulation. In some studies, too, an enlarged amygdala, likely involved in intense emotional re-activity when it is excessively differentiated, is found to become smaller with meditation practice.

A third region that grows with mind-training practice is the corpus callosum, building the connections between the differentiated right and left sides of the brain. In addition to these specific ways the head brain appears to become more integrated, a fourth finding emerges in studies that use new ways of looking at the integrative state of the brain. As mentioned earlier, the "human connectome studies," by utilizing advanced technology to show how distinct areas are linked throughout the brain, reveal that mind-training practice makes the brain's differentiated regions more interconnected. Part of this more integrated neural system growth is also revealed in the finding we've discussed about the default mode network, loosening the tight linkages within an excessively differentiated and isolated default mode system. Even studies of the connection of the head brain to the heart brain (the neural network surrounding the heart) show more functional linkages, especially with the compassion training programs that support the growth of kind intention, as we've seen.

Studies of compassion in expert meditators reveal that the brain's functioning has high degrees of electrical signals of integration during practice—in the baseline state while awake, and even while asleep. As stated earlier, these gamma waves emerge as differentiated areas of the brain become coordinated and linked with one another. The finding of gamma with compassion supports the notion that a possible mechanism beneath statements of kind intention is that they are promoting states of neural integration.

As integration appears to be the basis for healthy regulation, we can see that meditative practice may work at the brain level in how it promotes the growth of integration. The Wheel of Awareness, as we've seen from the beginning, has each of the three pillars of mind training, cultivating focused attention, open awareness, and kind intention, and so with future research we would anticipate that across subjects we would find these same neural correlates of growth and integration.

We come now to the experience of open awareness. While being aware of the contents of awareness helps us to let go of distractions in the focused attention training, redirecting our attention when it has become distracted, the state of pure receptive awareness with open monitoring may involve something a bit different than salience monitoring and redirection. At one level, enabling anything from the rim to arise and simply being aware of that from the hub is clearly a form of metaphoric integration, differentiating and linking the knowns and the knowing. But what might the mechanism beyond the metaphor possibly be here? While there is no one neural signature of being mindful because so many neural firings underlying the awareness of rim points might emerge with any given focus, we can ask what simply being open to whatever arises might involve—what's the mechanism of pure awareness?

If the rim points of the Wheel practice are, in mechanism terms, forms of energy and information flow as we've been exploring, what might the hub itself actually *be*? How does the hub become connected to the rim as we focus the spoke's focal attention and become aware of a rim point? So far, the notion of energy has fit well with our exploration of possible mechanisms beneath the wheel's rim, and even its spoke. But what is the mechanism of the hub? *If* pure awareness is related to energy flow, what might the wheel's hub of knowing—the experience of being aware—and the spoke of focal attention streaming energy into the hub actually arise from, if *arising* is even the right word?

To attempt to address these fascinating and practical questions of what the mechanisms of mind underlying awareness might actually be, let's continue in our next sections with a deeper dive into what findings from brain research reveal and then focus on the nature of energy itself.

INTEGRATION IN THE BRAIN AND THE SPOKE OF FOCAL ATTENTION

HOW AND WHERE DOES AWARENESS ARISE?

We come now to the question of how we become aware of these patterns of energy and information, these knowns of consciousness. How does the metaphoric spoke of attention—of focal attention— actually make the energy pattern of the rim enter the knowing of the hub? What might be the mechanisms of mind underlying our subjective experience of focal attention and being aware? If subjective experience is the felt texture of lived life we have within awareness, what might this awareness actually be? What is the mechanism symbolized by the metaphor of the spoke and the hub?

The simplest response to these fundamental questions about the mechanisms of mind underlying being aware, as we've seen, is that at this point we do not have an absolute answer. We have ideas, yes, but a final answer, no.

Being aware seems to involve a linking of differentiated parts in the brain. The overall perspective derived from this kind of pattern, as we'll discuss soon, is called the *integrated information theory* of consciousness and proposes that some degree of integration—the linking of different parts of the brain—is needed for awareness of something to arise. For example, when we hear a sound and become aware of the felt texture of the sound, the brain has achieved a certain level of coordination of a range of areas at the moment we know we are hearing the sound. How and why this degree of integration would determine the subjective experience of being aware, we just don't know.

In reality, we don't really know if the causal sequence is in one direction, as many believe—that brain creates mental experience. That is an assumption that needs to be questioned with, well, an open mind.

Even if the mind needs a brain to exist, we can still envision how the mind can get the brain to function in ways the mind initiates and the brain then follows.

These practices teach us that with intention, using our attention, we can develop our awareness—each aspect of the mind—to actually get the brain to become active in new ways that change and strengthen its physical structure. That capacity to use the mind to train the brain is the basis for the notion that where attention goes, neural firing flows, and neural connection grows. *Attention and awareness are mental processes that enable the mind to shape the brain in integrative ways that strengthen the mind itself.*

Using consciousness, we can cultivate the structure of the brain in helpful ways. We can understand these research-established steps with which the mind can change brain by realizing an often-dismissed view: Mind and brain, while related to each other, are in fact not the same. Does the mind need a body? From a scientific perspective, many would say yes. But does this mean the mind is the same as the body's brain? Not at all. And it does not even mean that the mind is limited to the brain, or perhaps even the body, as we've seen in our discussion of an inter mind.

We're not saying mind is independent of the brain or the body; we're merely pointing out that the mind is not a passive rider on the brain's firing patterns. The mind's subjective experience is simply not the same as neural firing, even if it turns out to be completely dependent upon it. Mind can direct that firing of its own accord.

But what exactly is the mechanism of this consciousness, our mind's experience of being aware, our capacity of knowing subjective experience, and how might it relate to the brain?

A broad overview of consciousness perspectives encompasses a spectrum of viewpoints that include seeing mind and consciousness as only enskulled and a function of the head brain; viewing them as fully embodied, not just in the head; thinking of them as being extended into our culture and embedded in our social connections; and seeing consciousness as a more universal process related to all objects or to a larger force of a god, as in theism. We will not resolve this wide spectrum of intensely held beliefs here, but simply invite you to realize that scholars continue to debate the nature of mind and consciousness with a wide range of perspectives.

Some contemporary science-trained writers and thinkers, such as the physicians Neil Theise, Larry Dossey, and Deepak Chopra, along with neuroscientist Rudy Tanzi and physicist Menas Kafatos, have suggested that consciousness is not limited to our brains or bodies. Kafatos, Theise, and others discuss the notion of *panpsychism*, the proposal that the mind is in all things. In these views, consciousness arises in the universe and not in the head brain or only from the body. Buddhism proposes a universal, background consciousness that underlies everything and shapes how we live our lives and repeat our lives with reincarnation. This larger consciousness is an inherent fabric of reality. In some of the other views shared by ancient wisdom traditions and many of the world's religions, such as Christianity, Judaism, Hinduism, and the Islamic faith, a related notion of a god or gods who are all-present and all-knowing is also at the heart of what is believed.

Carl Jung wrote about a collective unconscious that unites us in ways we cannot see. As I mentioned earlier, the former Irish Catholic priest John O'Donohue's view, which was also rooted in Celtic mysticism, embraced the perspective that the world is filled with unseen forces that shape our lives each glorious and mysterious day. The unseen nature of reality fueled Michael Faraday's proposal in the 1800s of invisible electromagnetic waves, a disbelieved view that is now an accepted aspect of the universe, even if we cannot see these waves of energy. John and I would wonder and wander in our various travels and teachings together in the United States and Ireland, reflecting on what a consilience between a spiritual view and a neuroscience-based view of consciousness might include. Sadly, he died before I could articulate to him much of what you and I will be exploring soon, a view that suggests a possible way to bridge the fields of science and spirituality. If John were still alive, I think he would have loved to join us on this journey—and we would have "had the craic" doing it, as they say in Ireland, laughing and having a grand old time.

We will not solve the issue here of *where* exactly consciousness rests or where the mind arises from—be it in the head, in the body, between people, in the universe—as it is a yet unanswered (but important) question. Resting in the uncertainty of where mind arises may itself be a part of understanding the true nature of mind. After all, we are using our minds to understand our minds, a venture worth a lifetime but likely not solvable even if the journey is fruitful. The name of our species, after all, is *Homo sapiens sapiens*—the ones who know we know. Exploring the mind's true nature, which we experience each time we do the Wheel of Awareness practice, is something that can help our lives in a powerful way even without final answers about its origins and even if the journey leads to ever more questions about the nature of who we are and why we are here.

As we move into the next section's exploration of the nature of the possible mechanisms of the hub, let's keep in the front of our open minds that you will have your own direct experience within both the reading of these ideas as well as in your continued practice with the Wheel. You and I can throw ideas back and forth—I into these pages, you from the pages into your mind and back into the further reading. How the Wheel unfolds for you now as you take in these concepts and let them wash through you as you do the practice on a regular basis will enable you to feel, sense, and experience which of them might be of help, or not, in illuminating the nature of your mind and opening awareness in your life.

One of my students in Ireland, working on his degree in the philosophy of mind, was recently told by his advisor to narrow his focus from the topic he and I were working on—what is the mind—to a "more attainable discussion," and they chose as his new dissertation topic "the meaning of life." We both laughed at the supportive suggestion that the question of what the mind actually is was far more challenging than defining the meaning of life!

Although we do not yet fully understand what scientists refer to as the "neural correlates of consciousness," exploring what we do know or even what has been theorized can be useful in getting one sense of the neural mechanisms underlying our Wheel practice. Philosopher David Chalmers has called the question about mental subjectivity and neural objectivity the "hard problem" of truly understanding how the material experience of neural firing could become the mental subjective experience of being aware. Some scientists find this view unhelpful in that they see neural correlates as the only way in which mental experience arises—for them there is no problem, much less a hard one. Somehow, consciousness simply arises from brain activity. For example, Antonio Damasio views our basic felt texture of consciousness—our feelings—as simply bodily states that we become aware of. There's no hard problem; there's just the reality of living in a body that has a drive toward homeostasis.

As stated by Oliver Wendell Holmes in the epigraph to this book, "A mind that is stretched to a new idea never returns to its original dimension." One idea to consider is that the mind's consciousness can get the brain to change its function and structure. Knowing how the brain and mind interact is a way we prepare our minds to take this new idea and apply it in practical ways. With this quote as inspiration to stretch our minds and our awareness—to make larger that container of water I mentioned at the beginning of this book—we'll explore some of the theories about the correlations between the brain's neural firing and our mental experience of consciousness so that we can best use these ideas to bring well-being into our lives. But even if we did find all the correlations, all the neural patterns activated during the experience of being aware, would we truly understand how neural firing "turns into consciousness," or would we still not have the answer? That's a wonderful and fascinating big unknown in the field of knowledge about our lives. For that reason, after we explore some of the notions of the brain and consciousness, it may be helpful to turn to another form of science to address this question about the mechanism of awareness—the science of energy itself.

The linear question "How does the brain create consciousness?" may not even be the right question to ask. Why? Because the experience of consciousness on the one hand may simply be an emergent property of the *whole body's processing* of energy and information flow and in this way cannot be reduced to neural firing in the head. Even if we have scanners examining only neural activity inside the skull, these understandably focused studies may be missing the ways the rest of the body, sitting outside the scanner, are crucially participating in a body-based consciousness. That would be missing the larger bodily system from which consciousness arose. And for those scientists and others who consider even broader systems involved in being aware, even the body might not be providing all the insights we need to understand the mechanisms of consciousness.

As we move ahead, let's try to keep an open mind about it all.

Let's also try to be consistent with science, but not constrained by it. What I mean is that the fact that science says this or that at this moment in our understanding does not make that the final word or the absolute truth about a given issue. Let's also keep in mind that correlation is not causation. Just because science reveals some observation, it does not mean it is the origin of something—like consciousness, for example, being correlated with various aspects of the brain's activity. Let's also recall that our beliefs, as mental models, can also selectively sample what we become aware of, whether it is in our interpretation of the meaning of experience, or how we make sense of empirical findings. Those mental models can be built from a sense of self in the world that prides itself on knowing what the world is, what the self is, what to anticipate, and how to survive with that self-in-world view. For this reason alone, we may cling to our viewpoints with an implicit sense of survival being at risk—and that may be why for some, if not many individuals, these proposals especially about the nature of the mind, and consciousness in particular, have such fire behind them. Let's let the flame of our passions light the way but not burn down our capacity for collaboration and seeking consilience— a common ground across usually independent pursuits.

AWARENESS AND THE INTEGRATION OF INFORMATION

There are many fascinating hypotheses about the correlation between brain functioning and the experience of consciousness. Here we will review concepts relevant for our exploration and practice of the Wheel of Awareness and continue to connect these proposals to our immersion in the practice itself.

One view, supported by the writings of scientists such as Giulio Tononi, Gerald Edelman, and Christof Koch, is that there is some degree of simultaneous neural activity among the firing of distinct regions of the brain and how they connect with one another in the head, resulting in the experience of being conscious. This is the integrated information theory of consciousness. Consistent with this theory, Judson Brewer and colleagues, for example, have studied something called "effortless awareness," akin to open awareness and the open monitoring process, and found it arises with states of neural integration.

There are various forms of consciousness, with a range of names, that have distinct correlations to the activity of specific neural networks. For instance, if someone has a stroke that impacts the brain stem region, a coma is likely to ensue. In the brain we'd correlate *basic* aspects of consciousness with the brain stem area, deep in your brain (at the palm of your hand model). Basic consciousness—being awake—requires brain stem integrity. Another example would be *interoceptive awareness*, those "gut feelings" and "heartfelt sensations" we all have wherein the "knowing" is accompanied by distinct sensations from the body. Scientists have monitored subjects' experiences of this form of consciousness and have measured neural activity in the particular regions of the brain, including the anterior insula, which we've discussed. As you move up your hand model from the basic brain stem toward the limbic thumb and prefrontal regions of the fingers above it, you'll find the neural regions that correlate with this interoceptive awareness of bodily states. As we've seen, the neural maps that are created by the limbic-prefrontal insula support this representation of the body in awareness. We call this process a feeling. And yet consciousness has so many shades and colors that to measure them all as actual occurrences in the brain is not possible—and so we look for broad patterns that help give a sense of the fundamental aspect of neural activity that is associated with the subjective experience of being aware. One of those broad patterns is the process of neural integration—the linking of differentiated areas to each other.

Further up in the brain, the various proposals suggest, a higher degree of complexity is achieved in the cortex, the fingers in your hand model. Working with a range of regions such as the dorsolateral prefrontal cortex (the side top of the prefrontal region correlating with the ends of your fingers) and the anterior cingulate cortex bridging the limbic and cortical regions (where the thumb meets your fingers), brain activity correlates with the "chalkboard of the mind" or working memory, with which items can be reflected upon, sorted, and then processed further within consciousness. More midline areas involving the medial prefrontal area (the middle two fingernail areas in your hand model) and other aspects of the default mode network, such as the posterior cingulate cortex, which we've discussed, participate in the awareness of our own or others' inner, mental states, something involving meta-awareness enabling our awareness of awareness, introspection, and theory of mind. When we direct that focus on our own inner state, scientists call this self-knowing experience "autonoetic consciousness." This *self-knowing*

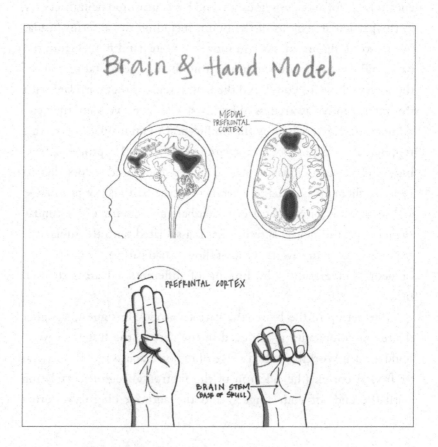

awareness involves insight, or mental time travel—connecting the past, present, and future. This is how the midline DMN activity correlates with a "sense of self" and is involved in the autobiographical narrative of our lives.

This brain-based view of the integrative complexity of information giving rise, somehow, to consciousness, fits well with our Wheel experience. We move attention around the rim, systematically directing the spoke of focal attention, as we integrate what we'd call energy patterns that are the mechanism beneath the integration of information that these views propose. We are consistent with the scientific findings, extending them by speaking directly about what information is, a pattern of energy. As we've seen, some mathematicians and physicists might suggest that it is the other way around, that the universe comprises information that then gives rise to energy. If we stay close to the concept of *energy and information* we can see that both groups, proponents of energy-as-primary and those of information-as-primary, will have their viewpoints met. And each of them agrees that things change, which is what the term *flow* indicates.

Okay, so we continue to be consistent with the science in suggesting energy and information flow is the fundamental mechanism of the Wheel. Now we can add the notion that integration may be fundamental to being aware.

ATTENTION, CONSCIOUSNESS, AND THE SOCIAL BRAIN

This perspective of integration of energy and information flow is also supported by another brain-based proposal, one that builds on the integration-of-information view and extends it to the social realm. This is how that extended perspective can be understood. Our evolution as human beings is dominated by our social nature. Sarah Hrdy writes in her anthropological explorations of *alloparenting*, that we as human mammals have the unusual feature of sharing the care of our young (parenting) with others (allo). What this meant in our evolution is that our ability to survive and thrive as a species depended upon us looking to others to figure out where their attention was being focused, what their intentions were, and if we could trust them with the care of our most precious resource, our young. At the behavioral level, this made us collaborative in our fundamental nature. It also made us "mind readers" in that we had to take the signals from others, noting their expressions, gestures, and behaviors, and interpret their mental states of intention, attention, and motivation. To protect our infants and ensure that they would be well taken care of by our chosen alloparents, we needed to be able to ask and attempt to answer some basic questions. How was this potential care provider's mind functioning in this moment? Could we trust this person or not? To answer these questions that were essential for the passing on of our genes, we needed the neural machinery to sense the mental states of attention, intention, and even awareness of another person. This view suggests that our capacity to sense the mind began as an activity directed to the other person—not to our inner selves. Theory of mind, mentalization, mind-mindedness, psychological mindedness, and even mindsight are all concepts indicating our capacity to make a map of the mind—of the other and of the self.

Mindsight's insight and empathy, then, may have their origins in first needing to know the mind of another, to have empathy skills, and then learning to focus that skill of mapping the mind onto our own inner life. Mindsight's third aspect of integration may be fundamental to awareness, and even to kindness and compassion, so we can see that our social nature and our experience of consciousness may be woven from a similar cloth, as revealed in these three aspects of mindsight skills—insight, empathy, and integration.

In our development as a species, this perspective on the social brain suggests empathy came first, and then insight followed. That order seems to fit with our view of an individual's development within attachment relationships as well, a pattern in which we view the communication with the caregiver as the mirror with which an infant first learns of her own inner state. We learn to see ourselves first in the responses of the caregiving other. This interpersonal origin of who we feel we are and how we come to know our "selves" is a key to imagining how the social world may become embedded in the structure of the brain, and perhaps how the default mode network circuitry that mediates our sense of self develops from our earliest days. In other words, our social lives—within families and likely within cultures—directly shape the neuroplastic growth of the neural structures of self.

When we say that our attachment experiences shape our sense of self, the neural correlate of this is how our energy and information flow sharing—our relationships—stimulate the activity and growth of our mindsight circuitry, including our DMN, which shapes our sense of self and others.

The neuroscientist Michael Graziano has built a model based on a social view of the brain. His proposal about the social brain and the origin of consciousness is relevant to our exploration of the Wheel and can be summarized in the following way. In our evolution, as we've seen, we needed to know how another person was *focusing her attention* in order to trust her mental state: Would she be focusing attention on our baby to protect him? As we built on this collaborative nature, our social structures became more complex and our need for collaboration beyond child-rearing was crucial for our survival. How we communicated our needs to others and read their signals to know their state of mind could become a matter of life and death. Homeostasis as a social species required mapping the mind. Would another villager be focusing on the saber-toothed tigers around us so that our collaborative hunting would help us all survive? Could we read another's signals and know when to run for cover? Making a map of another's attentional focus was of profound survival value.

What part of the brain do we use to map out the focus of another's attention? The brain uses an area called the *temporoparietal junction* (TPJ), which is the bridging region between the temporal and parietal lobes of the cortex. Communicating with the TPJ is another area important for theory of mind, called the *superior temporal sulcus* (STS), a groove in the temporal lobe of the cortex, just beside the temples of our forehead. On your hand model, these areas would be represented between the second and third knuckles of your folded finger-cortex. The TPJ and parts of the temporal lobe are considered as some of the non-midline parts of the DMN—and they are directly involved in our sense of the mental state of ourselves and of others.

While neuroscientists generally view these areas as important components of the social brain's circuitry, clinicians have found that when they are damaged, aspects of consciousness are disrupted. This suggests that the TPJ and STS are essential components of the neural correlates of consciousness. Other regions of the brain are also important in mediating consciousness, as we've discussed.

The names of these regions don't need to be held in working memory or even committed to long-term storage unless you like to "geek out" on them, but here they are: the *dorsolateral prefrontal cortex* (dlPFC) as part of the chief executive network and the *anterior cingulate cortex* (ACC), which along with the anterior insula is part of the salience network. These areas are more commonly studied when exploring the nature of focal attention—how we have a focus within awareness—and are adjacent to the forward-most parts of the DMN. These two more distant social brain zones, the TPJ and the STS, work closely with a distinct frontal midline cortical region, the medial prefrontal cortex (mPFC), in creating maps of others' minds as part of the default mode circuitry. (This medial prefrontal area is represented in the middle of your two fingernails of your hand model.) Recall that the mPFC is a fundamental part of the DMN—its most forward midline node—that links with the *posterior cingulate cortex* (PCC) as the posterior node of our default mode circuitry.

All these terms and abbreviations may get you dizzy, but the ideas we're about to explore are quite elegant, so while the neural data is complex, let's see how it is used to create a fascinating theory. Michael Graziano uses these findings to propose an *attention schema theory* for the origins of consciousness. At the heart of this proposal is the notion that awareness itself is information. We construct a symbolic representation of attention, a re-presenting of the process of paying attention—the object we focus our attention on and the presumed awareness of that object—as we create a representation of awareness. In other words, the information about awareness—about the focus of attention and what is being attended to—is simply an inference; it is inferring what it may be like for another person to be aware. We can never know the other's actual experience; we can only construct an imagined sense of their awareness. That ability to have a symbolic representation of the attentional focus and inferred awareness of another is then used by our brain to create the same inference about our own mental experience of being aware. In this direct way, the proposal suggests, awareness is simply a piece of information: there is no real awareness except the inference that awareness is happening. I know this may sound odd, that there is no actual awareness, so let me offer my own understanding of this unusual proposal.

When we look at another person, we make a map in our own neural machinery—a re-presentation in our brain—of what we imagine might be going on in that person's mental state, in their mind. In this way, we can have the constructed sense that another person has a conscious experience, as mapped out in our TPJ and STS regions, among other areas, including the medial prefrontal cortex. These are all a part of what I've called the *resonance circuitry*—a set of interconnected areas that allow us to feel another's feelings and to map another's mental state, to have mindsight. Interestingly, these same resonance circuits become activated during mindfulness meditation and reveal how being attuned internally and attuned interpersonally both seem to involve the social circuits of the brain that, as we can now see, are also part of the circuitry underlying consciousness.

The take-home message is that we use similar neural machinery of the social brain for insight that we would use for empathy into another's mental state.

You may have become aware of an interesting finding. Both the integrated information and social brain views of consciousness are about focal attention—about an object of attention becoming a part of consciousness. These views are fascinating proposals that relate to the Wheel experience perhaps directly in a possible mechanism underlying how the spoke connects with the rim—how we focus attention *on something* and then, somehow, it is in our awareness. In this way, our metaphoric spoke might have the mechanism of the degree of integration of energy flow achieved within the social circuits of the brain and other regions involved in the focus of attention and in being aware. These are helpful potential mechanisms offering insight into the spoke.

But what exactly is this awareness that the attention streams energy and information "into"? Is there in fact an "into" in the process of being aware? Is this metaphor of the hub of the wheel misleading us when it comes to considering mechanisms of awareness itself as a container, something that can be narrow or broad, that receives rim elements through the funnel of a metaphoric spoke of focal attention? Let's dive further into the science of consciousness and see where we go on our journey to illuminate the nature of the hub, of being aware.

THE HUB OF KNOWING AND POSSIBLE MECHANISMS OF THE BRAIN BENEATH PURE AWARENESS

Let's build on these two basic brain-based theories of integrated information and consciousness of the social brain and see how they fit with our own reflections and discussion of the Wheel experience. In the Wheel practice, we move from taking in sensory flow into our bodies, to inner bodily sensations, to mental activities, and then to our relational connections. This flow from outer to inner to inter is paralleled by these brain-based views of consciousness. Integrated information views support the notion of differentiation and linking— the basis of integration—in the emergence of conscious experience. And we can see the deeply intertwined nature of our *social* sense of reality and our *internal* sense of identity in the ways the consciousness of the social-brain perspective views the origins of awareness.

Ironically, as deeply rooted in the brain's modeling mechanisms as it is, this view of the social brain's role in consciousness illuminates the profound ways in which the mind is relational as well as embodied. Michael Graziano's view has some fascinating implications for how even our relationships may impact the experience of consciousness. For example, here is what he says about the notion of consciousness surviving death of the brain:

> If consciousness is information, if it is a vast informational model instantiated on the hardware of the brain, then it actually can survive the death of the body. Information is in principle possible to move from device to device. The irony is that the materialistic view makes mental survival beyond death much more likely, rather than less likely. Far from grinding its heel on the prospect of existence after death, the attention schema theory, an entirely materialistic theory, suggests that the mind's survival after the body's death already happens in a perfectly ordinary way. We get to know each other. We build models of each other. Information is transferred from brain to brain via language and observation.*

When we feel another inside us, when we feel that connection with someone we know well, we may be sensing this neural model-

---

* Michael Graziano, *Consciousness and the Social Brain* (Oxford: Oxford University Press, 2013), 222.

ing of that person's mind in our own neural machinery. These may be some further mechanisms of our sense of connection to those we are closest to.

So far, we can see that even the "private," "inner" practice of the Wheel of Awareness may be harnessing neural circuitry of "social" and "shared" aspects of our lives. Consciousness may be built upon profoundly social processes even if we think it is a purely privately held experience.

In the Wheel practice, when we come to the third segment of the rim, we open to whatever arises. In that segment's review, you may have felt the bombardment of many things arising or, in contrast, the spaciousness of few things entering the hub of awareness. The space between mental activities may have offered a glimpse into the nature of "pure" awareness metaphorically represented as the hub.

When we explore the practice of bending the spoke of attention back around to focus on the hub, of retracting the spoke, or of simply leaving it in the hub and resting in awareness itself, we have a number of visual metaphoric moves we can try in order to experience awareness of awareness itself. We've referred to this step as "hub-in-hub" and have reviewed the many common statements made about this experience opening the individual to a sense of expansiveness in which time disappears and a feeling of being connected to a larger whole frequently arises. How can the many descriptions of this aspect of the Wheel practice be understood?

What might the experiences of awareness being wide open and expansive mean in terms of a potential mechanism underlying this hub-in-hub experience? What might underlie a shift in the mind to a sense of timelessness? Many told me that they had a sense of connecting to people and things beyond the boundaries of their own bodies. Still others said simply that they felt a sense of joy and love. What might these universal reports actually mean? If these statements so consistently across the planet came up during the hub-in-hub part of the practice, what might the hub as a metaphor be illuminating in terms of how consciousness arises in our lives? What might the mechanism of awareness itself actually be?

In the integrated information approach, we might say that what is being integrated when nothing from the rim is being focused upon is oddly the integration of wide-open possibility, rather than one particularity of a singular thing being focused upon with attention. In other words, if linking differentiated elements—integration—is needed to become aware of something, then the hub-in-hub experience may simply be linking the infinite possibilities when there is no specific focus of attention, and that's where the sense of being wide open and timeless may arise from.

The consciousness of the social-brain perspective that proposes the mapping of attention itself might have a similar way of viewing the hub-in-hub portion of the Wheel practice. From this view we might propose that the modeling of attention on the attention to nothing in particular, no specific firing pattern of the thing you are aware of, the rim point, might be a kind of *mapping of infinity.* In other words, if a particular neural firing pattern—a rim point—were the focus of attention, as in the majority of the Wheel practice, we'd have a very specific subjective experience that would enter awareness as we mapped that attention. For this awareness *of something,* we are focusing the spoke on the rim for the experience of focal attention. But when we bend the spoke around, when we initiate the hub-in-hub experience, we now have a modeling on the non-object attention, paying *attention to possibilities* that have not yet become manifest in this state of open awareness. The awareness of this awareness—trying to utilize this social brain attention schema viewpoint—might be a modeling of the mapping of a non-object focus, and it feels wide open. In other words, mapping attention on only what is potential versus what is actual gives this information-about-attention model at that moment a sense of the infinite.

The neuroscientist Richard Davidson's work on meditation practice and brain firing may hold some additional clues as to how these perspectives of the integrative information and the consciousness of the social brain attention schema viewpoints might be supported in exploring open awareness studies and the nature of the hub and awareness. In his summary of that work with his colleague Daniel Goleman, here is what these two leaders in the field of contemplation say about what might be at the heart of open awareness and kind intention training, and perhaps the very neural correlate of receptive awareness itself as seen in longtime practitioners, called "yogis":

"All the yogis had elevated gamma oscillations, not just during the meditation practice periods for open presence and compassion but also during the very first measurement, before any meditation was performed. This electrifying pattern was in the EEG frequency known as 'high-amplitude' gamma, the strongest, most intense form. These waves lasted the full minute of the baseline measurement before they started the meditation."*

To get a feeling for the role of gamma waves in our life of awareness, Goleman and Davidson offer this exercise:

"Gamma, the very fastest brain wave, occurs during moments when differing brain regions fire in harmony, like moments of insight when different elements of a mental puzzle 'click' together. To get a sense of this 'click,' try this: What single word can turn each of these into a compound word: sauce, pine, crab? The instant your mind comes up with the answer, your brain signal momentarily produces that distinctive gamma flare."†

That moment of insight is the subjective experience of something emerging into awareness, associated with the "gamma flare" of knowing that correlates with high degrees of neural integration. We can propose that this integrative state is the neural mechanism of

---

* Daniel Goleman and Richard J. Davidson, *Altered Traits* (New York: Penguin Random House, 2017), 232.

† Ibid.

something from the rim being connected to the hub of the Wheel. Gamma waves can emerge at moments when the brain's firing becomes coordinated—when it reaches a certain level of complexity— and we then have the subjective sense of being aware, of being conscious of something—like when you see that *apple* is the word in the example above. Goleman and Davidson elaborate by offering this example:

"You also elicit a short-lived gamma wave when, for instance, you imagine biting into a ripe, juicy peach and your brain draws together memories stored in different regions of the occipital, temporal, somatosensory, insular, and olfactory cortices to suddenly mesh the sight, smells, taste, feel, and sound into a single experience. For that quick moment the gamma waves from each of these cortical regions oscillate in perfect synchrony."*

This is consistent with the integrative information view and might also correlate with a way in which attention is being modeled on the focused processes of various neural firing patterns involved at that moment in recalling the peach within awareness.

This helps us see the neural synchrony of being aware of something, of how the spoke of attention connects rim to hub. Again, *the spoke of focal attention likely represents a state of neural integration.* But what of pure awareness, the hub-in-hub experience? What might the correlate in the brain be of receptive open awareness itself?

Here we have some unique and potentially relevant insights from Davidson's lab study of a number of yogis, including Mingyur Rinpoche:

The contrast between the yogis and controls in the intensity of gamma was immense: on average the yogis had twenty-five times greater amplitude gamma oscillations during baseline compared with the control group. We can only make conjec-

---

* Goleman and Davidson, *Altered Traits*, 232.

tures about what state of consciousness this reflects: yogis like Mingyur seem to experience an ongoing state of open, rich awareness during their daily lives, not just when they meditate. The yogis themselves have described it as a spaciousness and vastness in their experience, as if all their senses were wide open to the full, rich panorama of experience."*

Such descriptions of the "spaciousness and vastness" of their experience are quite similar to what even newcomers to reflective practice describe about their subjective experience, even if brief, as an awareness of awareness, hub-in-hub, during their Wheel practice. These descriptions from workshop participants match what Goleman and Davidson note was documented over five hundred years ago: "As a fourteenth-century Tibetan text describes it . . . a state of bare, transparent awareness; Effortless and brilliantly vivid, a state of relaxed, rootless wisdom; Fixation free and crystal clear, a state without the slightest reference point; Spacious empty clarity, a state wide-open and unconfined; the senses unfettered . . ."†

This vastness of awareness may have the neural correlate of high degrees of integration in the brain, summarized by Goleman and Davidson this way: "The yogis' pattern of gamma oscillation contrasts with how, ordinarily, these waves occur only briefly, and in an isolated neural location. The adepts had a sharply heightened level of gamma waves oscillating in synchrony across their brain, independent of any particular mental act. Unheard of."‡

As we've discussed, neuropsychiatric researcher Judson Brewer and colleagues also found similar electrical patterns in a range of

---

* Goleman and Davidson, *Altered Traits*, 233.

† Ibid., 234, quoting from Third Dzogchen Rinpoche, trans. Cortland Dahl, *Great Perfection, Volume II: Separation and Breakthrough* (Ithaca, NY: Snow Lion Publications, 2008), 181.

‡ Ibid., 234.

meditative practices that are broadly labeled "effortless awareness"—
a state of being aware of whatever arises as it arises.

In a review of meditative practices, researchers Jonathan Nash
and Andrew Newberg suggest that such open awareness may be described in the following ways.

> This enhanced state is much more challenging to define as it
> infers the absence of affect and cognition—an empty state with
> no phenomenological content. This notion of emptiness has
> manifested in a host of semantic constructs derived from di-
> verse spiritual/religious traditions and languages, i.e., nirodha-
> samapatti (Pali), samadhi (Sanskrit), satori (Japanese), dzogchen
> (Tibetan). However, attempts to translate these terms into En-
> glish have struggled to capture the essence of this ineffable and
> nonconceptual state of consciousness. As such, many different
> terms have evolved depending on cultural/religious belief sys-
> tems, linguistic perspectives, and perceptions of the underlying
> ontology of meditation practice. The examples are numerous
> and include such ideas as: God Consciousness, Christ Con-
> sciousness, Buddha Consciousness, cosmic consciousness, pure
> consciousness, true-Self, non-Self, NDA [Non-Dual Aware-
> ness], absolute unitary being; and other terms such as Formless,
> Void, emptiness, and undifferentiated "beingness" or "such-
> ness."*

Studying "expert meditators" who have been doing reflective
practices of focused attention, open awareness, and kind intention for
over ten thousand hours is interesting and useful in revealing the
ways the brain can be trained with intensive practice. But even pre-

---

* Jonathan D. Nash and Andrew Newberg, "Toward a Unifying Taxonomy and Definition of Meditation," *Frontiers in Psychology* 20, November 20, 2013, 4, 806, https://doi
.org/10.3389/fpsyg.2013.00806.

liminary practices may create similar states of activation, if only briefly accessed during the practice itself. These studies help illuminate the nature of the mind and its relationship to the brain's integrative functioning. While most of us cannot devote tens of thousands of hours to formal practice, we can learn about the potential fundamental mechanisms that we can indeed train toward a more open state of awareness. That is a direction the Wheel practice can offer you in your daily life.

It may be possible, for example, to access pure awareness as you practice the Wheel and differentiate the hub. And once you learn to differentiate the hub from the rim and learn the skill of accessing the hub-in-hub experience, a new kind of freedom and clarity may await you more readily than you imagined was possible. Could it be that with ongoing practice we might gain more access to what we all naturally have beneath our patterns of recurrent rim points, a vast spacious awareness ready to be experienced?

A general statement about the neural correlates of consciousness we can make here is this: Awareness seems to have something to do with integration in the brain. This view is consistent with these exciting findings at the cutting edge of contemplative neuroscience that studies the impact of meditation on neural function, as well as the perspectives of integrated information and the consciousness of the social brain.

What we'll explore in the next section are some notions that build on these brain-based views of consciousness but are not constrained by them. We'll consider some possible mechanisms of the Wheel that take us into the notion of energy and information flow itself. You may find that what we explore next will both surprise you and relieve you.

THE NATURE OF ENERGY, THE ENERGY OF MIND

SCIENCE, ENERGY, AND EXPERIENCE

If mind emerges from energy flow, understanding as much as we can about energy would help us in understanding the mind and awareness. But what, actually, *is* energy?

One of the main scientific fields studying energy is physics. Imagine the excitement that arose when I received an invitation to participate in a weeklong gathering with 150 scientists, mostly physicists and mathematicians, in a workshop on the topic of science and spirituality. Trained as a researcher, I had little direct experience with formal spiritual education. By this time, my colleague John O'Donohue had died, and the direct teaching about things related to spirituality and religion and their connection to science that I had been doing with John had stopped. Surrounded by these physicists, I found every opportunity to explore these notions I had been wondering about regarding consciousness, the Wheel of Awareness, and the mind by repeatedly asking them a basic question: What is energy? I must have seemed to these scientists like either a broken record or a kid in a candy store, so energized and focused was my enthusiasm to follow this line of inquiry.

I was fascinated by their responses, and will summarize in the pages that follow the relevant ideas and their implications that emerged during our discussions over meals, on walks, and in informal gatherings. Though these scientists were physicists, not psychologists, for me what we discussed illuminated the possible mechanisms of mind and opened a new way of thinking about the experiences people were describing with the Wheel of Awareness. The questions I carried to this conference about the nature of being aware, of consciousness, of what the hub was all about, began to be clarified with physics-inspired insights I couldn't have imagined before.

Please keep in mind that the framework I am about to propose to you that arose from those discussions with the physicists and mathematicians is consistent with science but not constrained by it. In other words, this proposal about the nature of consciousness builds on and is consistent with what physicists, mathematicians, and others—as experts in their fields—have told me they "know" about reality, even though these notions have not been applied by them to understanding the mind. I don't want to misrepresent what physics or any other related field might say, or imply to you that these ideas are accepted or stated by traditional fields of science at this moment. They're not. What we're about to explore is how the science of energy, a focus of physics, *might* illuminate the mechanisms of mind and apply to what we've been exploring about the Wheel of Awareness and your direct, first-person immersions in your own subjective experience of mind. The key word in that last sentence is *might*.

Since first formulating this view, years ago now, and then teaching it in workshops, courses, and books, and applying it in my clinical practice and in my own life, I have found the framework fits with a wide range of experiences we all seem to have. It might just be accurate; it might not. A number of physicists who've taken the time to hear the proposal have been excited about its possibilities, including those who are expert in both quantum physics and meditation.

As we'll also see, a variety of contemplative and spiritual practitioners from a range of traditions have found the framework quite resonant with their own viewpoints. Here, I am using the term *contemplative* for deep, inner reflective practice. *Spiritual* is a term that may be used in various ways, often referring to the basic human drive to live a life of meaning and connection, as we've discussed. "Meaning" here refers to the sense of what has purpose and significance. "Connection" relates to the experience of belonging, of being a part of something larger than one's skin-defined sense of self. Meaning and connection can be illuminated in some fascinating ways with the ideas we're about to explore.

Interestingly, the framework appears to also be consistent with how friends, family, and the patients with whom I work closely discuss their inner, mental lives. I love reading autobiographical accounts, and these reflections, too, often fit with the framework. Inspired by John O'Donohue's poetry, I've also found that the poetic reflections of many writers on the nature of our mental lives can be sensed with a new perspective utilizing these ideas.

Now, these observations of the model fitting with the various descriptions of human experience could all just be a coincidence, or perhaps even an example of confirmation bias, my own mind's justification of its beliefs, letting into my awareness only interpretations of findings that affirm what I want to believe, twisting what I perceive to confirm what I want to think is really true. In other words, the framework may not be accurate. You'll need to see for yourself how it fits with your own experience.

Yet I keep coming back to the shared reflections I hear from people I have discussed these ideas with, and the ways this framework expands and deepens their understanding of the Wheel practice and their lives. This perspective seems to fit with science, subjectivity, and spirituality, perhaps helping construct a bridge linking these three ways of experiencing and understanding reality, helping them find common ground in our lives.

Try these ideas out for yourself with an open and questioning mind, discarding what doesn't work for you, and holding on to and building upon what does. This is a framework you may find helpful, or you may not. Let's see how it goes as you take it in and try applying it to your life.

I have a very doubting mind—I question even my own questioning. As we move ahead, it might be helpful to bear in mind that any doubt you may have, I likely have much more of—and yet we both can take on a willing, momentary suspension of disbelief to see if there might be some truth and practical applications in these new ways of envisioning our minds we're about to explore. There is always a part of my mind that regardless of the enthusiasm I may have—for this framework, as an example—I have my own measure of skepticism. Keeping that questioning alive is a healthy approach we can take, without letting uncertainty impede our progress. As a wise professor once advised me, insight and understanding move forward only when we have the courage to be wrong.

So what is this model? How does this framework fit in with your own experiences of the Wheel, in idea and practice? Each of these questions will be addressed as we move forward on our journey. Ready to go? Let's dive in.

THE ENERGY OF NATURE

We live in at least two levels of reality. In one level—the level of large objects—we have energy experienced as forces, such as gravity, pressure, and acceleration. When you ride a bicycle, you are using energy in your body to pedal the bike, feeling the force of gravity pull you toward the ground, the force of acceleration as you race across the street, the feeling of pressure as you jump off the bike and your feet hit the pavement. You live in a world of energy you are familiar with each moment of the day.

You also live in another level of reality—the level of very small entities, such as electrons and photons. Unlike with your bicycle or the pavement, you cannot see a single electron or photon, but you are nevertheless surrounded in a world of electrical energy and light energy.

We are born into large bodies, large in the sense that they are much bigger than an electron or a photon. We get used to thinking of energy in large-body terms, as forces and power that enable us to do things like work and move. Even the way our bodies function consumes energy as we take in food and breathe oxygen-rich air to utilize the energy from that food. Energy, as we've seen, is everywhere.

But *what* is energy?

This is the question I kept repeating to my scientific colleagues at our meeting. Energy isn't really a thing, they'd say; it's a name for a general aspect of our reality.

Okay, I'd say, what is this general aspect? What is the commonality among all manifestations of energy that then get expressed in a range of forms, frequencies, intensities, locations, and contours? *What* is manifesting across the CLIFF of energy? *What in the world is energy?*

You might imagine that there was a lot of energy in my questions directed to them.

Oh, a number of them ultimately would say in one way or another, *energy is the movement from possibility to actuality.* That's it.

Say what?

Energy is the movement from a *potential* to *that potential being realized.* That's what they mean by the basic statement that energy is the movement from possibility to actuality. Energy is the actualization of possibility.

My mind was spinning with this simple statement, and perhaps yours is, too.

Let's pause for a moment and reflect on this broad statement of possibility transforming into actuality.

One view, from a branch of physics called quantum mechanics, is that the universe has an underlying "quantum vacuum" or "sea of potential"—a mathematical space of reality representing the full range of possibilities that may arise into being. In other words, there is an aspect of reality—called a "mathematical space"—that is one way of describing where all things potentially able to become realized in the world rest; it's where they reside. This space is called a sea of potential, as it can be envisioned as a vast sea in which all potentially realized actualities float. It is from this sea, from this quantum vacuum, that anything that might become actually arises.

For those new to quantum physics, this may sound just plain odd. And for those who have an aversion to mathematics, this may feel intimidating. After years of moving beyond this initial trepidation with my colleagues and fellow travelers into the mind, I can offer you reassurance that what may feel strange at first can come to feel quite exciting, familiar, and even useful with just a bit of patience.

At this level of analysis of our world, and in this moment of our journey, we come to a view that for many is difficult at first to comprehend, or even to get an initial feeling for. Because we live in relatively large objects—our bodies, which interact with objects at a large scale, such as other bodies, cars, and buildings—we are used to thinking of things, including energy, as absolutes, not probabilities. If you feel this way, you are not alone at all. In fact, large objects operate, at least on the surface, by a set of principles of physics that are more readily apparent than the laws governing how small things interact. The large things in the world are sometimes referred to as "*macrostates*" and the small things as "*microstates*." Microstates include electrons and photons. Macrostates are our bodies, cars, and buildings.

The way the large-object world functions is the focus of what is called "classical physics," which Sir Isaac Newton proposed 350 years ago, and so these principles governing large objects are sometimes also called "Newtonian physics." With large objects, which are really large assemblies of microstates called macrostates, such as planets and airplanes, rules about these objects, such as the laws of acceleration and gravity, have been quite useful in the large-object lives we lead, and so we can fly in an airplane or drive a car and have mechanical engineers build the systems of wings and wheels and brakes to fly the plane or stop our automobile and restrain our bodies with protective seat belts to keep us as safe as possible. That's all engineering based on classical Newtonian physics. My father was a mechanical engineer who designed helicopters and automobiles and based his entire career on this accepted world of Newtonian, classical physics. There is a set of rules about these manifestations of energy in the interactions of macrostates, rules that determine a certainty in function so that we, hopefully, will stay up in the airplane or helicopter even in a storm, or come to a full stop when we step on the brakes in our car. Newton set the laws out in mathematical formulas that still hold to this day, enabling us to stay afloat in the air or stop at a red light. That's a wonderful feeling and usually a reliable experience of certainty in the macrostate world.

But quantum mechanics deals with a smaller, deeper level of analysis than is readily seen in such large macrostate objects. (It turns out that the quantum laws also apply even to macrostates; they are just much, much harder to detect at these larger sizes.) Initially formulated about a century ago, quantum physics explores the nature of probability in the universe, rather than the certainties apparent at the macrostate surface studied by a Newtonian or classical view of the world. A quantum is a unit of experience that is the basis for interactions—and so from the quantum view, life and reality are a matter of unfolding interactions based on a wild but empirically established set of findings that shape and shift based on *changes in probability.* As physicist Art Hobson states, a quantum is "a highly unified, spatially extended, specific quantity or bundle of field energy. The word derives from 'quantity.' Every quantum is a wave—a disturbance—in a field. Examples include photons, electrons, protons, atoms, and molecules."[*]

---

[*] Art Hobson, *Tales of the Quantum* (New York: Oxford University Press, 2017), xi.

Put simply, quantum insights reveal the verblike nature of reality based on potentials or probabilities; classical physics focuses on a nounlike certainty of objects interacting in the world. I've had some encounters with colleagues who ask me why I'd turn to quantum physics to understand the mind—why not just stick with the brain? Their concerns are often fueled by having heard lecturers use quantum terms without much reference to the actual empirically established scientific findings. Wild things can be asserted, they would say, in the name of quantum mystery. Even physicists themselves have heated debates about certain aspects of the field. Here is Hobson's view: "At least since the days of the early Greeks, philosophical people have wanted to know the ultimate constituents of the universe. What is the stuff of reality and how does it behave? . . . Atoms and everything else are made of things more fundamental and even more intriguing than atoms, namely 'fields' that are bundled into 'quanta.'" He goes on to cite the interaction between two of the leaders of the field, founder Niels Bohr responding to colleague Wolfgang Pauli's presentation: "'We are all agreed that your theory is crazy. The question that divides us is whether it is crazy enough to have a chance of being correct.' Nature is far more inventive than is human imagination, and the microscopic world is not what Niels Bohr or anyone else could have guessed. Quantum physics is indeed strange, and some have rejected some aspects of it on the grounds of this strangeness, but strangeness alone is not a compelling reason to reject a scientific theory."*

Several quantum ideas established by careful and repeated empirical studies may be useful in our exploration of the mechanisms of mind and the Wheel of Awareness. We will attempt to use these ideas as close to the science as we can, but then out of necessity we'll let our imagination build on that science to create a bridge to our own Wheel experience. In other words, there may be useful insights about

---

* Hobson, *Tales of the Quantum*, xiii.

the nature of energy—as a microstate process in our universe—that will help illuminate aspects of our mental lives.

We are not turning toward a quantum view to assert some kind of wild knowledge that might make things more complicated than they need to be. As the philosopher Jagdish Hattiangadi suggests, "Quantum mechanics is not being invoked because it is authoritative. This is not an argument from Bohr's authority. It is relevant to study because it lies at the lowest level that physics itself addresses."*

Let me highlight four principles from the empirical science of energy that we will explore and apply throughout the rest of our journey. Quantum physics invites us to examine:

1. the probability nature of reality;
2. the potential influence of measurement and observation on probability;
3. the relational nature of reality and the entanglement of quanta and its nonlocal influences; and
4. the arrow of time or directionality of change that may manifest only at the macrostate level of reality.

In case you are feeling concerned about where this may all go, let me start with a very controversial point that raises a lot of emotional reactions. This is the first of these four topics we will briefly review here—the questions regarding how observation influences the probability of energy.

The point that is of concern is when individuals offer a definitive statement to the effect that quantum physics has "proven" that consciousness *creates* reality. Among physicists, it appears that this is a highly debated inference regarding how to interpret an accepted,

---

* Jagdish Hattiangadi, "The Emergence of Minds in Space and Time," in *The Mind As a Scientific Object*, C. E. Erneling and D. M. Johnson, eds. (New York: Oxford University Press, 2005), 86.

noncontroversial finding in science—that the act of observation of an electron passing through a double-slit metal barrier alters the outcome of what is detected. Some suggest that the act of observation "collapses the wave function," meaning it makes the electron act as a particle—a certainty—rather than a wave, a set of probabilities. You may recall this finding from high school physics. What *is* controversial is not that discovery of a different outcome with measurement, but what to make of it—what it means about why the act of observation would be associated with something shifting from a range of probabilities to a singular certainty.

A perspective called the orthodox Copenhagen interpretation proposes that the act of observation changes this probability function, but this is only one of many interpretations; alternative views suggest that observation merely selects from a vast array of realities within the multiverse or that there in fact are no waves and particles, but some other way of imagining the nature of quanta. How that selection might occur or exactly what these basic units of reality might be and how observation influences them is not clear. Others suggest that this is a measurement issue, not the impact of consciousness. Quantum physicist Henry Stapp, a student of the founders of quantum theory, furthers the orthodox Copenhagen interpretation that proposes the general notion of the influence of mental activity on what we observe in physical reality, by suggesting that beyond the observation created by consciousness, the mental state of intention can also influence probability functions. At a quantum physics think tank with Stapp, I was struck by the clarity of his thinking and the passion of his conviction. You might imagine how a potential interpretation that places human consciousness at the center of the organization of the unfolding of probabilities into actualities in the universe might be quite appealing—and perhaps even accurate. But the scientific community is still filled with intense debate about this important issue. We will honor the controversy, and explore possibilities rather than assert absolutes.

Even if the orthodox Copenhagen interpretation holds true, or Stapp's fascinating extension of it to include intention as well as awareness in the influential factors, the finding seems to me to reveal that observation alters a probability function—it does not *create* that electron; it merely "requires" that the probability distribution of that electron's wave emerge as one certainty from a spectrum of possibilities. In other words, awareness might shift the probability of a microstate, but it won't create the quanta itself. But even if *that* were the case, it's fascinating. Here's a spoiler alert: We will not solve the double-slit experiment interpretation debate here by any means, but we will embrace the controversy and respect the scientific reasoning around these differing points of view in our discussions, open to at least considering how mind, including attention, awareness, and intention, *might* shape the unfolding of possibility into actuality.

You may be getting a feel for why this dive into quantum views might be quite relevant to understanding our experience of the Wheel. We train the three pillars of focused attention, open awareness, and kind intention. These mental skills could have some direct impact on how a possibility becomes an actuality—what the very flow of energy actually is.

In our journey ahead, we will keep this controversial notion in mind, considering that the mind's attention, awareness, and intention *may* alter probabilities—or they may not. Again, let's try to keep an open mind, respectful of doubts and discerning about how to interpret science and carefully apply it to understanding subjective experience, as we build a bridge between these mind-bending scientific views from the empirically verified study of the microstate world and what we experience with the Wheel practice.

Here is one of the big challenges we have as beings that inhabit our big, macrostate bodies. We do live in a *body*, yes. Wonderful. Our body is something to cherish and care for. And we have a *mind*. It may just be that some aspects of energy flow of the mind have properties that are determined sometimes by macrostate, body-size stuff—like when we feel the breeze on our cheek or soak in the glory of the sunset—*and* dominated at times by microstate fundamentals, the quanta of energy fields such as electrons and photons (as when we immerse ourselves in emotions, thoughts, memories, or imagination—or even in awareness itself). Unbound by the constraints of a certainty-dominated, macrostate, body level of existence, our mind can become freed to experience a broader and more flexible band of reality within the microstate world of probabilities. As we'll see, embracing this potential of possibilities and probabilities transforming into actualities as one aspect of the nature of our mental lives may help us more directly offer a view into the mechanisms of the mind beneath the experience of being aware.

Another fundamental and challenging notion from quantum physics is the relational nature of reality. As the physicist, philosopher, and physician Michel Bitbol explains, "Science made a momentous step forward as soon as it was understood that certain explanations have to be given in terms of relations rather than in terms of absolute properties. . . . Bohr said it's true that all these quantum concepts seem very awkward, but maybe in order to transform them into something less strange, we have to change our very concept of understanding. Bohr's idea was that we have to change our idea of understanding the world into an idea of understanding our relation with the world."*

The Wheel of Awareness practice invites us to experience directly these different aspects of energy flow in our subjective immersions. Someone who had done the Wheel and experienced these distinctions between a macrostate feeling of certainty and the microstate world of probability, especially in the hub-in-hub part of the practice, invited me to come to England and offer the Wheel of Awareness at the birthplace of Sir Isaac Newton. We gathered around the original apple tree that inspired Newton's proposals about the

---

* Hasenkamp and White, eds., *The Monastery and the Microscope*, 54–55.

nature of gravity. No apples fell on us on that misty June afternoon. On the wall of his birth home, where he had also returned during the plague when he was a student at Cambridge University, was the following quote: "I can calculate the motion of celestial bodies but not the madness of men." Could it be that the mind operates, in part, by quantum probability functions that Newton was simply unaware of before our contemporary views? As we did the Wheel and then discussed the ways the practitioners had experienced a subjective shift from rim to hub, we offered a connection across time to thank Sir Isaac for his powerful contributions and invite him to join us in this new level of exploration into the nature of reality. We will need to embrace these two "levels" of apparent reality, the classical and the quantum, as we try to understand the deep mechanisms of energy that may be at the heart of our experience of mind and awareness.

As the physicist Jacob Biamonte suggests in his work on a theory of quantum complex networks, the higher level of complexity—the classical level—can be seen as an emergent phenomenon of the lower-level components, the quantum level. And so these two levels are not independent; they are interdependent. Even if we experience them as distinct from one another, and are often more aware of the classical level in our everyday lives, both levels are available to us and influence one another. Biamonte states, "One of the oldest examples of emergence, and arguably the most important, is the question of why the world around us seems too often well described by classical physics, while the world we live in is, in actual fact quantum."*

Keeping in mind this fascinating scientific perspective that we have these apparent dual levels of reality, classical and quantum, or macrostate and microstate, we can then open our discussion to the reality that the subjective experience of our ever-emerging minds

---

* Carinne Piekema, "Six Degrees to the Emergence of Reality," Fqxi.org, January 1, 2015, https://fqxi.org/community/articles/display/197.

may reflect this macro and micro layering of our emergence, moment by moment. This first quantum principle of the probability nature of energy and the way we can become aware of it, and the second principle of how our minds may influence it, will be a primary focus of how we dive into the nature of the hub.

A third finding from quantum physics is that entanglement, as mentioned earlier, has been established as a real, *empirically proven* aspect of our world. What this means is that microstates can be coupled with each other—like two electrons pairing up—and their pairing leads to relational influences on each other that are not impeded by spatial separation. For example, if one electron spins clockwise and the other spins in the complementary counterclockwise direction, then when one electron of the pair is made to spin in a new direction, its entangled partner spins in the complementary and opposite direction in response. That shift in spin can occur when the electrons are directly in physical proximity, or it can occur when they're separated by long distances. Spatial separation does not change the relational coupling, the entangled relationship—in this case, the complementarity of their spin directions. This is how the odd but real property of entanglement has the feature known as *nonlocality*.

In the classical Newtonian view, macrostates that are spatially separated—like the bodies of you and a friend being thousands of miles apart—naturally have a sense of space separating the influences of those large objects. But entanglement research reveals that spatial separation for entangled microstates does not impede their relational influences on each other. Yes, of course, close friends are not the same as paired electrons—and entanglement may not apply to the minds of those friends; or it might, if those minds have features with microstate energy properties of quanta.

Paired electrons can influence one another no matter the distance apart. Odd, I know, but proven as real in this universe we live in. The physicist Abner Shimony even called this "passion at a distance."

Albert Einstein called it "spooky action at a distance" when he thought entanglement meant that there must be an incredibly fast traveling of energy. Entanglement happens virtually simultaneously no matter the spatial separation, traveling faster than the speed of light, and thus if it *were* an energy moving, it would have violated one of Einstein's essential notions—that nothing in the universe travels faster than light. That maximal speed remains an accepted aspect of our universe. This quantum property is not about energy *traveling*; it's about an entangled relationship not being affected by physical distance. I know, I know—odd, and from a classical big-body perspective, just plain weird and seemingly impossible. Entanglement, as classically challenging as it is, requires that we open our minds to the very notion of space and what that dimension of reality may mean at both a macrostate and a microstate level. As much as it invites us to consider things we may never have considered, entanglement is now established as a real part of our world, even for matter—which, after all, is condensed energy, highly packed microstates of energy that form the dense macrostate accumulations called mass, as we've seen in Einstein's famous formula: energy equals mass times the speed of light squared.

Whether this proven aspect of entanglement in microstates is a part of mental states, we just don't know—and we won't be answering that question on this leg of our journey together, either. As the quantum physicist Arthur Zajonc suggests, "At a very subtle level there is also a hidden connectedness, or entanglement or quantum holism as we call it. Things are apparently discrete, and at one level that's true, but at a more subtle level they have interconnections with one another. . . . One can begin to think every particle that has interacted with another particle has a connection to that particle that propagates and goes further and further; it branches. From a logical standpoint it would make sense to think that many, many parts of the universe are connected in ways that are hard for us to imagine. In simple cases, we can actually do the experiments to show the connectedness."*

As we've discussed, people sometimes describe their experiences of accurately sensing the mental life of someone they are close to in relationship but far from physically, and it just might be (*might*, again, being the operative term we will use in our questioning and exploring journey) that our minds indeed sometimes reveal the quantum energy property of entanglement with some relationships. Given that entanglement and nonlocality are now proven aspects of our world, if energy is what the mind emerges from, then wouldn't it actually be odd if entanglement were *not* an experience of certain close, mind-to-mind relationships?

A fourth issue we'll explore is the way we experience time. For some, entering the hub-in-hub part of the practice simply feels different, in terms of a sense of timelessness, from what is felt when focusing on the rim, with its sense of things coming and going in a time-bound sequence of before and after. This contrast is so commonly described with the Wheel of Awareness that it naturally invites the question, What might be going on in the hub versus the rim that could offer an insight into the mechanism beneath this common subjective experience? What might be the explanation of this shift in our subjective sense of time? Quantum physics views on the directionality of change might offer us insights that help put the big picture about mind and time together in some new and useful ways that could deepen our understanding of the Wheel experience.

Some physicists have suggested that time, as something that flows, may not exist. However, what does exist is an *arrow of time*, a term for the directionality of change. In our large bodies, we live with a Newtonian set of laws of certainty, a level of macrostates that do have an arrow-bound quality to how we experience the unfolding

---

* Hasenkamp and White, eds., *The Monastery and the Microscope*, 35.

of events. If we crack an egg, we cannot uncrack it. That's the arrow of time. But if you spin an electron one way or the other, it is free to move in any direction independent of what went before, given that before and after—a directionality of change—may not exist at the microstate level of reality.

It may be that as we rest in awareness, when we enter the hub-in-hub experience of the Wheel, we are experiencing an arrow-free quantum level of microstate conditions that do *not* have a directionality of change. If our mental experience of time, which we often call "time flowing," is actually our awareness of change, then the Newtonian, arrow-bound level of mental life *will* have a sense of time, and our quantum, arrow-free level will feel timeless. In this way, the various aspects of the hub or the rim may reveal some microstate or macrostate configurations of energy that could explain why some aspects of mental experience feel arrow-free while others feel arrow-bound, a subjective experience of a timeless present or a time-flowing movement bridging what we call past, present, and future.

Finally, the fundamental quantum finding we will explore in great depth in the pages ahead has to do with the general probability property of energy. Energy, as we've seen, can be broadly described as involving the movement from possibility to actuality. This notion from quantum physics basically states that energy emerges from a sea of potential, the mathematical space called the quantum vacuum. We won't need to do any mathematical equations or get lost in complicated numbers to gain a visual sense of how energy may be seen as moving along a spectrum of probabilities, along what some call a probability distribution curve, from open and vast in potential, to specific and narrow as an actuality.

To create an actuality from the sea of potential, energy must flow from the quantum vacuum.

To honor a specific detail emerging from discussions with my physicist colleagues, it's important to state that energy itself, according to some of these scientists, may not exist in this pool of possibilities, the quantum vacuum. To *transform* a possibility of that sea of potential into an actuality requires energy, and so energy "arises" from this mathematical space, so to speak. Sometimes this flow of energy can contain symbolic meaning; we call that flow information. Others see the universe comprising information, and energy arises from that. We can picture that view as a sea of potential containing all possible symbolic configurations we are calling information. This *generator of diversity*, this quantum vacuum, is then the source of all information that could possibly exist. Energy in this view arises from this sea of potential information, and its unfolding patterns of energy let the potential information become actualized in the world. As we've seen, the phrase "energy and information" respects both approaches of sensing the primacy of energy or of information and their ultimate intertwining in our experience of reality.

Since the reality of our world appears to be more about interactions than about fixed entities, the universe being more like a verb than a noun, this energy and information *flows*—it changes ceaselessly; it unfolds; it moves; it is an ever-evolving set of interacting energy fields that comprise the emerging world we call reality.

At this moment, you and I can take a deep breath with our macrostate bodies. Yes, we live in a body, and energy flows in that macrostate level of reality. It's real, and really important. When you press on the brakes of your bike, you want it to stop. Energy flows, too, as microstates, and so examining the quantum nature of our reality that explores these microstate properties most directly may be an important addition to the more familiar classical view of large-object macrostate reality. I rode my bicycle today thinking about how you and I would discuss these issues now, and I am grateful for both the macrostate, classical world that carried me through space and time and the imagination and awareness that may arise from our microstate, quantum world. That's an embrace of two levels of reality I invite you to breathe into in this moment, letting the classical macro world and the quantum micro world each be respected and welcomed into our sense of discovery in the journey ahead.

For some, focusing on something as elusive as energy or these quantum properties of reality may feel distinctly unscientific. Let me reassure you, however, that beyond the magnificent energy of holding someone's hand or gazing into their eyes in our macrostate, romantic bodies, beyond the energy of seeing or hearing these words with your macrostate sensory systems, there is another aspect of energy that is not as concrete or familiar as that which you touch, see, or hear. So opening your mind to this other, micro level of reality can feel a little strange, for sure. And for some people, talking about energy as the movement from possible to actual is just too much—they can't hold that idea, can't see it or taste it or touch it, and it just seems, well, too weird, too "out there," to be useful. Maybe it even seems unscientific to them.

Those who feel that a focus on energy and microstate levels of reality loses a basis in science are inferring that physics is not science. Rest assured, energy is a scientific concept, and an accepted reality of our universe. And studying the quantum nature of the universe over the past century has revealed surprising but empirically proven aspects of our energy- and information-filled world. If the mind is a part of this universe, a part of nature, then asking the question about the connection of mind to the nature of energy is, well, a natural thing to do.

But for some, exploring the nature of mind as part of the nature of energy becomes too abstract and feels, well, unnatural. It actually makes some of my professional colleagues visibly upset. Why not simply stay with the meditation practice of the Wheel, or just discuss the neural correlates of consciousness and be done with possible mechanisms beneath those neural patterns? Aren't the fascinating findings about neural integration and the power of neuroplasticity to change the brain with mind practice enough science for us to address? Why go further than that?

What fuels this decision to explore these science notions of energy in-depth with you here are the many experiences I've had revealing how even though what we are now exploring is a novel view most people are unfamiliar with and at first sometimes even uncomfortable with, in the end, with a bit of effort and new learning, the ideas become quite accessible, useful, and even fun.

In science, as we've seen, Louis Pasteur suggested that chance favors the prepared mind. This deeper dive into the mechanisms of energy will prepare your mind for the chance encounters life most certainly will throw your way. Diving deep into the probability nature of microstate flows of energy will also enhance the power of the Wheel practice to cultivate well-being in your life.

So let's go forward, as slowly as you need to, but progressively advancing into this fascinating and (I hope) useful way of thinking of the mind, of the Wheel, of awareness, and of our lives as we grow toward health.

ENERGY AS PROBABILITY

Let me offer an example that I hope will help make this abstract definition of energy as a movement from possibility to actuality as accessible as possible. Right now I am about to write a word. Let's say, just for our example, that there are about one million words in our shared vocabulary. What is your chance of knowing the one word I am about to write? Right, it is one in a million. Let's see how this might look in an illustration.

In the following image you can see a kind of map, which shows that at the bottom of this graph is an area depicting the million maximally possible words. Your chance of knowing that one word out of this pool of all possibilities, this sea of potential things, is one out of the number of maximal possibilities, which in this example is a million.

And so the probability of you knowing the word at this moment is pretty close to zero, and on the graph we see that as a "near-zero" position or value on the vertical axis, what in mathematics we call the y-axis. This y-axis can be called a *probability distribution curve*, as it includes the range of probabilities we have across the distribution of values, from zero or near-zero all the way up to 100 percent probability. Notice how the bottom of this y-axis is near-zero or zero, and the top is 100 percent. We call this lowest point "near-zero" because while it is quite unlikely you'd know from this huge pool the one word that I might choose, there is something more than zero probability. This moment in time, this particular moment of you not knowing and my not saying anything yet, is where we are now in clock-time, meaning how our time measurement indicates the temporal location of "right now." That shared place in time is indicated on the horizontal x-axis, which we can label as "clock-time" or, for simplicity, "time," even though as we'll see, time itself also has quite a fascinating story and may not be what we think it is as something that flows. And as you move from left to right along this axis, you are mapping how things "unfold across time"—which simply means how they change, or not, across clock-time. The position of the probability of you knowing the word at this moment on the x-axis, this moment of time, is near-zero on the y-axis, that correlation with its positioning or value on the probability distribution curve. That value is near-zero. Notice how we can mark this as a point on the map or graph—in this case, position A—that in this moment corresponds to the lowest probability, the "near-zero" point (as one in a million is near-zero, not quite zero).

On this two-dimensional graph so far, a position in the drawing—where the point is in our diagram—indicates two things: where in time the energy value is (x-axis), and where on the probability distribution spectrum the energy is (y-axis). A singular position—A at this moment—has two indicators, probability and time.

Now let's say I state one word of the maximal one million possible words, and the word I choose is *ocean*. At this moment we move a bit to the right on the x-axis of time and we label this new position as point A-1, corresponding to the 100 percent place on the probability distribution curve—the vertical y-axis. It is 100 percent because now, at this moment in time, the pool of maximal possibilities was drawn upon and one of those potentials became "actualized," in this case, as the singular, 100 percent actuality of the word *ocean*. At this position, A-1, you are filled with 100 percent certainty and you know the word because you've read the word: *ocean*.

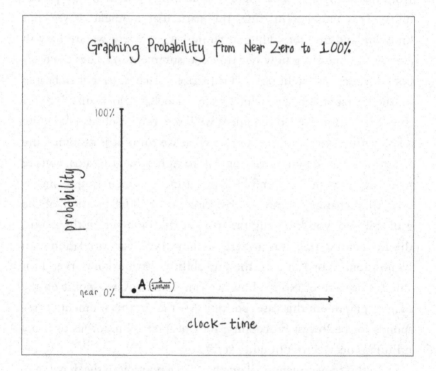

The probability at this moment that you'll know the right word is now up on the y-axis at 100 percent. You know what the word is.

Here you can see how probability and certainty are in a sense the same state or condition of energy. One hundred percent probability is maximal certainty. Near-zero percent probability is minimal certainty. If there are a maximum of one million words and I haven't

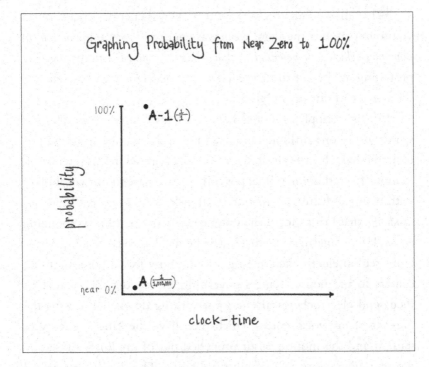

Graphing Probability from Near Zero to 100%

100% — •A-1($\frac{1}{1}$)

probability

near 0% — •A ($\frac{1}{1,000,000}$)

clock-time

spoken or written the word yet, it is maximally uncertain that you'll know the correct word. It's not quite zero, but one out of a million is very close to zero, so we call this near-zero. You may have noticed, too, that minimal probability and certainty is the same as maximal possibility. When no word has been chosen, there is both minimal certainty and at the same time, at the same position on the graph, it is equivalent to maximal, wide-open potential.

In energy terms, if you were a proverbial fly on the wall and watching with an open mind, you'd sense that something just happened in the universe, in the interaction between you and me, which involved the general movement from possibility to actuality. For me to say or write something and for you to receive that something required a flow, a change, an unfolding. *That movement in our universe from possibility to actuality is called energy.* From your fly's perspective, you've just sensed energy flow.

What allowed me to say or write *ocean* was energy; what allowed you to experience the word *ocean* was energy. *Energy is the movement from that which is a potential to that which is realized.* Energy, we are proposing, is also the fundamental nature of subjective experience—the essence of our mental lives.

In this example, you and I share a common language that has words, using one million as an example of the number of those potentially shareable linguistic symbols. Energy flows in this interaction to move from those maximal possibilities we share in our vocabulary within our culture and in our relationships to *something happening inside me* that brings forth the one neural firing pattern symbolizing *ocean*. I then manifest from electrochemical patterns in my head-brain region electrochemical signals that flow from those linguistic centers to my neural centers governing expression. Those regions then send electrochemical energy streaming down neurons to the muscles of my vocal cords, which then have the kinetic energy of tension and the motion of air propelled out of my lungs caused by the muscular movement of my diaphragm. That kinetic energy of air moving passes by those oscillating cords to say the word into frequencies of air molecules vibrating for sound and a word is spoken. If I am writing, energy streams from my head-brain to the muscles in my arms to make my hands and fingers type the words. You then receive the sound waves of air movement and create hearing from sound energy by way of your ears' acoustic nerves sending electrochemical energy signals up into your head-brain's sound and linguistic centers. Or you receive the patterns of photons bouncing from a light source off of a page or from a screen and into your eyes where the retina in the back of your eyes transduces that energy pattern with all its CLIFF variables into further electrochemical energy patterns in your head-brain, passing them on to the sight decoding centers, which transmit these to the linguistic regions and *you somehow mentally perceive in your subjective experience the word* ocean.

That's all energy flow. Together, we moved from possible to actual.

That something inside me is my inner mind; that perception of the word in your subjective experience is *your* inner mind. That sharing of energy—the sharing of possible into actual—is our relational inter mind.

Let's now take our emerging diagram and elaborate on it a bit.

If I were to have the intention to think only of words that began with an *o*, then the probability of your knowing that word would be higher than one in a million—let's say now it is perhaps one in ten thousand. At this moment, we'd indicate this state as a probability position at a higher location than the near-zero point. When I now say or write the word *ostrich*, we've moved from the higher probability at position B to the actualized 100 percent of position B-1.

Or let's say I am in the frame of mind to consider only words

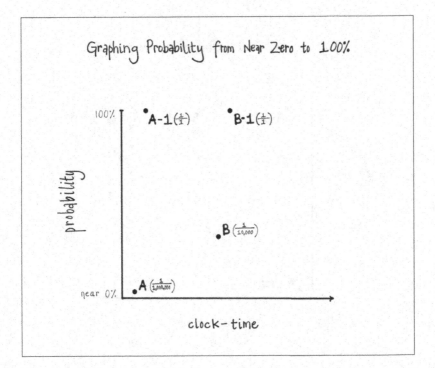

related to bodies of water—*ocean, lake, pond, pool, stream, creek, river,*
and so on—and that there are only thirty such words. Now your
chance of knowing is even higher—one in thirty—and we'd represent that moment at an even higher place on the y-axis. In this case,
when I would state a word—say, *sea*—you'd then move from that
elevated location along the y-axis, a position indicating a smaller
number of possibilities than the maximal number of all words in our
vocabulary, and so this smaller subset is at a position of *elevated probability* from which actualization arose. In other words, the group of
thirty water-related words is simply a subset of the maximal words
possible, and its probability position is higher up on the y-axis, closer
to actualization at 100 percent.

To be sure we are clear on this movement from some position of
maximal possibility as in example A, or elevated probability that
moves up into actualized certainty as in example B, let's consider two

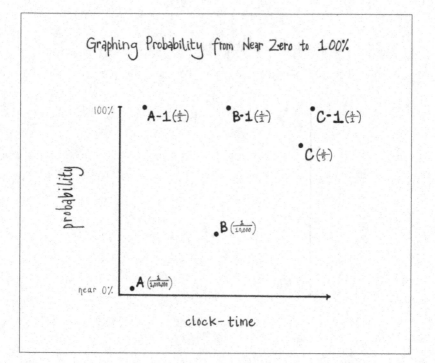

more examples. If I were to name one of the four or five oceans in the world, your chance of knowing would be higher still, one out of four or five (depending on whether we're including the Southern Ocean, around Antarctica, as some countries do). Once I said the name Indian Ocean, you would have moved from a *position of elevated probability*—in this case one out of five, indicated as position C on the diagram, a position far above the near-zero position—to a 100 percent position, C-1, once the word had been stated.

If I were to ask you if you knew if I was going to say left or right, the grouping of possibilities would now be two, and your probability of knowing would be one out of two, or 50 percent—even higher up on the probability curve position of the y-axis. This position of increased probability would be higher on the diagram but not all the way up to the 100 percent position of maximal certainty; once I say or write *left*, then we move once again up from the elevated probability position on the grid to what we can now see is a position of maximal probability, 100 percent certainty.

Here you can see in the diagram how *energy is flowing* as we move along the x-axis for the change that unfolds, and the change in probability in its position shifts along the y-axis. This is how our diagram visually depicts the movement moment by moment along the x-axis of time, as the probability variable of energy changes from potential to actual through a series of probabilities as revealed by the y-axis coordinates.

In this diagram, we've labeled each example's probability value, so that where we began in each case is one out of one million for A, one out of ten thousand for B, and one out of five for C. You can use your imagination to envision where you'd put the examples in the case of words related to water (a probability position of one out of thirty) and related to direction, left or right (a probability value of one out of two) on the diagram, too. I've left these two depictions open on the diagram so that your own mind can create the visual positioning and you can actually feel how energy can flow from what you read to what you can actually imagine—and then draw this visual image in the book itself, if you choose.

Each of these starting places of possibilities from which an actuality will arise—from maximal at A to various degrees of decreasing subsets in B and C—can then be seen as a kind of platform from which energy transforms into an actualized realization, as indicated by A-1, B-1, and C-1. As we move ahead and expand our diagram, we'll come to see that the starting platform from which energy emerges from a possible into an actual may play a special role in our lives. These examples reveal an important take-home notion that will help illuminate a mechanism beneath the Wheel practice. Sometimes the flow from possible to actual begins from a maximal source of options, as in case A. At other times, that flow emerges from a restricted pool of available choices, as in the cases of B and C.

The flow of energy, we can now propose, may be visually depicted on our diagram as the movement from these pools of maximal possibility at near-zero probability or from restricted subsets with

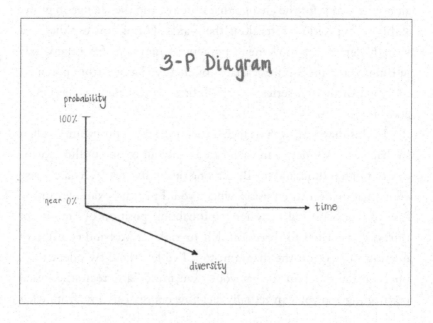

their various ranges of elevated probability into actualization, the realization of potential into manifestation in reality.

If we now take our two-dimensional grid and make it a three-dimensional diagram by adding a third axis, one that extends out of the plane of the page, we have a three-dimensional diagram that reveals a more complete view of how to envision these positions. Diversity along this new axis, what is termed a z-axis, indicates the variety of things that might be present in a given moment. A narrow range along diversity would indicate few things; a broad range extending widely along the z-axis dimension would indicate many things.

With this basic three-dimensional diagram, we can now look at how the position at the bottom of the y-axis of probability, indicating the lowest certainty, can be indicated as the geometrical shape of a plane, a figure bounded on one side by the x-axis of time and on the other by the z-axis of diversity. Take a look at the next diagram, and you can imagine that this framing of the diversity and time axes creates something that looks like a slanted rectangle, a trapezoidal *plane*.

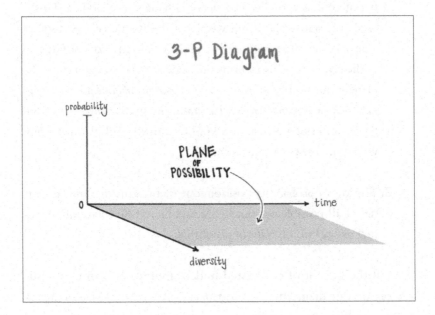

If we now draw in that plane, you'll see that it represents the position in which the maximal possibilities reside. This would be where we'd place the one million words in our example A. Whatever the kind of things being explored, if maximal options are available, that means that the probability of knowing what a particular one might be is near-zero, the lowest probability position. Notice, again, how the position of minimal probability and lowest certainty is the same as one of maximal possibility and highest potentiality. On the diagram, this position of highest potential of all options we can call the *plane of possibility*.

In the following illustration we can also provide other names for the basic probability positions we've been discussing, in addition to this plane of possibility. Here is a way to name the positions on our three-dimensional energy probability profile diagram.

1. The highest position of actualization is a *peak* of actuality. This is when a possible has manifested from potential into actual.

2. We can name the elevated places of increased probability not yet manifested as actuality *plateaus* of enhanced probability. This is when the state of probability is not at the 100 percent position of a peak of actualization, nor is it at near-zero, the lowest position of the probability distribution curve depicted on the y-axis, at the plane of possibility. In other words, *plateaus indicate a subset of options that are potentially realized as peaks*, and so the probability from the position of a plateau is a kind of jumping-off platform from which, in a sense, peaks may arise.

3. The lowest probability position, one that has the maximal potential of all possible options that could be transformed into an actual, is within the *plane* of possibility.

For the benefit of our shared understanding, we can now visually see on our diagram how *energy moves from plane or plateau to peak*

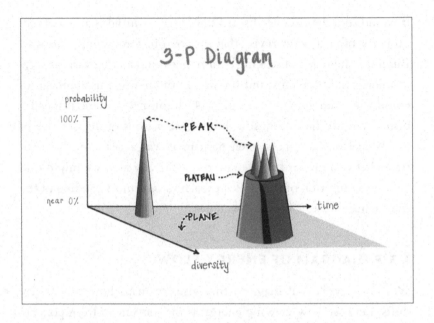

as it shifts from open possibility or elevated probability to actualization. This is one meaning of the term *energy flow*, and it is how we can visually attempt to display that movement between possible and actual. In other words, we are building on the notion of energy as the movement from possible to actual with the suggestion that energy also may move through a series of probability values as indicated by the plateaus. On the diagram, we can see that peaks sometimes arise directly from the plane, and sometimes directly from a plateau.

Plane, plateau, and *peak,* then, are our three grounding terms and describe the way we can visualize what energy flow may involve. For this reason, we will name this diagram, and this overall framework, a *3-P* perspective.

This 3-P diagram is an attempt to visualize a consilience or common ground between a physics view of energy and our emerging findings of the subjective experience people have with the practice of the Wheel of Awareness. Back when I first heard of this view of energy, I thought that if this consilient approach did not work, maybe it would soon be time to discard the idea that mind is an emergent property of energy, or revise that proposal in some significant way. But if this approach of seeking common ground among various ways of understanding reality and the nature of energy, this approach of consilience, did apply, if it could help illuminate potential mechanisms beneath the findings of direct observations of the practice of the Wheel of Awareness, then perhaps it was at least on the right track. Let's go forward and see more specifically how we might find a useful application of this 3-P approach to our understanding of the experience of the Wheel of Awareness.

A 3-P DIAGRAM OF ENERGY FLOW

We now have a 3-P diagram that visually maps how probability shifts. Let's see how viewing energy as the movement from possible to actual may directly correlate with our experience of the Wheel— and the mind in general.

Our diagram has three coordinates, like a three-dimensional mapping we might use to indicate the location of something in space. That something is a particular variable of energy we are now naming directly, the variable of probability. The vertical, y-axis can be called a probability distribution curve indicating where the probability value is between near-zero and 100 percent. We can let go of the specifics of our introductory examples of you knowing a word I might think of, and now view the diagram as a more general mapping of energy—and as we'll soon come to see, of the mind and the Wheel of Awareness.

Our map is a diagram delineating probability, time, and diversity. *Probability* ranges from lowest at near-zero in the plane to 100 percent, the highest at a peak. *Time* really means *change*, as we've seen, and so this is measured as "clock-time," how things unfold as our measurements of time, our clocks, move forward. *Diversity* is how many potential items are present at a given position, ranging from zero to infinite. These coordinates of the map, these three axes, indicate the values of each of these three variables as we locate a position in the three-dimensional diagram. A position, then, a point on the diagram, corresponds to the y-axis of probability, the x-axis for a moment in time, and the z-axis for diversity. As energy change unfolds across clock-time, we move along the x-axis. A simple way of thinking about energy change, one that we will emphasize in our discussions here, can be shown on the diagram as a position that moves along two of our three axes—the y-axis as it changes along the probability distribution value, and the x-axis of where we are in clock-time.

Our third axis represents the variations or diversity that may exist at a given moment, from a narrow range to a broad distribution. In any given moment, there may be a diversity of things possible, indicated as the width of the z-axis coordinates, so a position might be not just a singular point, but a broad expanse. This z-axis, then, is a visual indication of not which particular things, but rather how many things are possible in a given energy state.

By definition, the plane of possibility is at the near-zero point in probability and is filled with a nearly infinite array of potentialities, so its diversity is maximal in the plane. The plane has that two-dimensional appearance of a huge z-axis breadth—a visual depiction of infinity—that defines one dimensional edge of the figure of a plane by this z-axis. Notice, too, that the other dimension of the plane is the x-axis of time, which extends without end, implying eternity. This implies that the mathematical space of the plane is both infinite and eternal—extending along the diversity and time dimensions maximally. As we've noted, this lowest-probability value of the plane is identical to having the qualities of highest potential. The equivalent of near-zero probability is virtually infinite possibility. And so this can be called an *open plane of possibility*. Notice that in mathematical terms, this plane of possibility represents a boundless state of eternity (maximal time), infinity (maximal diversity), and open potential (maximal possibility).

In our diagram, we can see energy flow as moving between maximal possibility in the plane to maximal probability in a peak.

The plane of possibility in physics terminology would be similar to what the quantum physicist Arthur Zajonc, when I presented this model to him at a meeting, said he likes to call a "sea of potential." And he said that without knowing our example of *ocean* as a term! Or, perhaps, even more likely, Arthur made that suggestion of the sea of potential, and my daughter is doing work related to the health of the oceans, and my family and I just had a birthday celebration near the ocean—so all of these water-related experiences, embedded in memory, which itself is a probability process in our embodied brains, made it more likely I'd be primed to say or write *ocean* instead of something else. In this case, you could map that state of my mind as having some priming, some readying of my responses, some in-creased probability we can now name as a plateau, leaning toward a word more likely to be related to seas or oceans. This enhanced probability, this increased certainty about a water-related term being chosen, is our plateau of elevated probability created because of each of these diverse and interrelated experiences over time shaping the energy state of my mind at that moment of choosing the word. This might be specifically an energy state of my brain, or it might be an energy state of my body, or it might also be an energy state of each of these and my relationships in the world, including with Arthur, and now including with you. Energy state—however it might man-ifest itself, we can propose—involves a probability position, and now we have a diagram to visually illustrate just that.

Physicists also refer to this notion of a mathematical location such as the plane of possibility, a probability space that contains all that might arise, this sea of potential, as the *quantum vacuum*. As we men-tioned, to continue to stay true to the science, it's important to recall that for some scientists, this vacuum is not energy itself; it is *where energy comes from*. In other words, the sea of potential, the quantum vacuum, what we're naming on our diagram a plane of possibility, is not energy; it's just the ground of the universe or the mathematical space of all possibilities from which energy arises. We'll try to be as careful in the use of our terminology as we can, referring to the probability position of the plane on the diagram as the source of energy arising, not the energy itself. When energy flows, it is emerging from this plane of possibility and arising as actualities, visualized on the 3-P diagram as peaks and also, we are proposing, as plateaus of elevated probabilities. It's at that moment of arising from the vacuum that energy is happening.

For our discussion here, let's keep this notion that energy per se is not in the quantum vacuum or sea of potential in the back of our minds, but we won't need to worry too much about these distinctions of the plane as not being energy itself, and simply that it is the source of energy. Our attempt here is to prepare your mind with science, and extend that science into applications in understanding our subjective experiences. The plane of possibility is related to energy, for sure, even if it isn't energy itself but the source—a probability space—from which energy emerges.

It may be that neural processes in the body harness these energy movements of probability and directly shape our subjective experience of mind and the ways we experience our relationships in the world. The fundamental concept we are now exploring is the view of energy as the movement from a sea of potential toward the realization into actuality.

By the way, these notions about a plane of possibilities that only get manifested into actuality by the flow of energy do not mean that there is no *actual* quantum vacuum. We are using the phrases *actualization* or something being *actualized* or *activated* or *realized* to simply mean "manifesting as a form that came from a potential." Even the term *realization* implies that when something is an idea or potential it is not real until it is realized. Possibility *is* real. In other words, *energy is the movement into form that arises from a formless pool of potentialities, of possibilities, from which all forms emerge*—they become realized, activated, actualized. Potential becomes manifested. Possibility becomes actual. Formless becomes form.

That's one take on the physics view of how energy flows in the world we live in. It seems mystical, spiritual, and perhaps even magical. But it's really the mathematical mechanisms beneath a physics view of energy and our universe. The formless sea of potential, the quantum vacuum, may not be energy itself but it is the real aspect of the universe from which all energy is thought to arise.

MAPPING THE MIND AS PEAKS, PLATEAUS, AND A PLANE OF POSSIBILITY

Do you ever get that feeling of continual emergence into form from the formless when you let your mind simply wander? In the Wheel practice, when we experience open awareness, we may be becoming aware of how actualizations bubble up from a plane of possibility. That space of the plane isn't really anywhere as a physical space per se; as we've discussed, it's a mathematical space of potentiality from which anything that *could* be comes to be. I know the notion of a mathematical space may seem unfamiliar or even odd, but it's a way we can try to articulate the mechanisms of our universe and how energy is a real process in our world that may emerge from it. The subjective feeling of mental activities "bubbling up" that is so often described may reveal the fundamental mechanism of how possible becomes actual, how formless becomes form—which is exactly what the science of physics states energy flow is all about.

The potentiality of possibility is real; it is simply formless.

What arises from the plane of possibility is an actualization. Potential in the plane or probable in a plateau does not make these nonrealized states unreal or unimportant; it simply places them in a different position in energy's unfolding.

Moving from possible to actual, this proposal and the 3-P framework expand this notion of energy to include a range of probabilities resting between the extremes of maximal potential at the near-zero probability position of the plane to actualization at a peak of 100 percent. If there were truth in both the disciplined studies of the universe and careful observations of the mind's awareness, wouldn't we expect to find some sort of consilience across these usually independent fields? Wouldn't there be a common ground between science and subjectivity? How might a view of energy as moving from possibility to probability to actuality correspond to your experience with the Wheel of Awareness?

If the mind is indeed an emergent process of energy flow, and energy changes not only through shifts in the CLIFF variables of contour, location, intensity, frequency, and form (variables we are familiar with at the classical Newtonian, macrostate, large-body level of experience) but also in its probability and even its diversity values—what we may experience more at the quantum, microstate level—then we should be able to map out aspects of the mind and the experience of the Wheel from this 3-P perspective. Let's reflect on your Wheel of Awareness practice and see how mental experience might correspond to this 3-P diagram.

A *peak* might be a thought. As the many possible cognitive processes transforming energy into information unfold, one may become manifest and available for awareness as a specific thought. Possible thoughts emerge into reality as one particular thought.

The area just beneath a peak but above a plateau, what we can call a *sub-peak position*, might be thinking. This could be seen as a kind of cognitive *cone*, a functional funnel through which the unfolding of energy patterns called thinking can flow and become focused and narrowed into a singular thought.

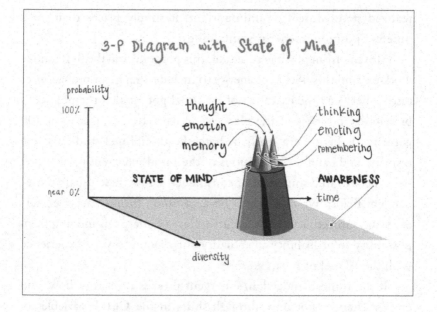

Likewise, a memory would be a peak, and remembering a sub-peak position. Here again we'd envision the cone arising from sub-peak toward peak values as a funnel through which the many layers of memory would be shaped and shifted toward a singular memory, or, if diversity were high, a set of memories activated simultaneously.

In a similar way, an emotion might be a peak; emoting or emotional processes would be a sub-peak position.

Emotions are a complex set of processes, and the feelings underlying them that arise from the whole body interact with neural processes of thought and memory to form our emotional processing in the moment. In other words, we have terms for these mental experiences that imply their separate nature when in fact they may be inextricably intertwined as emotion-thought-memory and more. When we become aware of that intricate subjective feeling state, we can view this as the emergence of possible feelings into one actualized state, the bubbling up of a peak of an emotion, thought, memory, and more from the feeling funnel that on our diagram is depicted as a cone underneath the peak.

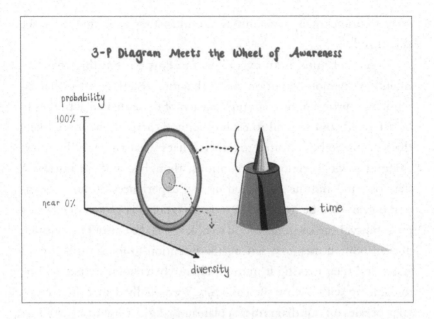

Here we have the notion that the rim points of the various segments of the rim on the Wheel practice might correlate with our peaks and sub-peaks that form the cognitive cones or funnels that direct the potential and probable into becoming actualized. For ease of reference, we'll simply use the singular term *peak* for the thought and the thinking, memory and remembering, emotion and emoting that are the ways these rim points become realized in an intertwined manner. In other words, we've come to a suggestion that the combined sub-peak and peak positions of the 3-P diagram might correspond to the rim of the Wheel of Awareness.

Beneath a peak rest probabilities that are higher than the plane but lower than a peak, like the *state of mind* of choosing only words beginning with an *o* or naming one of five oceans. Such states of mind include intention as a mental process, one we've discussed that sets the direction of energy and information flow and the ways it will be processed. Now we can envision how such a state of mind may be correlated with a *plateau*. From a given plateau, a given state of mind, cones moving up toward peak positions of actualization serve to funnel many possibilities into ultimately a selected few to be actualized.

A state of mind is an overall energy flow pattern that coalesces intention, memory, emotion, and behavioral reactions into what essentially is priming, or readying, of each of these mental activities to be activated, and to bind to each other and therefore be more likely than chance to be activated together. That's what we mean by intertwining mental events like emotions, thoughts, and memories. A state of mind and the associated mental experiences of mood or intention can each be mapped onto our diagram as a *plateau* of elevated probability. I can be in the mood to talk about the ocean I just visited, present now in memory, setting the intention to focus on bodies of water and then making it more likely my behavioral output will be to come up with a word such as *ocean*. We visually depict these mental processes on our diagram as a plateau that gives rise to a particular set of peaks, this one peak that arose being the realization of the word *ocean*.

What might a plateau on our 3-P diagram correspond with in our Wheel of Awareness practice? At times, it may be possible to have a state of mind enter our awareness, and then in this case the plateau may itself correlate with a rim element—something that is able to enter awareness when linked with a spoke of attention. At other times, plateaus may be quite difficult to detect, serving as *filters of consciousness* outside awareness that give rise to only particular cones and their peaks. Such filters may enable only certain elements to enter awareness, determining which rim points can be linked to the hub by a spoke of focal attention. In this way plateaus serve as filters for what does or does not become a part of the peaks of actualization we can experience as the objects of awareness.

It may be, too, that plateaus as filters also shape what becomes a part of our nonconscious mental life, restricting and shaping what becomes actualized from a very specific subset of potentials it enables to become a peak—even if these are not a part of consciousness. In

other words, possible becoming actual may occur without our becoming aware of it. We know from a range of studies that many
mental activities—thoughts, memories, emotions—occur primarily
outside our conscious experience. This might be depicted on the
metaphoric image of the Wheel simply as a rim element without
being linked by the spoke of attention to awareness in the hub. What
might this mean in terms of how nonconscious mental activities
would be viewed on our 3-P diagram? We'll address that question a
little bit later in our journey, so let's see what we come up with as we
move forward in our discussion.

The plane of possibility on our 3-P diagram represents the generator of diversity, the source of anything that might be possible, a
sea of potential, the quantum vacuum. Emerging from the source of
potential processes and forms, our plateaus and peaks arise from the
formless sea of potential, our plane of possibility.

The plane of possibility is a real, mathematical probability space,
even if it is not in the kind of classical Newtonian physical space our
embodied minds are used to encountering, and even conceiving.
Cognition, the way we think, is said to be *embodied* and *enacted*,
meaning the way we process information is shaped by these bodies
we live in and how we move around in the world. Since the body is
a big collection of microstates assembled into a large macrostate that
interacts through our five senses with other macrostates, naturally we
all think, as Sir Isaac Newton did, in these classical physics notions
of space and time. At the quantum, empirically established level of
microstates, however, space and time are simply not the same entities
as our Newtonian embodied and enacted minds might think—or
even perceive. Add to this the view that our cognition is also *extended*
into other information-processing forms in our classical world and
embedded in our shared cultural meaning systems, and we can see how
our views may also be constrained and reinforced by conventions of
common communication—of shared notions of reality. To move beyond these understandable patterns of embedded, extended, enacted,

and embodied cognition, we can take a deep Newtonian breath and open our minds to a microstate perspective on probability that comes from a scientifically grounded, quantum level of viewing the nature of energy flow. Our 3-P diagram maps out a quantum notion of probability and now we are attempting to find correlations of this framework with our Wheel experience.

The value of these three aspects of the diagram—plane, plateau, and peak—is that we can see how their probability position may illuminate mechanisms of the mind underlying the Wheel experience.

The plane represents a wide diversity of possibilities. A plateau is a more limited set of potential activations from which a more constrained pattern of peaks can arise. A high and narrow plateau would indicate a narrow state of mind; for example, a mental filter that would only give rise to a limited number of peaks of thought, emotion, memory, and images as they become actualized. A lower, broader plateau would indicate a more open state of mind, but a particular mind frame that is still a filter permitting a wider but nevertheless constrained set of mental activities as peaks or even states of mind as

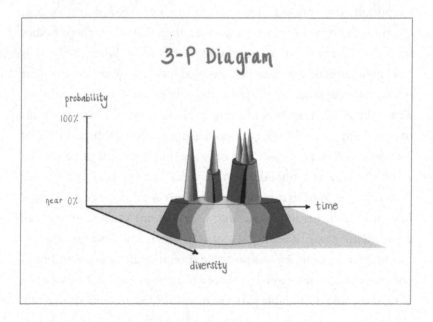

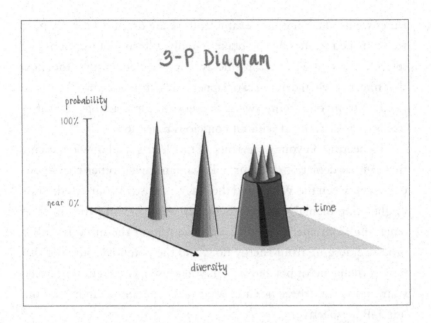

particular plateaus arise from it. Plateaus function as filters, helping us learn from the past and to be efficient in the present so we can prepare for the immediate future. There is great survival value in being able to construct filters—plateaus are a helpful function of the mind, if they can be flexible and adaptive.

A low-lying plateau may be a way of visually depicting a frame of mind, such as a self-defining mindset that who I am is separate from the world or my identification with one in-group or another, that embeds a mental stance with a specific range of states of mind seen as particular plateaus and their respective thought patterns arising as peaks.

We can even see on our 3-P diagram how some peaks might emerge directly from the plane, and perhaps this is a wide-open mind, not constrained by a particular frame of mind and mental states that filter what is able to become actualized from the pool of possibilities. Perhaps this experience of peaks rising up directly from the plane of possibility is what is meant by a "beginner's mind." Sometimes it is great to have that state of a filterless mind; at other times we need a filter—for example, if we are driving a car, we need to be primed to step on the brakes rapidly, filtering our options to a select few so that we can stop quickly when needed. Notice, too, how that filtering when driving can happen on "automatic pilot," without needing to involve being aware. Sometimes, rapid action—a peak—needs to be actualized without conscious reflection.

Reflecting on your experience of the Wheel, and now reviewing these visual depictions on our 3-P diagram, what other correspondences between the Wheel and the diagram arise in your mind? How might your mental experience match with viewing the mind as emerging from energy flow? If a mechanism of the mind is truly a process emerging from energy flow, and the potential source of that flow is the plane of possibility, can you sense a connection between your subjective experience and what this experience might be from our 3-P perspective?

Can you feel how a thought arises with a certain intention, moves forward as thinking, and then becomes crystal clear, suddenly, within awareness—as a peak of activation? Can you feel the sometimes less clearly demarcated experience of thinking—a sub-peak position? And how does a mood or intention feel to you—what is the sense of a plateau? These mental activities of the third segment of the rim might be positions above the plane, as plateaus, sub-peak positions, or peaks themselves. The mind's activities, the rim points along the third segment of our Wheel of Awareness, can now be mapped on our 3-P diagram.

And what of the first and second segments of the rim? These may come to us as peaks of activation as well. When we focus directly on hearing and sight, taste, touch, or smell, a possible is transforming into an actual. As we take in these forms of external energy flow, they influence our sensory receptors and the downstream circuitry that ultimately links us to sensory awareness. When we coalesce a given sensory channel with others, and combine this with the filtering process of prior knowledge we call perceptual bias, we develop a more complex perceptual awareness, a process capable of being shown on our 3-P diagram as plateaus of filtering possibility into peaks of activation. These above-plane positions of plateaus and peaks would be the rim points of our first segment of the Wheel, too.

The second-segment input of bodily states can arise as movements from possibility to actuality as we sense the energy state of the body. In all the ways the body's signals can form and transform, it is energy that flows—the movement of these possibilities into elevated probabilities of a state of the body, and then into the particular actualities of that moment. This might be sensed as plateaus of general bodily states or peaks of specific feelings that are the manifestations of the energy state of the body, what would be rim points on the second segment of interoceptive awareness on our Wheel. Rim points here, again, would include plateaus and peaks, the above-plane values of energy along the probability distribution curve. We might experience a broad, restless feeling in our body, as when our awareness takes in the signals of our heart and gut. As we scan our body's state, the feeling of our gut and heart can become clearer, moving perhaps from a plateau to a peak, and we can then sense in a specific way what our heartfelt and gut-based intuition might guide us toward as a course of behavior to be taken. Our body's state can serve as a helpful guide to our overall actions, opening us up to the plateaus of our internal states of mind so that we use an internal compass to adjust the peaks of action in more adaptive and, we could say, integrative ways.

Energy states in general can be revealed as conglomerations or profiles of any combination of the variables of CLIFF that can shift and change as possible becomes actual, as energy flows. That set of CLIFF profiles is magnificently diverse and rich in its complexity. Now we can name probability and diversity as another two facets of energy that can also be identified as shifting variables beyond these five of contour, location, intensity, frequency, and form. Let's focus primarily on the variable of probability in our discussions ahead. We may only get a glimpse of this probability-state facet of energy at a quantum, microstate, reflective way of being aware, as we learn to become sensitive to where energy is along the probability distribution curve. We indicate the characteristic of this probability variable by its vertical position on the 3-P diagram.

Have you ever felt in your body a sense of something emerging? Could you sense a mood not quite manifesting as a feeling but instead as a vague but real overall frame of being in that moment, a leaning, a propensity? Have you ever had that sensation in your mind of something "wanting to happen"? Each of these sensations may be energy in the plateau position. A plateau is an increased likelihood, a priming, a propensity. A plateau in general serves as a filter, making certain peaks of activation more likely to arise than others. That may be the mechanism of how a plateau serves as a *priming filter.* We'll simply use the term *filter* to designate in our 3-P framework how a plateau selects only certain aspects of the wide array of possibilities of the plane to be available for actualization. What is actualized? A particular bodily sensation, a specific emotion, a mental idea becoming crystal clear—these would be the movements toward peaks from our filtering plateaus of energy in that moment. It may be that becoming aware of an energy pattern is more easily achieved when it is at a peak position; when energy is at a lower-probability state, such as a plateau, it may have a less distinct quality when we do come to sense it directly. In other words, we may be able to sense peaks in awareness much more readily than sub-peak processes or filtering plateaus.

In your body and its brain, we can imagine the neural mechanism accompanying this sixth facet of energy's probability shifts as arising from the electrochemical energy state of our nervous system and our body proper. For example, some scientists believe that when we are experiencing the recall of memory, neurons fire in a pattern linked to the past event. That's how we've come to store a memory created by a past event that influences the *probability of neural firing at some future time.* This is what memory storage and retrieval means—

an altered probability of firing now based on what happened then. This would mean that the actual manner in which we store our memories and perhaps even think our thoughts is embedded in our nervous system as a probability function. Our emotions, too, influence the likelihood of the unfolding of thought and memory in what are called "state-dependent" processes—the emotional state we are in directly shapes the nature of the information processing that unfolds. Information arises from patterns of energy, and we can now see how part of that emergence is shaped by probability—in both our brain and the sensation of our mental experiences. We can see that our 3-P framework focusing on the variable of probability is actually quite consilient with the neuroscience view of how the brain functions and the mind emerges.

We also have something called "memory of the future," in which we anticipate what is coming next by priming the way we are likely to act. Researchers think these priming processes involve alterations in the interactions and interconnections among linked neurons. These shape our prospective mind, creating the experience of self-fulfilling prophecies, the way our sense of self in the world reinforces its own becoming. We've discussed these self-defining and sometimes self-confining processes—part of our mental time travel and prospective thinking—as functions of the default mode network, the DMN.

These neural processes may be the embodied mechanism of our plateaus that serve as *filters of consciousness* creating our sense of self and shaping our states of mind. We may have patterns of a range of plateaus that organize how we process information in various states, influencing the ways thoughts or emotions or memories come to be available to us within awareness. We can sometimes feel our filtering plateaus directly, but more often we sense the shadows they cast on the states of mind they prime us to feel and the particular set of selected peaks they permit to arise.

Our filters of consciousness shape our experience of mind and, in turn, shape the actualizations that can emerge, defining and sometimes confining our experience of the feeling of being alive.

When our filters are free and flexible, we are efficient and live in harmony with the world, having a fluid sense of self arising from a dynamic set of plateaus adjusting to the ever-changing needs of the world around us and within us. This is what it means to live with presence. When a particular filter is frozen and rigid, or chaotic and without a coherent core of its structure, these characteristics can make us prone to the rigidity and chaos that an unrealized and unintegrating self-defining set of plateaus can create. In these situations, being present and showing up fully for life are compromised.

Peaks, plateaus, and plane—these are on a continuum of probability values and depict how our body and mind may function based on shifts in energy.

We've identified the above-plane values of peaks and plateaus of the 3-P diagram as corresponding to the rim points in our Wheel map of the mind. That's a useful and grounding way of seeing how the energy mechanism of this 3-P framework correlates with the visual image of our metaphor of the Wheel—especially the rim. Let's now build on our ongoing direct experiences with the Wheel practice and focus on the hub and spoke directly in order to further anchor this 3-P diagram in our understanding of awareness and what it means to live with presence.

AWARENESS, THE HUB, AND A PLANE OF POSSIBILITY

AWARENESS AND THE PLANE OF POSSIBILITY

When you do the Wheel practice, what does the space between mental activities feel like? What is the sensation for you when you bend the spoke around to rest in the hub, when you are aware of awareness in the hub-in-hub portion of the practice? In this section, we'll explore how the mechanisms of your mind's awareness may correspond to the properties of energy from our 3-P framework.

When I guide individuals through the Wheel practice and we come to the third rim segment review, I suggest that they allow any mental activities on the rim to enter their awareness. Ironically, many have reported to me that few or even no mental activities arose, and if they did, they were much less intense and frequent. One description of the experience is that it feels as if waves are lapping on the shore of awareness. For some, this is the first moment in a very long time that they have felt peace of mind—lapping waves instead of pounding surf. Words used to describe this state in which "very little was arising" or "nothing was coming" and feeling as if awareness exists in the "space between mental activities" are parallel to those used to describe the hub-in-hub step of becoming aware of awareness. As we discussed at the end of part I, these descriptions commonly include terms like open, expansive, vast, peaceful, serene, clear, infinite, time disappearing, at ease, God, love, joy, and spacious. Other descriptions include the sense of emptiness and fullness all at once, a sense of feeling complete and open. What do these direct immersions in the hub, in awareness itself, illuminate about possible mechanisms of mind and what might correlate with our 3-P understanding?

When I first began to notice how similar people's descriptions of the hub were, I thought it might be some kind of fluke, some interesting though odd finding particular to the individuals I happened to be working with. But then when my colleagues began reporting similar results in themselves and with their clients, and when more and more workshop participants, without knowing of these findings, would say virtually identical things—regardless of their background education, culture, or experience with meditation—I began to wonder what these universal experiences might be revealing.

You may at times have a different set of sensations; I do as well. Our experiences with the Wheel may vary from practice session to practice session. Yet the commonality of these reports across such a large variety and number of individuals—consistent with those in other practices from the distant past, as we've discussed earlier— invites us to consider what common mechanisms may be tying these together.

When we take the Wheel reports of the subjective experience of the space between mental activities and of the hub itself, might the descriptions of this spaciousness correspond to the plane of possibility?

Perhaps—underlined a thousand times—*perhaps* the source of the knowing of consciousness, the subjective experience of being aware, emerges from the plane of possibility.

If this proposal is true, then here is what it might explain. When we bend the spoke around and become aware of pure awareness, the reason we experience a sense of vastness is that we are experiencing infinite possibility—the sea of potential—that is the mathematical reality of the plane.

This view would help explain what might be going on in awareness that many would describe as having both a sense of emptiness and fullness at the same time. What might be happening that could be both empty and full at the same time, as so many describe? The plane is empty of actualities yet full of possibilities. The plane is devoid of forms but filled with the formlessness of potential. The plane is both empty and full, simultaneously.

Actuality and form emerge at above-the-plane positions along the probability spectrum. Energy flows and gives rise to probabilities and actualities; the plane represents all that might arise though it has not yet arisen. And this plane of possibility might just be the source of awareness. If the knowns of the rim correspond to peaks and plateaus, those above-plane positions on the 3-P diagram, the plane itself might correspond with the hub—the knowing of awareness.

Let's pause for a moment, or several moments, to consider this proposition.

Here's a very brief overview to consolidate what we explored in the previous section. A thought, emotion, and memory might be a peak. Thinking, emoting, and remembering might be a sub-peak value, just below the peak. The cones leading up to these peaks would serve as funnels that narrow down the possibilities arising from particular plateaus—and sometimes arising directly from the plane itself. An intention, mood, or state of mind might be a plateau. These plateaus would then confine and define the kinds of thinking, emoting, and remembering we experience as they give rise to specific thoughts, emotions, and memories. These plateaus are the filters of consciousness that shape how the knowns of our minds unfold, directing the nature of the rim elements and shaping what we can become aware of within the hub.

The new component of our proposal we are introducing here is that the experience of being aware itself emerges from the plane of possibility. The knowing of the hub would correlate with the plane. The knowns of thought and thinking, emotion and emoting, memory and remembering and states of mind, intentions, and moods would be above-plane values, our peaks, sub-peak positions, and plateaus.

BRAIN CORRELATES OF PURE CONSCIOUSNESS

Modern neurobiology, including its branch of contemplative neuro-science that studies reflective practices such as meditation, as we've seen, suggests that the subjective description of a vast and spacious awareness might correlate in time with the finding of highly integrative neural firing patterns in the brain.

Our suggestion from the 3-P perspective is that this "spacious, empty clarity" arises as the mind's open and receptive awareness occurs when the energy probability position is immersed in the plane of possibility—a probability position of near-zero certainty that we've seen is not energy itself, but the source from which energy arises.

Merging these three separate approaches of subjective experience, empirical brain measurement, and our energy probability framework of the mind, what might we propose as the neural correlate of our plane of possibility?

As we have explored in previous chapters, many brain-based theories suggest consciousness arises from *integration of information within neural activity*. Electroencephalogram studies support this notion of integration across neural circuit activations in the process of being aware. We've placed an energy lens on these statements, viewing *neural integration as a pattern of linking differentiated energy states together*. Gamma waves are one way to assess such states of neural integration as differentiated regions are firing in synchrony. Let's see how these views of integration might in some way correspond to the plane of possibility proposal of awareness.

Could this sea of potential, represented as the plane of possibility in our 3-P diagram, be considered a linkage of infinite diversity within that mathematical space of potentiality? In other words, if the plane represents the physics-established notion of a sea of potential, then within that quantum vacuum rests infinite potentiality—that's simply how it is scientifically defined. From an integration point of view, this space could be interpreted as the ultimate level of differentiation—all that could be rests there—as well as linkage, as it all rests in the same interconnecting probability space. That linkage of differentiated potentials could then be seen as a huge degree of integration from our 3-P framework.

In the brain, how would we measure such massive diversity and linkage all in one neural energy state? Might this be some electro-chemical energy profile reflecting a form of integration, the open linkage of ultimate differentiation? Could this state of massive integration be how the brain mediates the process of awareness?

Recall that gamma oscillations are patterns of electroencephalo-gram (EEG) findings that are measuring highly integrated electrical activity in the brain. In contemplative studies of subjects who were expert meditators, neuroscientist Richie Davidson has found these gamma waves to be associated with a "spaciousness and vastness in their experience, as if all their senses were wide open to the full, rich panorama of experience."* Recall, too, that other researchers in this new branch of neuroscience studying contemplation, including Judson Brewer and his colleagues, found that effortless awareness, created by a range of ways of having a receptive awareness to whatever arises, was associated with network integration in the brain of experienced meditators.

In seeking a consilience among the other brain-based notions of consciousness, from the point of view of the integrated information theory of neuroscientists Tononi and Koch, mentioned earlier, could it be that when states of integration are achieved in the brain, the

---

* Goleman and Davidson, *Altered Traits*, 232.

subjective experience of being aware arises as it is entering this plane of possibility position during that integrated brain state? In other words, could these EEG findings of receptive awareness and the brain's integrated firing patterns during consciousness reveal an over-all probability position of the brain's energy state as being in the plane of possibility?

From the attention schema theory perspective of Graziano in discussing the consciousness of the social brain, as we discussed ear-lier, we could propose that modeling attentional focus—making a map of attention itself—on the experience of paying attention to pure awareness might create a certain kind of spacious schema, a wide expansive mapping of that specific state of attention on aware-ness. Integrated complexity in the brain creates awareness. Letting go of a particular object of attention and simply focusing attention on the modeling of attention—what this view suggests awareness ulti-mately is—would then amplify a kind of modeling of modeling, in-creasing a state of neural integration at that moment.

Under usual circumstances, what these two theories offer is a view of focal attention—the experience of being aware of *something*—not really the experience of pure awareness itself. Could the contem-plative neuroscience views of integration with vast and spacious receptive awareness be combined with these two cognitive neurosci-ence views of integration and focal attention, perhaps revealing the brain's activity involved with being aware not only of something, but of pure awareness itself?

Staying with the broad field of brain science, we can turn now to the work of neuroscientist Rodolfo Llinás, who proposes that a forty-cycle-per-second, or 40-hertz (Hz), electrical activity sweep from a deep area of the brain, the thalamus, up to the higher cortical regions gives rise to our experience of being aware of something. In other words, somehow this observed 40-Hz energy sweep is thought to be fundamental to becoming aware. We'll explore this neural sweeping process more soon, but here just note again that a common view of some kind of linking of different regions within large-scale networks seems to be at the core of how the brain is involved in consciousness. How and why the subjective experience of being aware actually happens in this view, as with all of the brain-based views, as far as I can tell, we simply do not understand. And even how and why the subjective experience of being aware might arise from our proposed 3-P framework of the plane of possibility—whether this state is in the head-brain, the whole body, in our relationships, or, as some have suggested, in the cosmos—we just don't know, either.

If this plane of possibility view on the origins of awareness is correct, if it is an accurate though necessarily incomplete description of a possible mechanism of mind and consciousness, then our journey ahead is a potentially fruitful consilient attempt to link science with subjective experience, an effort worthy of our continued exploration and application.

In the section that follows, we'll deepen our discussion of this proposal that the plane of possibility corresponds to the hub of the Wheel of Awareness by exploring the distinct subjective experience of "living from the hub" versus "being stuck on the rim." The plane may be experienced more at the quantum microstate level than the rim, which may be dominated more by the Newtonian, classical physics macrostate rules including certainties and an arrow of time. This view may help us understand our direct experience with the Wheel and how facets of the hub's sense of limitless potential and the presence of possibilities devoid of an arrow of time may fill our subjective experience with a deep sense of freedom arising from the plane of possibility. This shifting from the spacious hub to the certain rim, from plane to above-plane plateaus and peaks, may in this way reveal the contrasts between the quantum and classical levels of reality in our day-to-day lives. Understanding this contrast more fully is aided by illuminating the nature of the plateaus that serve as our above-plane filters of consciousness in the next step of our journey.

FILTERS OF CONSCIOUSNESS

FILTERS OF CONSCIOUSNESS AND
THE ORGANIZATION OF EXPERIENCE

A question before us right now is how it might be that we become aware of some fragments of energy or information and yet do not become aware of others. In other words, why and how do only some peaks and plateaus enter awareness whereas others, even perhaps the great majority of them—our nonconscious energy and information flow patterns—do not?

When we dream, for example, we have a kind of awareness that we may not recall later on. However, we have all experienced instances when we awoke from a dream quite aware of what we were just experiencing. Writing a dream down at that moment gives you a chance to recall the dream world later on. Neuroscientist Rodolfo Llinás has written about the notion that all states of consciousness can be compared to dreaming. Sigmund Freud also wrote extensively about dreams, suggesting that they served as a "royal road to the unconscious." He referred to dreams as a form of "primary consciousness," in contrast to our waking state, which he called "secondary consciousness," in which our awareness of our true feelings and motivations is hampered in some way. Both Llinás and Freud allude to the quality of dreaming in which there is a shift away from any sense of a tightly demarcated self. It is as if we are looking at the action in our dreams as both the seer and the seen; in this sense, there is so much we can discover about ourselves, and perhaps about reality, by examining our dreams. If we can remember them upon waking we can use these insights consciously, but dreams—and nonconscious mental life in general—affect us even if we are not aware of their existence.

You might have noticed that I am using the term *nonconscious* instead of *subconscious* or *unconscious*. I do this consciously because I have found that these terms have particular meanings in a range of domains—including psychoanalysis, and even within our popular culture—which tend to build the conception that there is a certain uniform structure to what underlies our minds. Quite to the contrary, these nonconscious processes are anything but uniform. *Nonconscious* is a more fitting term in my estimation, as it communicates that, in fact, a vast array—perhaps even the majority—of diverse mental activities are transpiring in any given moment without ultimately linking to our awareness. When we awaken in the morning, we often have no recollection of any dream having occurred, though there is a great deal of research on the brain states associated with sleep that reveal that the brain is quite active during certain phases of sleep. What is this "work" that our brain is doing while we sleep that requires us to be "unaware" later on of so much of this neural activity and the energy and information patterns it creates?

A similar experience of this dream reality, in which we have a more loosely defined self who can perceive the action of the dream from many angles, can be felt under the influence of some psychedelic drugs. And perhaps not surprisingly scientists who have recently studied the brain's activity under the influence of certain drugs, such as psilocybin and MDMA, have compared this pattern of neural firing to certain aspects of the dream state. In these brain states, the tight functional linkage of certain higher cortical regions with the integrative functions of the lower limbic areas, including the hippocampus, loosens. This decoupling of one set of areas from another may allow for a much broader range of neural firing patterns to be released in these states. The possibility these empirical findings invite us to consider is that the usual "waking brain state" may in fact limit us to one set of neurally constructed experiences of what we deem to be real. In this manner, our waking state may have a confined set of what we are calling *filters of consciousness* that carefully orchestrate what we experience in awareness and hence believe is the only perspective that is real.

As William James stated in his classic text, *Varieties of Religious Experience*: "Our normal waking consciousness, rational consciousness as we call it, is but one special type of consciousness, whilst all about it, parted from it by the filmiest of screens, there lie potential forms of consciousness entirely different. . . . We may go through life without suspecting their existence; but apply the requisite stimulus, and at a touch they are there in all their completeness, definite types of mentality which probably somewhere have their field of application and adaptation. No account of the universe in its totality can be final which leaves these other forms of consciousness quite disregarded."*

Related studies have revealed lasting clinical improvement in medically ill individuals or those with trauma who are suffering from anxiety and depression after just a few treatment sessions with these primary-consciousness-inducing substances. This seems to indicate that releasing the brain from its habitual filters of consciousness may be therapeutic for certain conditions. These research findings suggest that shifts in consciousness in the moment, and then in how we experience awareness in the long run, can have profoundly beneficial

---

* William James, *Varieties of Religious Experience* (Boston: Harvard University Press original, 1895; CreateSpace Independent Publishing Platform, 2013), 388.

effects on a person's life. For someone facing death or having experienced severe trauma and who is now stuck in rigid or chaotic dysfunction with states of helplessness or terror, it may be that offering new ways of enabling the brain to perceive a wider reality of life offers profound relief, literally freeing their mind from their prior suffering. These studies invite us to consider the possible mechanisms of the mind by understanding how the brain participates in the experience of suffering and how shifts in the brain's neural firing patterns underlying states of consciousness and the experience of self may be transformed in the healing process.

Neuroscientist Selen Atasoy and colleagues have suggested a way of understanding the role of widening the experience of consciousness by exploring how the whole brain's interconnected circuits called the connectome may be functioning, something they call a connectome harmonic: "In other words, during loss of consciousness neural activity becomes locked to a narrow frequency range, whereas in wakefulness a broad frequency range of the connectome harmonic spectrum constitutes the neural activity. A broader range of connectome harmonics are enabled for activation for increased excitation that is known to occur in the psychedelic state (Glennon and others 1984). Hence, following the musical analogy, consciousness can be compared with a rich symphony played by an orchestra, whereas loss of consciousness would correspond to a limited repertoire of a musical note played repetitively."* The question for us is this: Could accessing the hub of the Wheel of Awareness, gaining access to the plane of possibility, offer a way to open consciousness and increase the variety of plateaus that might arise? Without such access, the restricted set of plateaus may potentially be serving as constraining filters of consciousness and limiting which peaks we might have access to experiencing.

---

* Selen Atasoy, Gustavo Deco, Morten L. Kringelback, and Joel Pearson, "Harmonic Brain Modes: A Unifying Framework for Linking Space and Time in Brain Dynamics," *The Neuroscientist*, September 1, 2017, 1–17, doi: 10.1177/1073858417728032.

Many people I have spoken to who have experience with the Wheel practice have described an opening of awareness that may have the mechanism of a similar freeing of the filters of consciousness. They speak of feeling a new sense of freedom from depression, anxiety, and trauma. Reduction in chronic pain is also a common finding. A prior set of filters that kept someone constrained to certain dysfunctional nonintegrated states—ones that might be plateaus imprisoning a person via traumatic intrusions of pain, anxiety, and fear, or leading to the experience of depression, helplessness, or despair—might now be dissolved by giving the person more access to the plane of possibility and freeing him or her from these constraining filter-created states of chaos or rigidity.

As we can see, major growth can occur if we can live more from the plane of possibility and lose or loosen some of the filters—the plateaus—that arise in our lives. To strengthen our minds and prepare them well to meet the challenges of life, let's explore more about this 3-P perspective on growth. Let's first look at how our proposed filters of consciousness may be an above-plane, usually nonconscious mechanism that shapes the nature of our state of being aware.

Let's assume, for now, that the hub is the hub no matter what state of consciousness we are in. In our 3-P terms, we experience awareness from the plane of possibility, and the plane is simply the plane. From a brain mechanism point of view, this would mean that the subjective experience of being aware, however it is mediated, is *not* actually shifting, though our state of consciousness might. What the common experience of dreams may reveal is that there is not a change in the mechanisms of being aware, but a change in the filter of consciousness occurring in that state. A particular state of consciousness, then, would be a change not in awareness itself, but in what shapes the overall experience of being conscious—the contents of what we are aware of and the characteristics of that state of awareness itself, as we'll soon explore.

Filters shape what emerges as contents of our awareness, which in turn influence further flows of information. This unfolding sometimes flows like a stream, sometimes like a waterfall with such force it can displace everything in its path. The quality of a given state of consciousness is shaped by the nature of the above-plane energy patterns that arise.

What are these above-plane filters that construct states of consciousness and organize our life? Can we get more than a brief glimpse into their structure and function in our lives so that perhaps we can free ourselves from their incessant hold on how we experience being aware? Instead of avoiding these filters in the opaqueness of our nonconscious minds, can we befriend them and become freer, knowing what they are and the role they serve in our conscious experience of life, and then learn to live more fully through this befriending?

What might brain science illuminate for us about this process of mind that usually operates beneath the surface of our awareness?

HOW TOP-DOWN AND BOTTOM-UP SHAPE OUR SENSE OF REALITY

Is it possible that these filters of consciousness are somehow related to a fundamental mechanism that links awareness to self-organization?

A number of neuroscientists are exploring how to apply mathematical principles to understanding the complex functioning of the brain. Karl Friston has reviewed some of these approaches that examine what is known as the "free-energy principle" of the brain's functioning. Concepts such as free energy, homeostasis, and entropy are explored in great detail. Free energy is "an information theory measure that bounds or limits (by being greater than) the surprise on sampling some data, given a generative model." Homeostasis is "the process whereby an open or closed system regulates its internal environment to maintain its states within bounds." And entropy is defined as "the average surprise of outcomes sampled from a probability distribution or density. A density with low entropy means that, on average, the outcome is relatively predictable. Entropy is therefore a measure of uncertainty."* Certainty is related to self-organization.

As we explored earlier, complex systems have the emergent property of self-organization, one we can suggest is like our river of integration we discussed in part I, with a harmonious flow between order and chaos. This self-organization is an emergent property reflected in John O'Donohue's poetic aspiration, "I would love to live like a river flows, carried by the surprise of its own unfolding." We can let self-organization arise and flow takes care of itself. When given freedom within a complex system, integrative harmony naturally emerges as it travels that edge between familiarity and unfamiliarity, certainty and uncertainty. A systems view of this state is called *criticality* and refers to this state between chaos and rigidity. As M. Mitchell Waldrop suggests: "Criticality is the constantly shifting battle zone between stagnation and anarchy, the one place where a complex system can be spontaneous, adaptive, and alive."† Criticality is the mathematical space of our river of integration and its FACES flow of being flexible, adaptive, coherent, energized, and stable.

It may be that the plane of possibility is the source of that integrative flow of harmony emerging with optimal self-organization.

But sometimes experience constructs our learned plateaus that create impediments to harmony, blockages to integration that lead to peaks of chaos and of rigidity. A rigid peak would be one that stays for long periods of time along our horizontal time axis of change—revealing a highly predictable, unchanging peak of actualization. Or we may have chaotic states arise in which the z-axis of diversity is quite full, with lots of things chaotically arising in a given moment.

In the usual state of consciousness in our everyday adult lives,

---

* Karl Friston, "The Free-Energy Principle: A Unified Brain Theory?" *Nature Reviews Neuroscience* 11, no. 2, 2010, 127–38.

† M. Mitchell Waldrop, *Complexity: The Emerging Science at the Edge of Order and Chaos* (New York: Simon and Schuster, 1992), 12.

most of us have learned to live in world as best we can by having the five aspects of a FACES flow as a part of how our minds work. To stay in the central flow of harmony within the river of integration allows us to be flexible, adaptive, coherent, energized, and stable. To achieve this way of being, we need to attain knowledge, learn skills, and then apply that knowledge and those skills to everyday experience. If we don't acquire these energy patterns and the symbolic forms of information they create as concepts and categories, and instead live as if we have perpetually just arrived anew, everything will be fresh and novel, yes, but we will be extremely inefficient and ineffective in getting things done. We will stop to smell every rose as if it is the first time we've seen and inhaled that magnificent flower—but we will never make it to work or the gym.

Now I imagine you are asking yourself, "Dan, what is wrong with that?" And I am fully on your side about the need to have this beginner's mind, for sure.

Yet there is another side to the story of life. The other day, as an example, I saw a dog on the street on my way to work. To be efficient and effective at getting to work, I needed to note the dog, perhaps taking a moment to appreciate its cuteness; note its type; be cautious of it if it was being aggressive; and then move on. Having the familiarity with the entity—the animal, the mammal, the domesticated canine, the dog—is a way of taking what I'd learned in the past as concepts and categories and *filtering* what I was experiencing at that moment. There is nothing wrong with filtering—with having plateaus. The question is, are we serving them or are they serving us?

One useful term describing this filtering process is *top-down*, which is in contrast to the *bottom-up* of a beginner's mind. This is different from a common use of these terms for the anatomy of the body, with top-down meaning how activity from the cortex (the fingers of your hand model) influences the lower structures (your limbic thumb and brain stem palm). And the reverse, bottom-up, is sometimes used to describe how the anatomically lower structures influence the higher ones. That's a fine use of these terms. But we'll be using these same words in an equally valid but distinct way.

Bottom-up means that the flow of energy and information is fresh and new and as unconstrained as possible, given that we do live in a body. Being a conduit of sensory flow is a bottom-up experience.

In contrast, *top-down* signifies that we are experiencing the construction of information representations shaped by prior experience. In brain terms, the "top" of top-down means that some embedded neural connections that have been formed by prior experience and stored in memory are shaping present energy and information flow and preparing us for the future. Such top-down connectivity makes the brain's current state of firing, what is sometimes called its *spatiotemporal configuration*, directly influence global brain function in that moment. In energy terms, top-down influences can shape the global energy state of the brain in any given experience. Mental construction is a common top-down experience in our lives.

There are a number of views of how prior experience may constrain the types of brain states that are created in a given moment. Whichever mechanisms ultimately apply, the notion is similar: Energy patterns from the past are stored in memory, activated with a given context or experience, and then these reactivated energy patterns—what we can suggest are energy states across the full spectrum of the CLIFF-PD (where the *PD* stands for *probability and diversity*) variables—directly influence incoming streams of sensation so that what is perceived, conceived, and behaviorally enacted is shaped by a top-down filter, automatically preparing us for what comes next.

This is what a plateau does: filter energy and information flow.

A filter funnels possibilities into a set of particular energy patterns and the specific information they convey. Even what we *perceive* with sight is more intricate and influenced by the past than what we *sense* with the receptors of the retinas in our eyes. In short, *there is no such thing as immaculate perception.* We might get as close to bottom-up conduition as we can with sensation; once we perceive, we are prone to the pressures of prior probabilities *filtering* our present experience of what we are aware of. Filters are a top-down process.

Sensation in its purest form may be as bottom-up a flow as we can get, given that we live in a body; perception and conception are already influenced by prior experience through top-down filters of what are sometimes called schema or mental models. What this may mean is that we humans, with our intricately experience-shaped brains, have a great deal of top-down influence on bottom-up sensory input.

This may be why as we move into adolescence and beyond, life can become dulled. We begin to filter too much through the concepts and categories acquired through prior learning and lose touch with the novelty of "beginner's mind" and the freshness of seeing the distinctions among things. The social psychologist Ellen Langer, in her studies of a different kind of "mindfulness" than what is studied with contemplative practices, has revealed that being open to these fresh distinctions is a source of well-being and vitality. In Langer's work, appreciating novel distinctions enhances our health. We can see this finding as revealing a more vital and integrated way to be in the world, freed from the common developmental prison of being a human whose brain restricts the freshness of life via top-down dominance in our moment-to-moment awareness. As I and Madeleine Siegel, my daughter and the wonderful illustrator of this book, have written in a chapter for Langer and her colleagues' handbook on mindfulness, her creative form of mindfulness—and perhaps the contemplative form as well—is a way of learning to thrive with uncertainty. We used the plane of possibility as the link between these two forms of being present for life, both of which research has established to be health promoting.

In other words, as we grow and accumulate experience with age, our cortical capacity to learn is accompanied by the growth of stronger and more refined filters of consciousness. Learning to free ourselves from this top-down restriction of bottom-up may be one positive and shared outcome of being mindful in both Langer's view and the contemplative mindfulness practices. We need to access the plane more fully and not be limited by prior knowledge or expertise embedded in our plateaus and allowing only certain peak streams of energy and information to arise.

One view of top-down and bottom-up might relate to the default mode network, the DMN. Let's explore this network a bit more here, as it relates to a possible filtering process for consciousness that may illuminate the mechanisms beneath the Wheel experience in more detail.

PLATEAUS, "SELF," AND THE DEFAULT MODE NETWORK

Recall that the DMN is a mostly midline set of circuits that goes from the front of the brain (with aspects of the medial prefrontal cortex) to the back, with the posterior cingulate cortex, the PCC, having a major function. We've seen that one view of the DMN is that it plays a dominant role in defining our sense of self—our conscious, subjective sense of who we are, or at least of who we *think* we are. When this set of conceptualizing circuits is excessively differentiated and not linked as a network to other regions as part of an overall integrated system of the head brain, as we've discussed, we may develop a sense of inadequacy, isolation, excessive self-preoccupation, anxiety, and other elements of suffering such as depression and despair.

One possible way to view self, plateaus, and the brain is this: *Top-down concepts of who we are—of who we think we are and our "sense of self"—may arise from filters of consciousness that are constructed from the information patterns of the DMN's interconnections.* When we are able to loosen these top-down, self-defining filters of the mind, these cate-

gorizing and constricting plateaus, when we loosen the neural associations of the DMN that filter and shape how these energy and
information flow patterns are formed and enter consciousness, we
can change specific, personal meaning in our life to a larger sense of
purpose and connection, and a broader sense of meaning in how we
live and define who we are.

In order to attempt to delineate all the varying ways that energy
and information enter our awareness and have a sense of personal
significance that may arise from our top-down filtering process, how
we have an experience of individual *meaning*, I created the following
mnemonic of the ABCDE's of meaning in the mind. This is not by
itself the broad sense of how to live a meaningful life, but rather the
specific relevance of how any particular energy and information pattern has a unique, individualized, personal significance for each of
us—yours different from mine, but each of us with an overall state of
mind in the moment that embeds meaning for us. Being aware of this
personal meaning may become a way of living a more *meaningful life*
in the broader sense of how we use that term to indicate a life of
purpose and connection.

The ABCDE's of meaning include:

1. *Associations:* Sensations, images, feelings, and thoughts that emerge
   in tandem with each other, both spatially and temporally in the
   brain. This shapes what arises as we SIFT through the mind (an acronym within a mnemonic!) and reflect on what has meaning for us.

2. *Beliefs:* Our mental modes and perspectives on the world that
   shape what we see, as in "You need to believe it to see it."

3. *Cognitions:* The flow of associated information processing as it unfolds in cascades of concepts and categories with their avalanches
   of facts, ideas, and patterns of perceiving, thinking, and reasoning
   that shape our view of reality and our ways of problem solving.

4. *Developmental period:* The time in our life in which events have occurred, such as our early childhood, adolescence, or young adulthood, that shape the top-down influences happening in the moment.

5. *Emotions:* Feelings arising from the body, shaped by relationships, and spread through the head-brain, instantiating significance and value in our lives, and often involving a shift in our state of integration in any given moment, whether subtle or intense.

These ABCDE's of how the brain forms and recognizes meaning are filtered differently during the waking state and the dream state. It seems that when we experience a more open awareness in the dream state—when the brain's tight linkages of the waking state are loosened—we may be accessing more directly and more freely a different set of ABCDE's of meaning. What does this mean in terms of our Wheel of Awareness experience?

It may be that *plateaus construct personal meaning* in our lives by filtering the nature of these associations, beliefs, cognitions, how they are influenced by the developmental period in which they first arose, and which emotional states emerge under their funneling of energy and information flow in the moment.

The reason such self-defining filters of consciousness exist may be that they are serving to organize our mental life. Plateaus embed the ABCDE's of personal meaning, helping shape our individual identity and make sense of the inner and interpersonal world.

Plateaus serve as filters of consciousness shaping what we experience within awareness in ways that fit our expectations as we anticipate the future, attempting to make life predictable and appear to be safe and secure. They create a particular state of mind in that moment, a state that has its own particular meaning pattern.

From the brain's free-energy principle, plateaus help us achieve homeostasis by reducing entropy—reducing uncertainty. We've also seen that our inner consciousness may have its evolutionary and de-velopmental origins in our social connections. This overlap between inner and inter is a theme for the brain, for the mind, and for our relational lives. What our filters of consciousness "permit" to enter awareness may be an attempt to organize the contents of conscious-ness to fit our expectations. "We know what is going on" would be the subjective feeling of this self-reinforcing loop of filters of con-sciousness that construct a world we expect to experience.

Neuroscientists commonly call the brain an "anticipation ma-chine." Given the wild array of energy flow patterns of life, getting ready for what is going to happen next, being able to predict the unfolding of experience, may be accomplished best by constructing a perceptual filter that selects and organizes what we actually become aware of based on what we've experienced before. Even our percep-tual system can be primed to perceive what we conceive to occur. In other words, we see what we believe.

The DMN may enable us to shape who we think we are. Part of this circuitry gives us the ability to mentally time-travel, making sense of the linkages of past, present, and future. We have a running narrative about who we've been, who we are, and who we think we should become. Our capacity for a *prospective mind*, how we predict and plan for the future, is a bit different from anticipation. Projecting into an imagined future is also how these top-down filters enable us to get ready for what we think will come in a more distant next. Top-down DMN processes also include theory of mind, how we come to make a map of the minds of others and ourselves. These even longer-lasting representations that move beyond anticipation into self-reaffirming planning are more like the stories we tell about each other—our focus on others and the self that is embedded in our nar-rative views of the world. We learn about the nature of the mind from past experiences and then use that top-down learning to sup-port and constrain how we sense what is going on now—in this case, in the minds of others and ourselves. We perceive and make sense of life through the selective top-down process of these filters. These, too, are learned plateaus that come from past experience, shape our current contents of consciousness, and prepare us to experience— and to construct—future perceptions.

Filters help us survive. When you drive a car, you want the readiness of the top-down knowledge and skills of steering and braking priming and focusing your perception and behavior. Filters shape what we believe and how we mold what we sense into what we perceive, and they continually reinforce their own convictions about the accuracy and the completeness of their perspective. We might even see this as the basis of *confirmation bias*, selectively attending to only that which confirms what we already believe. If we were continually aware of these pervasive filters, or aware of their limiting perspectives, we might innately feel that their survival value would be compromised. So we often are not aware of our plateaus, and we usually don't even inquire as to their existence or validity.

The upside of top-down is that it helps us make sense of life and feel safe and secure in an often confusing, unpredictable world. A common phrase used originally by the military and now by various organizations is that we live in a time of VUCA—volatility, uncertainty, complexity, and ambiguity. One way we may understand some individuals' nonconscious strategies for adapting to this challenging moment in human history is that they harden their filters in an attempt to make the perceived world more certain and predictable and less threatening. Our top-down filters of consciousness, our plateaus, whether flexible or rigid, may reveal the mind's attempt to achieve some kind of homeostasis in the face of challenges to our survival.

The downside of such a filtering of reality is that we become limited in what we experience. Rigid plateaus may make it challenging to be present in life. We judge people and events before we allow ourselves to even experience them openly. And if we've learned from suboptimal experiences to construct plateaus that are themselves suboptimal for our thriving, then we are in a prison of our own top-down mind's making. Top-down has now imprisoned our lives. This is why balancing these filters with bottom-up, more receptive awareness may be necessary in order to have an integrating mind.

The plane of possibility might be the portal for balancing top-down with bottom-up.

Bottom-up sensory flow, of the inner or outer world, is a conduition experience that helps us loosen the constructive top-down filters that constrain how we live and what we are aware of. Perhaps this is visualized as peaks arising directly from the plane. Recall that attending to the flow of sensation activates the side sensory circuits that inhibit the mostly midline DMN dominating chatter of what we can now see may be a top-down self-reinforcing loop of constructed cognition about the self. Getting rid of a sense of self is not the goal; finding a balance by cultivating a more fluid and flexible experience of self and learning to be more fully with sensation can be a path toward integration in our lives. We want to learn to live with a range of peaks that arise from the plateaus or from the plane. The idea is the integration of top-down and bottom-up flows—not destruction of top-down so that we are only bottom-up—empowering us with both the benefits of top-down and the freedom of bottom-up.

ONE PERSONAL SET OF FILTERS

What might these filters be like?

Each of us is unique; each has our own above-plane plateaus and peaks that make us an individual. In this way, we differ along the rim, in the peaks and plateaus, yet we find common ground in our hub, our plane of possibility.

Let me share some of my own plateaus and peaks to offer one set of examples that can illustrate what filters can feel like and how they shape what enters awareness. Some filters may come and go; others may be persistent and take on the pattern of defining our experience of self. In my own experience, a persistent set of filters I've come to know has four dimensions that they screen for, and those spell SOCK: sensation, observation, conceptualization, and knowing. You may share some of these as innate aspects of our common humanity, such as the capacity to observe with a sense of identity or to create conceptualizations about the world around us. You will likely also discover your own unique set of filters that are specific to your history and ways of organizing reality, your particular patterns of construction that manifest as top-down plateaus in your life. Recall that we are each different individuals, and one way these differences are created is by our particular set of filters, our plateaus and their specific peaks of life, that shape what we experience in awareness. Let's simply work with this acronym of SOCK as one example of what one person, I, your companion on this journey, have sensed, observed, conceived, and even had as a feeling of knowing, and see how the brain might mediate such a top-down filtering process.

Sensation is how we stream our first six senses into awareness. In this filtering stream is the fundamental process of conduition. It's what we take in with the focused attention on the first two segments of the rim. As a filter, this would have the least top-down influences—but since we live in a body, the conduit "hose" that directs this sensory stream likely has ways that past experience shapes our personalized neural capacity to sense and then certainly to perceive the world around us and within us. It's a useful stream, as we've seen, for counterbalancing a top-down dominance of a chattering mental life.

Observation is how we are a bit distant from the direct sensation, having perhaps a large input from the DMN based on prior experience that initiates something that if it could speak might sound like, "This is who I am, and this is what my experience should be." The DMN anchors experience in the past, setting the pattern of brain firing in such a way to be sure that prior associations, beliefs, cognitions, developmental periods, and perhaps even emotions—the ABCDE's of meaning in the mind—all conform to prior expectation.

Conceptualization is a filtering layer that constrains our mind's experience by shifting and shaping rim elements to conform to beliefs and categorizations of factual information. What this conceptual filter does is make the world appear to be both understandable and, most important for our survival, predictable. We categorize the world into groupings with a sense of constructed notions of their essence— classes of animals that are appealing or not, for example, or views of what kinds of emotions are good or bad to experience. Concepts are our way of organizing information into categories that divide up the world. The way the brain constructs these conceptual filters likely involves the intricate layering of the cortex as it funnels neural energy patterns within a given region and then interconnects these patterns with more distant cortical areas, all while being influenced by a range of non-cortical regions involved in evaluation and homeostatic regulation. In this way, conceptualization is not merely an intellectual process—it likely involves a body feeling state that shapes the conviction and the tone of our beliefs, and how we respond to any threats to the accuracy of those viewpoints.

While the intention, in a sense, of concepts is to help us, the implicit ways that they filter what we are aware of actually reinforce our belief in their accuracy, the process called confirmation bias we discussed earlier. Notice that this, as with all the filter layers, happens outside awareness, outside the hub of the Wheel. These top-down processes can be called implicit mental models, as they filter and shape our subjective experience of being alive usually without our even being aware of their existence or influence on us. Conceptual filters directly shape how we think about the world and even constrain our imagination about how the world might be.

Knowing is more than simply having conceptual knowledge; it is a deep sense of feeling the integrity and authenticity of some inner state or interaction with the world. Knowing likely involves a wide range of areas in the embodied brain—the extended nervous system and our whole body—and how they relate to a global state of integration. Something may feel wrong in the gut, feel off in the heart, or feel incomplete in the head. These would be the ways the knowing layer of filtering may draw on sensation, observation, and concept and be a kind of global state filter beneath our other layers.

That aha experience of insight we described earlier that involves gamma waves emerging from highly integrated states may reveal some neural correlate of how this aspect of knowing comes into awareness. Knowing may be a filtering of ongoing events that both constructs a sense of what is true and serves as a conduit that simply gives us access to a clarity about what has meaning and coherence in the state of global integration—within our inner and our inter mental lives.

PURE AWARENESS AND THE FILTERS
OF CONSCIOUSNESS

These filters of consciousness reveal how prior learning alters what kinds of rim elements emerge into awareness. You will have your own experience of filters that shape what is permitted entry into awareness in a given state of mind—whether that is as conduition or construction. These filters may be useful to try to detect and describe, to get to know as your Wheel practice continues. It is these filters, which we all likely have but that may be quite distinct in their nature for each of us, that shape both what we are aware of and our present state of consciousness in any given moment. These filters shape our repeated states of mind, our parts of a self or aspects of our personality that may each have enduring patterns that shape and shift our experience of who we are as they filter the contents of consciousness, a regulatory process often occurring without our awareness or conscious intention. A set of filters may dominate our lives, like those DMN self-defining filters that reinforce our top-down sense of self during our waking hours.

It may be an important journey for each of us to take to free our minds to be more in a bottom-up mode, loosening the grip of those filters that are often simply trying to be helpful in organizing and orienting us to the real world we live in—or think we live in. Being playful, having a sense of humor about who we are, and cultivating access to our hub beneath the filters of our rim can be a part of freeing the mind. In our 3-P perspective, this means accessing the plane of possibility beneath the plateaus that serve as filters of consciousness so that we become aware with more openness and learn to live with more freedom. Why don't we simply do this more readily? The shift into a different state of being, that vast open expanse of the plane of possibility, that place where spontaneity can arise, may be so unfamiliar and so different from what we experience as a top-down predictive plateau-constrained set of filtered peaks that we avoid the plane even without knowing it. If we are looking for certainty, we certainly wouldn't naturally drop into the openness of the plane. In an uncertain world, we can understand the drive to retain the predictive self-reaffirming categories, concepts, and perceptual biases of our filtering plateaus. The problem is, rigid plateaus keep us from being present for life, a presence that arises from the plane.

Ironically, the self-organizing role of filters of consciousness may be helping us to survive but inadvertently creating restrictions in the movement toward integration that requires us to more freely access the plane. This may be especially evident in cases of unresolved trauma, anxiety, or depression—but it also may keep any of us from feeling meaning and connection in life. What may be needed in each of these situations is some kind of intervention that helps relax these restrictive filters so that they can loosen and permit the push toward integration—a push that naturally arises from the plane.

When we are living from the plane, we are present for life. From the freedom and spaciousness of the plane of possibility, integration naturally arises. In short, *presence is the portal through which integration emerges.*

Here we are shining a focus of attention on the paradox that filters may exist in our life to help self-organization, but in many situations of our human journey they may become too rigid or chaotic themselves to facilitate free-flowing integration. This dysfunctional effect of our filtering plateaus may be a result of a number of impactful factors, such as personal history, genetic inheritance, and social exclusion in society, that lead to an experience of not belonging and the pain of isolation.

Our human journey itself may be vulnerable to the development of rigid filters. Once we are adults—and perhaps even before, during adolescence or at the end of childhood—our constructed daytime self-defining filters take hold as we fit into whatever social worlds we live in, and whatever personal experiences we've been trying to adapt to as we make sense of life and strive to survive. Our top-down filters tell us who we are, sometimes in habitual patterns that reinforce themselves and construct that familiar sense of a "me" or "I" of lived experience. These learned filters of a self shape our waking consciousness. *Opening to who we can be* is an awakening of the mind so that we can know more fully and freely the wide-open nature of our possibilities.

THE OSCILLATORY SWEEP OF ATTENTION: A 3-P LOOP, A SPOKE OF THE WHEEL

If information emerging from neural processes arises but can remain outside awareness, what is the mechanism by which such information enters consciousness? Brain research can be used to imagine what might be happening from a neuroscience perspective, and though, as we've said, no one knows what is truly going on to create awareness, we can suggest the following process built from these proposals.

To be aware of something means, as we mentioned briefly earlier, to have some portion of a forty-cycle-per-second or 40-Hz sweep link various neural activities to each other. This fits with the integration-of-information theory, and it is supported by many brain studies that examine oscillatory patterns involved in attention, awareness, and thought. Oscillations are cycles of a process, a reinforcing loop of activity. In the case of the proposal that consciousness involves a 40-Hz oscillatory sweep through portions of the head brain as it links activities in various distinct regions, we can postulate that some similar process is built into our 3-P perspective. This would mean that an above-plane position—a plateau, sub-peak, or peak—that we become aware of gets swept up into the oscillation cycle, linking that above-plane energy to activity in the plane itself. This would be a proposal for how we become not just aware from the plane, but *aware of something* by the linking of the plane to that something. Our illustration reveals this image of a looping process that would symbolize this oscillatory attentional sweep.

If that something is a thought or emotion or memory, there would be a loop connecting plane to peak. If there was awareness of a mood or intention or state of mind, aspects of our filtering mechanisms we've been discussing, we would see a loop connecting the plane to these plateaus. A loop on the diagram would correspond to a neural sweep in the brain. The sweep has been demonstrated in

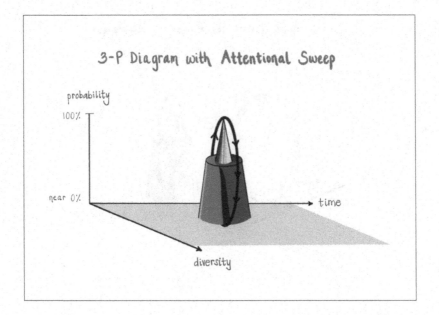

brain research to have a 40-Hz frequency; our proposal is that this sweep would have a corresponding looping process that links plane to plane for hub-in-hub, or plane to above-plane position for hub to rim. Sometimes our hub-in-hub experience might simply have no attentional focus—as when this step of the Wheel practice is carried out not by bending the spoke or retracting it, but by not sending the spoke anywhere, just resting in the plane.

The spoke of our Wheel image would correspond to the loop of our 3-P diagram. The illustration shows a schematic of this sweep as a loop *linking* plane to above-plane positions and corresponding to the spoke of the Wheel.

Without participation of the plane in this sweep of attention, the mental activity can exist but will not enter consciousness. That would appear on our Wheel drawing as an active rim point without a spoke, and on our 3-P diagram as an above-plane position of plateau or peak without a linking loop. These visualizations of rim or of peaks and plateaus without spoke or loop depict the nonconscious mind at work.

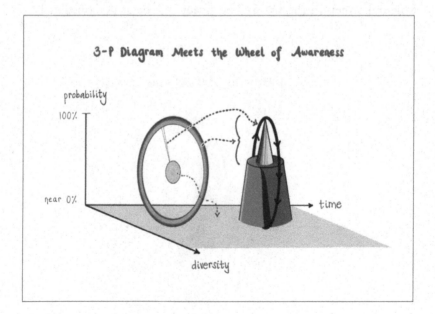

This general pattern of a sweeping process comprised of neural oscillations may be common in the functioning of the brain. I recently had the opportunity to speak with the Oxford University professor Morten Kringelbach, a computer scientist and now brain researcher, after a lecture he delivered at UCLA on trauma and the mind. Morten and I discussed how the scientific and mathematical terminology he himself had used of segregation and integration were parallel to our interpersonal neurobiology terms, differentiation and linkage. It soon became clear that an integrated state that for us means a balance of differentiation and linkage, for a mathematician's and computer scientist's view of brain function might correspond to a condition they discuss called "metastability" and may possibly overlap with the state of "criticality" we mentioned earlier. This complex systems' property in the brain can be understood this way: "dynamical systems such as the brain maximize their state repertoire when they approach criticality; that is, transition between order and chaos, which has also been proposed to be the neural mechanism underlying conscious wakefulness . . ."*

As Morten and I walked through the UCLA botanical gardens, we arrived at a point near a bamboo grove where, decades ago, several of my psychiatric patients I'd take there for a therapeutic stroll would pause and often come up with some new insights as we crossed the creek, the small stream still gurgling now all these years later. It seemed to me that our conscious mind can at special "times of criticality" come forth with some new access, some freer sense of who we are with new insights or recall into the past. Perhaps that was a mind whose revelations within consciousness might arise in a new "metastable state" that Morten suggested was like the bottom of a probability valley, an "attractor state" of a complex system's flow that drew energy patterns toward it. We discussed how one possible view is that

---

* Atasoy, et al., "Harmonic Brain Modes," 7.

when this metastable condition overlaps with the state of criticality—the balance of differentiation and linkage that flows between rigidity and chaos—awareness arises. Perhaps, I thought as we strolled along, such shifts might be inspired by the awe of the botanical garden as this opening mental state in connection with nature relaxed those filters of consciousness and permitted new combinations to arise within awareness. Perhaps this is how and why new perspectives emerged in the bamboo garden all those years ago. These states of insight, as we've seen, might be moments of new integration; ones that may arise as we make sense of life. And even as I share these ideas here with you on our journey, it feels like these views reach a new clarity as they rest in awareness. The criticality between chaos and rigidity along with the metastable state holding energy patterns in a prolonged but temporary state of firing may enable us to feel the clarity of new ways of seeing the world within us and around us within consciousness. This holding of new energy patterns in awareness gives us the ability to come to new insights and make new choices. So much to ponder about the potential overlaps of these characteristics of connectome harmonics and their states of metastability and criticality with our discussions about the Wheel and the 3-P framework. A wonderful walk it was, a wondrous journey with you and through life this is.

With emerging new technologies, such as magneto-encephalogram (MEG), which enable us to observe the fine-grained timing of neural firing in the brain, the central role of oscillations is becoming more evident in our understanding of mind and brain. Here is what Morten and his colleagues Selen Atasoy, Gustavo Deco, and Joel Pearson have to say about the central role of not only the importance of these oscillations in the brain, but how the whole brain has oscillating sweeps that link the widely differentiated regions into a connectome harmonic that is the core of how brain activity and mental states may co-arise:

The framework of elementary harmonic brain modes offers a unifying perspective and explanatory framework revealing the link between various seemingly unrelated findings on neural correlates of consciousness. The proposed framework links the spatial patterns of correlated neural activity, not only to temporal oscillations characteristic of mammalian brain activity but also to brain anatomy and neurophysiology. Hence, this framework goes beyond enabling a new dimension of tools for decomposing complex patterns of neural activity into their elementary building blocks, by also providing a fundamental principle linking space and time in neural dynamics through harmonic waves—a phenomenon ubiquitous in nature.*

From our perspective of plane, plateau, and peak and how these oscillations in the brain may help create various states of consciousness, we can envision a sweep as a way to express in simple terms what some of the brain's connectome harmonics may be revealing in any given state of mind in that moment and the accompanying experience of being aware. When the harmonics' metastable state—that deep attractor state of the complex neural system—overlaps with criticality—the oscillatory state emerging at the edge of activation between chaos and rigidity—perhaps, as Morten and I discussed, this was a convergence facilitating the emergence of consciousness. And perhaps, you and I can suggest, this oscillatory neural process might be the underlying neural correlate of what we're proposing as the quantum view of a plane of possibility—the sea of potential, the quantum vacuum. In this metastable state, energy patterns may be held in consciousness for a more extended period of time; in this integrated state of criticality, new possibilities can be accessed. And then the emerging energy and information flow patterns potentially could be

---

* Atasoy, et al., "Harmonic Brain Modes," 14.

consciously experienced and transformed within awareness. These two perspectives may be quite compatible, one at the level of complex systems and their metastable and critical states, and one at the probability level of quantum dynamics. Energy manifests at both the macrostate and the microstate levels of reality. Complex systems such as the brain might operate at the macrostate level while quantum properties are more readily apparent at the microstate level. In both levels of analysis of reality, dropping into the plane of possibility may be how to envision ways of opening awareness to enable a broader range of connectome harmonics to be created and free up a more unbridled arising of the filtering probabilities of plateaus and the actualities of peaks. Harnessing the hub, dropping into the plane, can free the mind. Connectome harmonics may be an exciting way to view the neural correlates of energy profiles underlying the plane of possibility. As the Wheel of Awareness enables us to harness the hub, to access the plane, this practice may help us become more fully present as we awaken the mind to the vast possibilities life has to offer that we may rarely tap into in our day-to-day lives.

SWEEP RATIOS, STATES OF MIND

For the conscious mind, this 3-P model enables us to also illustrate the wide variety of what are sometimes called *states of consciousness*. In a given moment, we can view the overall probability state as involving a combination created by the linking oscillatory sweep, which we can simply depict as a loop connecting plane to above-plane values. In other words, who you are in a given moment can combine the awareness of the plane's probability position—the knowing—with a loop connecting it to a probability position above the plane as plateau or peak—the possible knowns. This view of a loop of attention helps us resolve a confusing aspect of our 3-P framework you may have noticed, one embedded in this question: How can we be aware and also aware of something if that something is a probability position *above* the plane of possibility, but the awareness itself arises from the plane? Drawing on neuroscience findings regarding oscillation, we can see the commonality of such looping in brain terms in the 40-Hz sweep and in the connectome harmonics. A similar oscillation can be seen in the physics notion of fields of energy in which we can see, for example (and no pun intended), that light has a waveform in its probability distribution as a spectrum of values. When light is a wave, its spectrum is present. When photons appear as particles, a singular value has been manifest from a range of possibilities. Light can be both a particular value—a particle—and a range of values, a wave.

We can suggest that within this oscillating sweep that we are simply calling a *loop*, we can have an array of levels of involvement along the 3-P probability distributions. At one end, we can have virtually the entire sweep in the plane, and that might be a state of wide-open, receptive awareness, vast and spacious because so much of that state is in the plane of possibility. We could say from a Wheel perspective that this is a hub-dominant state and depict it as a high ratio of the loop in our 3-P diagram, meaning the percentage of the looping in the plane is dominant.

Being aware of something other than awareness itself means having some portion of the energy state, this spectrum of probability values from 100 to near-zero, including above-the-plane positions as they are linked through the oscillating looping to the plane of possibility. Part of that probability state at that moment of time is in the plane; part is above the plane—that's how we are *aware* (plane) of some*thing* (above-plane).

Let's say, for example, that you are intentionally attending to the breath. At one moment you can have 50 percent of the neural firings of the 40-Hz sweep *in the plane* (however the brain might be able to manifest that probability state), so you are aware; and 50 percent of the sweep is above the plane on the peak of the breath—the sensory conduit of that bodily sensation—so that the breath is the *thing* you are aware of. In this probability state combination of 50/50, there is a balance of hub and rim. This is how you know (plane or hub) the known (above-plane position or rim).

Here are some perhaps equivalent terms: 1) balanced oscillatory neural-energy-state *sweep*; 2) *mindful awareness* of the breath; 3) *spoke* connecting hub and rim; and 4) *loop* linking plane and peak. The chart at the end of this part reveals these various terms and how they might correspond to one another. Let's call this proportion or balance between awareness and the thing you are aware of the *sweep-ratio* or simply the *sweep*. You can have a plane-dominant sweep or a peak-dominant sweep, each term indicating the ratio of in-plane knowing and above-plane knowns shaping the state of consciousness.

Let's try out another oscillatory energy state. Let's say that a distraction takes over awareness, and you are now placing focal attention on a meeting coming up next week. You might say that you "got lost on the rim" as you lost track of your intention to focus on the breath and became absorbed in your preoccupation and worries about the meeting. Instead of a wide-open hub or freely accessing the plane, enabling mental access to your intention to focus on the exercise of breath awareness, you now have 99 percent of the sweep in the peak of the worries about the meeting and 1 percent in the plane. That preoccupation with the meeting took over awareness so much that you lost track of your intentions—you got lost in the worries, aware of only them and losing track of other issues, like the fact that you are doing a breath practice at this moment. Sound familiar? Before this occurred, you likely had non-focal attention on the meeting, placing value and nonconscious concern on the upcoming event *outside of awareness*. These concerns could be seen as activated rim points, having energy patterns of plateaus and peaks activated but not connected—yet, at least—with the plane. So this is what non-focal attention would look like, activations *without* being swept along with the plane.

With the Wheel as a metaphor, you got lost on the rim as that highly valued meeting worry pulled *focal* attention to it. That's the spoke of focal attention. Mechanism-wise, the sweep oscillated with the meeting's above-peak values and now you are *swept up* to the peak as your focal attention is pulled to the worries about the meeting. You have temporarily lost the spaciousness of the balance as your sweep-ratio now has become heavily peak dominant. But soon the part of your brain that monitors the relevance of what's going on— your salience circuitry, which includes your insula—activates and gives you a feeling that if it could speak, says, "Hey, the contents of your awareness are not on the intended focus. You've gotten distracted!" Recall that this simply means you are a human being with a mind. You are doing nothing wrong; you are just doing human. Fortunately, your salience network can monitor without you knowing it, as it, like so much of our minds, works outside of awareness. And the more you train that salience system, especially with the focused attention pillar of the training, the stronger it will get. What you practice with intention creates a repeated state that will then become a trait that can work in the background without your effort or conscious energy.

Consciousness uses energy, and holding things in awareness with focal attention not only requires precious resources, it is also limited in the number of items that can generally be well focused upon at a given time. When the worries take over focal attention and fill awareness, the breath leaves that spotlight of focal attention.

So now you have your strong salience circuit, which you've been training with the Wheel practice, a circuit that "has your back," so to speak, and it creates a peak of "let's focus on the breath" that competes with the peak of the worries about the meeting. That peak may at first not be linked to the plane, working in the nonconscious background. But soon it becomes a part of the sweep, too, linking the salience peak to the plane of awareness. You now might even hear this as two inner voices ultimately within consciousness—one worried about the meeting, the other saying to get back to the breath. These two peaks, these two thoughts, could be seen as two rim points, the meeting and salience monitoring input. And so you remind your self—bring back to mind—that you are doing a breath practice. Now it's time to redirect, and so, with a gear-shifting aspect of attention you are also training further as an important *skill of modifying* that strengthens the overall skills of your regulatory mind, the breath peak now comes back into focus, you let the meeting peak go, and you move back to perhaps a balance of 50 percent of the sweep on the breath and 50 percent in the plane.

You may even get into "the flow of the breath," and now have 99 percent of the sweep on the breath peak and 1 percent in the plane. *You've chosen to get lost in the flow of the sensation of the breath*, as that's what this task is inviting you to do—you are not getting distracted or lost on an irrelevant peak, a distracting rim point. *You are choosing how to arrange your sweep-ratio.* With your guided focal attention, you returned awareness to the breath and are now letting yourself get into the conduit sensory flow of the breath. Salience monitoring senses you are on track and doesn't intrude into awareness, watching from behind the scenes of consciousness, a plateau perhaps that is capable of filtering what arises or not, that at this moment is not involving the plane of possibility in its activities or interfering with the experience of being aware. Enjoy the flow!

In this manner, attention may be related in fundamental ways to the filtering of plateaus. When the plateau directs energy flow, it is what attention is doing. When the plateau determines how the loop will connect with the plane, when that filtering is activating and organizing certain possibilities and linking them to awareness in the plane, it is now not merely attention; it has become focal attention. In this manner, our 3-P diagram's loop may correspond to the 40-Hz oscillations in the brain that are themselves correlated with being *aware of something*—with focal attention. In this view, then, a plateau would be our 3-P view of how a state of mind can use attention to selectively direct energy and information flow, in this case shaping what we become aware of. When that flow enters awareness, it now has a loop connecting plane to above-plane value. On our Wheel image, we'd place a spoke connecting hub to rim.

Soon something shifts. Let's say your mind wanders again, to another point on the rim—thoughts about a dinner tonight. That dinner can also be a peak value, claiming the precious and limited territory of the 40-Hz sweep from plane to plateau. But the breath is still unfolding, as something you may even be non-focally attending to—you're still breathing, after all. You notice the distraction, let the dinner concerns go, and return to the breath. The practice continues, strengthening your ability to direct attention and access awareness. Your intention to do the breath practice is seen as part of the plateau that helps redirect your focus of attention to the breath.

With a balance of the plane and the above-plane object of awareness, this looping of knowing and known, we can visualize this as a 50/50 designation on the loop. Being absorbed primarily in the known would be 1/99, whereas being mostly in the knowing and just a bit on the known would be 99/1. If the sweep were only above the plane, we would be able to draw this out as a ratio of 0/100, which would be no awareness at all, zero consciousness. That's our nonconscious mental life. In strict neural-sweep terms, this might be a way to indicate non-focal attention. But if we leave the loop to mean focal attention, such a zero value wouldn't make much sense in a drawing, as it would basically mean no sweep, so why bother drawing any loop in this case? For the sake of convenience, if we wanted to draw out a particular nonconscious process that we were highlighting, this 0/100 indicator on a loop would at least be a useful way of visually depicting this mental activity outside of awareness.

Being aware with a wide-open expanse can involve a high percentage in the plane, even to the exclusion of anything in particular that we might have as a "thing" we are aware of in that moment. That's the experience many describe of hub-in-hub, and we might indicate it as a loop that stays only in the plane itself, perhaps a loop with a number of 100/0 if we wanted to depict the sweep-ratio. One hundred percent in the plane, none above the plane. And 100/0 is infinity—which corresponds exactly to the way many say this part of the Wheel practice and resting in the hub, or dropping into the plane of possibility, actually feels. What people describe of this state is a sense of joy, peace, and clarity.

With the loop revealing a sweep-ratio of 100/0, hub-in-hub, there is a vastness and spaciousness of awareness that is felt, an immersion that we are suggesting happens when we've learned how to access the plane of possibility and enjoy the capacity we have to experience pure, open awareness.

In my own life, at times I'll want to get lost in something, like smelling the roses along a walk I take regularly near our Mindsight Institute. I'll pause, take a deep breath, and then bend down over a rose. Then I'll let the air out, visualizing how on the next in-breath I'll let the aroma of the rose fill my experience, and then I let that conduit of the scents fill my sweep-ratio and dominate awareness at that moment. I consciously, intentionally choose to do this, and the flow of the fragrance of the flowers is fabulous. There is a feeling that there is no room in that moment for any other thoughts, any other senses, any other concerns. I am just with the rose. If I open my eyes, I can switch to the visual channel, intentionally, and let sight become the dominant conduition, soaking in the vibrant colors and subtle textures of the petals and stems. And in that moment, you may imagine using the term *flow* as flow researcher Mihaly Csikszentmihalyi uses it, as I let myself disappear and become, as fully as I possibly can with this body I live in, flowing with the rose. It's not an energy exaggeration to say that at that moment, the energy that is the rose and the energy that is "me" are essentially—in their essences—intermingled within my awareness. And perhaps I am now simply opening awareness to that fundamental reality of our interconnectedness. Could it be, as so many have experienced after the Wheel practice, that there is indeed no separation between us and the roses around us? It is in those moments of dropping into the plane of possibility that we can become aware of the reality, in that state of presence that arises from the plane, that the rose and this body are part of one flowing energy pattern. It's not that I need to construct that idea—it's more that I can let the idea of me and the idea of the rose go and open to this eighth sense, enabling me to feel our deeply interconnected nature. This reality can become a part of how I live, in that moment, and in my way of living even in moments beyond that flow.

At other times, I imagine how I might create a more balanced sweep-ratio, and I loop the plane with a particular peak with plenty of room for more diversity in that state of consciousness—to consider other ideas, bring in other facts, let my mind wander into unknown territory. I am not lost in the experience; "I" am there as a fully present but widely accessing being, balanced in the vastness of the state of consciousness that includes the thing itself—the rose—and the awareness. I am in a 50/50 loop of hub and rim, plane and peak, with lots of spaciousness within awareness to take it all in as well as reflect on things. Remember how we began our journey reflecting on that cup of water? As I take my walk smelling those roses, I've expanded my cup of water, and whatever salt life puts in or whatever savory sweets arise, I am ready to drink.

Focal attention is said to have a limited capacity—we can focus on only one activity at a time. It may be that learning how to regulate our sweep ratio permits us to intentionally place our precious attentional resources on exactly what we choose to focus on and fill awareness with in any given moment or setting. You can try this simple exercise yourself next time you are having a meal with friends or family. Meals, as we discussed in part I, are an excellent time to practice being present and exercise your new capacity to explore awareness. Let yourself and your companions know you are about to try a sweep-ratio shift. Let the experience continue with your social conversation for a while. Then suggest that you alter the ratio by letting the food you've been consuming go from its low placement in the sweep, something that was just in the background, to the majority of positioning. Let the sensory streams of the taste, smell, sight, and texture of the food fill awareness so that they become 99 percent of the ratio—1 in the plane, 99 in the sensation of the food. Such a focus on the food will exclude other elements from awareness, so continuing a conversation with this sweep-ratio won't be possible. Be in the flow of the food and your body's taking in of these nutrients. After a few minutes of this being with the food, return to your social conversation. What did you notice? For many, when we place focal attention with its limited capacity on a conversation, there simply isn't room for appreciating the sensory qualities of the food. We don't choke on the food, usually, nor do we put a fork into our cheek. We can have a small amount of the sweep ratio on the process of chewing and swallowing and using our utensils, but little will be available to fully feel the food itself. We generally can attend focally to only one process at a time—and you can now see how to shift this at will in your life. That's a shift in your sweep-ratio. As you practice the Wheel, you may come to find that this ability to intentionally shape the sweep-ratio and alter your state of consciousness and the chosen contents of your focal attention will continue to strengthen and enhance your experiences. There is a time for many different kinds of sweep-ratios, different states of consciousness, and now you can embrace that skill of further integrating them into your life.

The vastness of the plane of possibility gives us the capacity, when we've learned to access it more readily, both to have a more sustained focal attention and to hold on to a sense of freedom and flexibility to take in a wide expanse of emerging experiences. Perhaps this corresponds to what Richie Davidson found in his meditation research as ways in which we increase the ability to stay focused and aware even as the things we are attending to change. My own subjective sense of this with the Wheel practice is that there is a broader receptivity with which to experience and appreciate all that arises.

Part of this journey to intentionally shape our states of consciousness by altering our sweep-ratios also includes learning how to recognize and release the filters of consciousness that directly organize the knowns of present moment awareness. With practice, we can free up these plateaus to be more flexible and even experience how to let peaks arise directly from the plane. Integrating your life enables you to strengthen your mind by becoming more present through this source of being aware.

Having access to the plane fills us with a sense of choice and change, of tranquility and connection.

AWE AND JOY

Returning to the way that many have reported their experience of the hub of the Wheel—this sense of vastness, of being wide open—let us now consider how it might be that the plane of possibility can allow us access to so much joy, love, and even awe.

The plane of possibility can be thought of as a portal to integration. As we've seen, this plane from a probability perspective can be viewed as maximal integration—its inherent linkage of all the differentiated potentials that are possibly available. When we access the plane, when we drop the probability position down into the plane of possibility, we let the particulars of peaks and plateaus relax and enter a more spacious state of joining, connecting with the wide array of potential experiences life offers us without needing to control them or even understand them. We rest in what is, and are open to what can be. The majesty of simply being alive becomes the perspective from which we experience presence in our lives when we live from the plane.

From the *subjective experience of being in the plane*, we permit ourselves access to a state of awe as we let a sense arise of there being so much more than just our individual, private sense of self—the tender regard, the love for this amazing gift of just being here—and this joy, this gratitude, this awe fills our consciousness. Once this feeling is experienced, be it through the practice of the Wheel or outside of a formal practice, even for just brief moments when the plane may become accessible, our minds get a glimpse of this vastness with its feeling of peace and well-being, and we experience a sense of being alive that is so full, so natural, so at ease and complete. As we mentioned in part I, social neuroscientist Mary Helen Immordino-Yang has found that these states are activated with neural firing in brain stem regions associated with the deepest neural circuits involved in basic life processes. This state of awe and gratitude, this joy for life, is an inner sense of vitality and an inter sense of connection to the larger world around us. We can propose that the plane of possibility is the probability state that naturally gives rise to the subjective experience of joy, awe, and peace—of life-affirming meaning, love, and connection.

In the next part we will explore how we might access this state more readily in our lives by first returning to the stories of individuals we met in part I and how they used the metaphor of the Wheel of Awareness—as an idea and as a practice—to gain more access to the plane of possibility by harnessing the hub of the mind.

Expanding our awareness can free our minds to experience the plane itself in its vast and spacious potential. As we begin to spend more time in the hub of the Wheel, we may even get to sense how our filters are constraining and constructing our experience of being alive, shaping our sense of identity. When this new skill of dropping into the plane of possibility, accessing open awareness, and becoming more present for life is strengthened, new possibilities for choice and change become available as our minds become more integrative and aware.

Why integrative? As we find more differentiated ways of being— ways of accessing new potentials that become actualized as above-plane probability values—we link to a wider array of states than a particular set of plateaus that filter and restrict our lives may have allowed. In wondrous ways, the plane of possibility is both the source of being aware and the source of new options for living. Consciousness gives us choice and the capacity for change not only because it permits us to pause and reflect but also because it gives us access to the source of new options.

If this 3-P framework fits with your own experience, you may come to find that becoming more aware is also becoming free. Awareness and tapping into a wide-open plane of possible new ways of being in the world may come from exactly the same probability position in the journey of the mind's energy flow. As we let the natural self-organization of these newly available differentiated potentials arise and become linked of their own accord, as we "get out of our own way" and drop into the awareness of the plane, tapping into the experience of simply being present and trusting the process of being aware, the innate drive of the mind to cultivate more highly integrative states can be set free. Accessing the plane of possibility is the natural portal for more integrated states to arise.

A TABLE OF CORRELATIONS AMONG MENTAL EXPERIENCE, METAPHOR, AND MECHANISM

We've now come to the conclusion of part II and can provide a visual display of some of the ideas explored throughout our journey. The following table lists the terms and their conceptual framework. In the first column, you'll see our everyday, common use of words, labeled Mind as Subjective Experience. In the second column are terms from the Wheel of Awareness metaphor—in idea and in practice. In the third column, you'll find the ideas of the 3-P perspective, including plane, plateaus, and peaks. In the fourth column are ideas related to the neural correlates of consciousness, and in the fifth column is terminology related to our more general discussions about the mind.

Mind as Subjective Experience	Wheel of Awareness Metaphor	3-P Diagram & Mechanism	Neural Correlation/Brain Activity	Other Terms Related to Mental Life
Awareness	Hub	Plane	High Integration	Consciousness
Focal attention	Spoke of attention	Loop of sweep	40-Hz sweep from thalamus to cortex	Concentration
Sensation (first five senses of the outside world and the sixth sense of the body)	First two segments of rim	Peaks of activation with minimal filtering	Lateralized brain regions active, including sensory cortices and insula	Conduition
Mental activities (seventh sense)	Third segment of rim	Peaks often arising from plateaus	Cortical regions including midline default mode network (DMN)	Construction
Sense of interconnection: relational connections felt as conduition and construction (eighth sense)	Fourth segment of rim	Peaks directly arising from plane and/or plateaus	Memory, sensation, and/or resonance with energy states from other people and the planet— our relationships; energy input from the environment	Connection

PART III

STORIES OF TRANSFORMATION IN APPLYING THE WHEEL

Harnessing the Hub and Living
from the Plane of Possibility

I n part III of our journey, we will dive more deeply into how the Wheel of Awareness can be used in our lives—as a metaphor illustrating an idea and as a practice we can use to integrate consciousness.

Let's return to the example of the individuals I introduced you to in part I so that we can explore the ways in which the Wheel of Awareness supports actual growth and healing in our day-to-day lives. In summary, we will discuss: Billy, the five-year-old who learned not to hit; Jonathan, the sixteen-year-old with roller-coaster moods; Teresa, the twenty-five-year-old who had experienced early developmental trauma; Mona, the forty-year-old mother of three who was at the end of her rope and losing patience with her children; and Zachary, the fifty-five-year-old businessman who learned a new way of being in the world, which set him on a new path in his life.

After exploring their experiences, we will further illustrate the 3-P perspective introduced in part II, and prepare you to harness these ideas and practices in your own life as we come to our fourth and final part of the book.

OFFERING THE WHEEL AS AN IDEA TO CHILDREN: BILLY AND THE FREEDOM OF THE HUB, THE SPACIOUSNESS OF THE PLANE

Teaching children about the Wheel of Awareness, be it in the class-room or at home, or when coaching athletic teams or musical per-formers, is a wonderful way to support their growth. As a visual guide to the way the mind works, it can help children understand more clearly that they have the power to make choices about how they live their lives. With the ideas of focused attention, open aware-ness, and kind intention built into the visual metaphor of the Wheel, children are offered the major ways research suggests we can create more health and happiness in our lives. One of the most basic ideas of the Wheel as a drawing is that it becomes visually clear how what we are aware of—the rim—is distinct from the hub, our experience of being aware. This is an idea that can have profound empowering effects on children, as it did for Billy.

In my textbook *The Developing Mind* you'll find an extensive review of the research revealing how many of the regulatory circuits of the brain develop during the first dozen years of life, shaped by both our genes and the experiences we have, especially our relation-ships with others. A relationship is a pattern of communication—between two people, for example—that can involve a sense of being seen and understood, cared about and connected. Communication can also involve the transfer of ideas—ideas that can change how the mind develops.

Billy's story is an example of how a young mind can be stretched by a new idea that changes the course of one's life.

Recall that five-year-old Billy had been transferred to another school after hitting a peer in the school yard. Billy's new kindergarten teacher, Ms. Smith, taught him the Wheel of Awareness as an idea, one he could draw out on a piece of paper and then apply in his inner life and interpersonal actions. One day, Billy sought out Ms. Smith and asked that she give him a minute so he could put the brakes on his behavior and not hit a child who had taken his blocks out in the yard. Billy expressed this to his teacher by saying he was lost on his rim and needed to get back to his hub.

From a *mechanism point of view*, what do you think may have been going on for Billy?

One possible explanation we can now suggest is that the metaphor of the Wheel enabled Billy to realize that his inclination to hit Joey was just one rim point on a Wheel that offered him so many other choices in terms of his emotional response to his schoolmate's negative behavior. In other words, Billy did not have to follow this one impulse but could instead return to the hub of his awareness and take the time to consider what course of action he truly wanted to take. He found freedom in turning toward the hub to access other rim points; in 3-P terms, he could drop into the plane of possibility to pause and rest in the mental space in which other options existed. From this powerful pausing in the plane, he could now choose options other than those on plateaus of anger or habitual antisocial learned reactions, where he would have been on automatic pilot.

Consciousness is what allows us to forge spaces between our impulses and our actual reactions. It enables us to be more flexible in how we respond versus just acting automatically. The hub not only enables awareness, it also is the source of options empowering us to tap into the array of behavioral choices we now have available to us.

We've defined the mind as an emergent, self-organizing, embodied, and relational regulatory process. Energy and information, we've proposed, is the stuff of the mind—and so Billy was learning a new way to regulate this flow. Regulation depends upon monitoring with more stability so that we see with more focus, clarity, depth, and detail. As a self-organizing process, recall that the mind facilitates the unfolding of integration as the way its liberated emergence creates the FACES flow of being flexible, adaptive, coherent, energized, and stable. This new idea of the Wheel allowed a five-year-old little boy to differentiate between the knowing in the hub and the knowns on the rim. What does this mean? This means that the idea and visual image of the Wheel could free Billy's mind and enable him to integrate his consciousness and make new choices.

As we review this story of a young child realizing that his impulse to use his fists could be replaced with a more kind and compassionate response, it is important to consider how much kindness and compassion are in fact the emergent outcomes of integration. If the space between a negative interaction with another person and our response is quite literally opened up by greater awareness, our interactions with others become much more kind and compassionate—they become more integrated. However, sometimes things get in the way—moments when we feel we are not getting our needs met, or difficult social conditions in the home or community in which we live, for example. Even though integration may be an innate drive of every mind, various events, internal or interpersonal, can place a roadblock on this natural push toward integration—toward being kind and compassionate. Blockages to integration can result from developmental experiences, and these blockages may move us away from the flexible FACES flow of integration to the banks of chaos and rigidity. These banks are where Billy was before he came to Ms. Smith's classroom, and this central flow seems to be now where Billy is able to choose to go.

The mind is both within us and between us; it's both inner and inter. Ms. Smith created an emotionally and socially intelligent classroom environment so that both the inner and the inter minds of her students were engaged. Her classroom encouraged reflection and promoted integration. We might say that Ms. Smith cultivated a generative social field. Billy's inner mind now was set up with an idea, a metaphor, and an inter mind that found connection and acceptance so that the fullness of who he was, and who he was able to become, were each reinforced with these new integrative experiences.

Inner and inter, we are all shaped by the ways our mind is both embodied and relational.

We might say that by having the image and idea of the Wheel and being in this new environment, Billy could now access more possibilities than the learned patterns of behavior he experienced in his past. The pathway to such change involves reflection, an opening of the mind to the freedom of the plane. What that receptive awareness does is offer him a new spacious way to reflect on what his inner and inter mind is doing at that moment, and open him, too, to access a set of possibilities that were unavailable to him before. Who knows, it might even be changing his default mode network's self-shaping, self-selecting neural activities toward a more flexible and adaptive set of filters that permit a new sense of self and mode of being in the world to emerge. You go, Billy. And you go, Ms. Smith!

Here we see the power of knowing these potential mechanisms beyond the metaphor for our own understanding. Naturally, Billy was offered the image of the Wheel, a metaphor—not the image of the plane of possibility, our proposed mechanism. He could use the idea in metaphor form, and likely at that age these mechanisms would be too abstract. Even with the metaphor, Billy could be empowered to have a deep and hopefully lasting inner and inter transformation in his life. You may be priming your mind for what my son and daughter say I cannot communicate, a joke: Metaphors be with you, Billy.

As we grow past early childhood, into adolescence and beyond, knowing about the plane of possibility as a mechanism of the mind can be a helpful way to understand our inner, mental lives. But for some, this mechanism isn't necessary; the metaphor of the Wheel is all they need to help integrate consciousness. For myself, I find that the phrases "spaciousness of consciousness" and "consciousness creates choice and change" certainly apply to the Wheel image and the notion of "harnessing the hub" in our lives. The Wheel is a clear image of metaphorically visualizing key aspects of the mind.

Even more subtle details, though, are illuminated by our 3-P framework, and by viewing the 3-P diagram and the mechanism of the plane of possibility as the source of this spaciousness and freedom. For example, this framework enables us to see, and to say, why consciousness permits choice and change—because awareness drops us into the very mathematical space in which other options rest. As the scholar Michel Bitbol states, "the quantum vacuum, it's waiting for activation to give rise to 'particles,' in the same way that the air, once the sun and water are there, is waiting for an observer or a camera to give rise to a rainbow."* Although not stated by physics, our proposal is that awareness itself may emerge from the plane of possibility that may very well be the quantum vacuum, the sea of potential, from which basic energy patterns—the quanta called "particles"—arise in our world. The 3-P framework helps us understand how new energy- and information-flow patterns can be chosen from this plane of possibility. You and I can appreciate that there are different approaches for each of us, and finding what works best for you, or for the people you are working with at different ages, or speaking with at a dinner party, invites us to make important adjustments in what levels— metaphor alone, or metaphor with mechanism—we engage in a discussion about the nature of the mind and consciousness.

We have been proposing that awareness, the knowing of consciousness, emerges from a plane of possibility, a sea of potential, the generator of diversity, the quantum vacuum. With this 3-P proposal of a mechanism beyond the metaphor, it becomes clear how the awareness of consciousness is inextricably woven with the spaciousness of possibilities. As we've seen, giving Billy access to an expanded awareness is not just giving him time to reflect; it gives him new ways of responding instead of automatically reacting. Consciousness permits choice and change because the *reflection* on choices and the *resources* of alternative responses each arise from the same probability

---

* Hasenkamp and White, eds., *The Monastery and the Microscope*, 67.

position—the plane of possibility. That is a view only the discussion regarding mechanisms illuminates for us—and now we can apply this view to our metaphoric idea and practice of the Wheel of Awareness.

If you find these deeper discussions of mechanisms helpful, wonderful. I hope you are at least finding them of interest. As we move ahead with the discussions of others' experiences in the following narratives, naturally you may be reflecting on how their experiences relate to your own practice and ways you harness the hub or access the plane of possibility.

These changes that arose from Billy's growing access to his plane created a new set of learned probabilities above the plane. This new learning in his brain likely altered the probabilities of neural firing in new patterns; as we've seen, that's what memory and learning are all about—changes in probability. On our 3-P diagram, we would see this set of changed probability patterns as his newly configuring plateaus, sub-peaks, and peaks. The peak of actualization of his actions was now quite different, with his "getting back to his hub" and making new choices from his plane of possibility, which allowed him to not activate a peak of hitting the other boy.

Even Billy's self-defining consciousness filters, the default mode network plateaus of his sense of self, will likely be modified because of this new way of being in the world. Others will now respond to Billy's responses differently, and the system will reinforce his becoming a differentiated person now linked into Ms. Smith's classroom. Offering Billy the Wheel provided him the opportunity to become more integrated in his inner mind and his relational, inter mind. With continued positive reinforcement and the empowerment that comes along with his moving from a proclivity to be reactive to a trait of being reflective, receptive, and responsive, Billy will be supported in his growth toward a more integrated way of being in the world. He is learning to live from his hub, to access his plane, inside and out.

TEACHING THE WHEEL TO ADOLESCENTS: JONATHAN AND CALMING THE ROLLER COASTER OF PLATEAUS AND PEAKS

Adolescence is a period of great physical, physiological, neurological, and social change. In the book *Brainstorm: The Power and Purpose of the Teenage Brain*, I offer both adolescents and the adults who care for them an exploration of the essence of this period of life. I describe this essence with the acronym ESSENCE.

ES stands for the *emotional spark* of this developmental time of life in which the brain is remodeling itself. During this period, the limbic area of the brain is undergoing great changes that create more intense emotions and less predictable mood states. From a 3-P perspective, this looks like rapidly shifting peaks and plateaus that then give rise to turbulent thoughts, emotions, and memories. The downside of this emotional spark is moodiness and irritability; the upside is passion and vitality.

SE stands for *social engagement*. Adolescents are built for connection and collaboration, yet our modern schooling of teens often involves competition and a feeling of scarcity and inadequacy. The sad result is often a sense of pressure and isolation, which causes unhelpful stress and sometimes a sense of despair. Our social relationships are one of the most important ingredients to a healthy, happy, and long-lived life—and we learn social skills in a big way during our adolescent years. Yet with the sleep deprivation and tension many teens in contemporary culture experience, the adolescent period's time for connection is often cut short to the detriment of many during this age. We can only imagine how such experiences shape the DMN and reinforce a sense of a separate rather than interconnected self. The downside of social engagement is giving in to peer pressure and perhaps losing a moral compass to gain group membership; the upside is connection and collaboration.

The *N* in ESSENCE is *novelty seeking*. Changes in the brain's evaluative limbic circuitry and its reward system drive a young teen toward behaviors that may involve seeking the unfamiliar, uncertain, and at times dangerous. A change in the limbic system's evaluative appraisal may create something called "hyperrational thinking," in which only the positive aspects of a choice are considered important—making the dangers of a decision less pressing than the pleasures. This situation would focus attention, both focal and non-focal, on these thrilling aspects of a choice, plateaus of a state of mind creating particular positive spins on the peaks that arise. The downside of novelty seeking and risk taking is injury and death; the upside is courage to live life fully.

Finally, CE stands for *creative exploration*. While childhood is a time to soak in what adults know and to understand the world as it is, adolescence is a period when many begin to challenge adult knowledge and imagine not only how the world might be but also how it should be. The downside of creative exploration is a sense of disappointment, disillusionment, and despair as the adults who just a short while ago were revered as gods are now seen as "just people" or worse; the upside is imagination.

Downsides and upsides, the ESSENCE of adolescence offers both challenges and opportunities. The key to an approach that helps adolescents grow well is to help support the upsides of passion, connection, courage, and imagination.

How we approach adolescents during this period—as parents, as mentors, as teachers and coaches, and as a society—will directly influence not only their individual development but also the future of our world. Adolescence is a period of great opportunity, yet we often treat it as a time to just get through as quickly as possible. We are often filled with false statements that give us a misunderstanding of this important life period; common myths, such as raging hormones being unavoidable causes of crazy teen behavior, are found throughout the world. The good news is that the truth about adolescent brain remodeling means that we can empower adolescents to actually engage their minds and their lives to optimize how their brains grow and change during this period of rapid transformation.

We can only imagine from the 3-P perspective how different the filtering plateaus of an adolescent are from what they were during childhood, and even what they may become with adult responsibility. Plateaus are the filters that determine which peaks arise, and so we can envision the ESSENCE of these shifts altering not only what adolescents do in their behaviors but also what they experience in their inner sense of awareness. Plateaus serve as filters, shaping what can arise as peaks of actualization from their selected subset of possibilities. These filters can shape our nonconscious information processing, and they can influence what enters awareness as they serve also as filters of consciousness constructing our sense of self in the world. You can imagine how such shifts in plateaus during adolescence would help us understand the rapidly changing sense of self that this important period of life often involves.

The overall goal of adolescent brain remodeling is for the pruning down of neural connections to create more differentiated circuits and then the later myelin formation to establish more linkages. Yes, you may have seen this coming: The purpose of the adolescent brain being a construction zone for a while is to ultimately create a more integrated brain.

I offer the Wheel of Awareness as both idea and practice in the book I wrote for adolescents themselves to use. This mindsight tool, building insight, empathy, and integration, is part of a larger toolkit that helps construct an internal compass to help youth of this age navigate their lives during this challenging period, and set them up for emerging into the adult years with a more integrated brain and a stronger mind.

Jonathan, from the first chapter and also described in the book *Mindsight*, was a sixteen-year-old who had a powerful set of emotional storms running and almost ruining his life. Beyond simply the passions of an emotional spark as part of his ESSENCE, these mood instabilities turned out to be the early signs of a serious psychiatric illness, what I and two other board-certified child and adolescent psychiatrists diagnosed as bipolar disorder. Later studies at UCLA and Stanford would begin to explore what a few colleagues as well as I had found in individual cases, that offering a form of mind training such as mindfulness and the Wheel of Awareness could alter the course of the illness.

The remodeling of the adolescent brain involves the pruning of important regions involved in mood regulation. This finding, combined with the very real possibility that stress may enhance the pruning process and lead to further dysregulation—especially in a genetically vulnerable person, who then experiences further stress, further pruning, and on and on—means that the brain's ability to integrate is compromised. Integration, recall, appears to be the basis of healthy regulation—regulating mood and emotion, attention, thought, and action. This compromised state of integration, of not having the linking of differentiated areas, may be at the core of psychiatric disorders such as manic-depressive, or bipolar, disorder. Genes may often play a role, as may chance events, in making the brain vulnerable to impaired integration, the results of which may only become apparent during the remodeling period of adolescence. In fact, the majority of psychiatric disorders, including addictions and disorders of anxiety, mood, and thought, are most likely to first appear clinically during this important period of brain pruning and myelination. Jonathan seemed to be at the early stages, where brain remodeling was being shaped by a genetic vulnerability. As it turned out, the Wheel became an important mind-training, likely brain-integrating, practice for him.

Jonathan's Wheel practice ultimately enabled him to remain more firmly in his hub and sense his rim with more clarity. As his open awareness developed, he learned to access the vast spaciousness of the plane of possibility. Resting in the receptivity of the hub, accessing the clarity and tranquility of the plane, is exactly what

Jonathan needed as a sanctuary from the storms of shifting moods and states of mind. This newly learned capacity to live more from his plane of possibility enabled Jonathan's plateaus of intense states of mind and the chaotic and rigid peaks they'd create to become less controlling in his life. From this newly accessed plane—what Jonathan would call the power of his hub—he could sense the rim points of his mood swings with more distance and learn to calm the storm with more clarity. He had mastered the Wheel of Awareness, and felt a new sense of hope for his life. In many ways, learning to live more from the plane of possibility gave him options for how much of an attentional sweep he could choose to have for his emotional reactions. The spaciousness of his awareness now available to him was his enlarged container, and the previously overwhelming salt of his stormy emotions became calmed and diluted in this vast and now accessible source of being aware. Learning to live with the presence of the plane, harnessing the hub, empowered Jonathan to stabilize his mind and, in turn, to have the self-reinforcing experience of his own personal mastery of these emotional storms, making him feel that he could rely on himself, lowering his sense of helplessness, and then teaching him that finally he could count on his own mind.

On the fourth segment of the rim during the Wheel practice, Jonathan began to further cultivate kind intention. We say "further" here because the very practice of focused attention, as we've seen, begins that process of being kind to ourselves as the mind becomes distracted and we turn the focus of attention back, again and again, to the intended known. The fourth segment builds on this grounding in kind intention. The disappointment Jonathan expressed with himself, the feeling that he could not trust even his own mind to function well, and the stormy ways his relationships with peers and family members would naturally unfold with his accelerating emotional upheavals and "breakdowns," left him feeling quite hostile toward himself, and also toward those close to him. He was at a breaking point when we met.

We can only imagine from a 3-P perspective how these patterns of being out of control and the negative attitude he developed toward himself during those stormy months built a set of plateaus that created a pattern of hostile inner dialogues about himself, internal conversations that likely only worsened his way of dealing with an oncoming emotional storm and increased the intensity of its effects. Reinforcing such filters of consciousness with these repeating experiences of being out of control, Jonathan's own mind would now have a structure of rigid plateaus from which only negative, helpless, and hopeless peaks of thoughts, feelings, and memories could arise. When he first came to see me, Jonathan felt imprisoned by these experiences and in despair about what he could possibly do to escape. There were no plateaus of hope, no peaks of thought or feeling that gave him trust that things would work out for him.

Although standard treatment would almost always involve medications for someone with these experiences and this diagnosis, for understandable family medical history reasons, Jonathan's parents refused the suggestion of a prescription, and instead we chose to carefully try what at that time was considered a nonstandard approach. Fortunately it worked, both in the short run, as he became more stable, and in the long run. Now, over fifteen years later, he is stable, medication-free, and thriving.

For a genetically at-risk brain struggling toward integrative growth, an integrative practice like the Wheel of Awareness is a natural suggestion. But such mind-training strategies may not work for all individuals with integrative challenges, and if used, should be done so with careful clinical assessment and monitoring. Mind-training practices in general lead to increased integration in the brain, and so it may make sense to use such approaches with individuals with compromised neural integration at the core of their difficulties. Research has shown that in the general population, mind training increased neural integration in many ways with increased growth of: the corpus callosum connecting left and right hemispheres, the hippocampus linking memory systems together, and the prefrontal cortex connecting widely separated regions to one another. In addition, meditative practice increases the interconnectivity of the connectome, meaning the linking of those more subtly differentiated areas distributed throughout the brain. Further, the DMN becomes less tightly bound and isolated in its functioning and therefore more integrated into the overall neural system. And for those with an enlarged amygdala, which is involved in excessive emotional reactivity, mind training leads to a decrease in this overly differentiated neural node of our emotional life.

When we also recognize that the Human Connectome Project has revealed that one of the best predictors of well-being in mind and body is how interconnected our differentiated connectome is, we can see why mind trainings that promote neural integration, especially during this period of brain remodeling, would help cultivate health in our lives.

If adolescent brain remodeling is happening to create a more integrated brain, and if we know that mind training with the cultivation of focused attention, open awareness, and kind intention cultivate more neural integration in these ways, why not offer all adolescents such integrative practices during this formative period? The answer seems simple: There's no reason not to. Let's work together to help support the growth of the next generation to care for each other and the planet, supporting the ESSENCE of adolescence so that adolescents can develop well, live happy and productive lives, and make positive contributions to our society.

If you could meet Jonathan now, you'd feel the power of integration to liberate an adolescent's natural capacity for passion, connection, courage, and imagination. Now in his thirties, Jonathan is no longer an adolescent but he still possesses these important qualities. His ESSENCE was clearly nurtured by his Wheel of Awareness practice. The hub became a sanctuary from which he could learn to experience his mind and its inner storms in a new and more regulated way, and this ability continues to support him as he moves through life. From these new experiences, a new set of plateaus with more optimistic and hopeful peaks could be created in his life. In addition, accessing the plane of possibility opened a window into Jonathan's passions that allowed him to take the fuel of his interests and creatively channel them into productive plateaus and peaks in his personal and professional pursuits. In doing this resilience-building and at times hard work, Jonathan gave himself a gift that will keep on giving for all the journeys in his life that lie ahead.

THE WHEEL FOR PARENTS AND OTHER CARE PROVIDERS: MONA AND THE FREEDOM FROM RECURRENT PLATEAUS AND PEAKS OF CHAOS AND RIGIDITY

Raising children is one of the most challenging as well as rewarding relationships we can choose to engage in. How we as infants, toddlers, children, and adolescents connect with our care providers— our parents and others in our lives—in part shapes the trajectories of our growth and development. The field of study called *attachment* offers us a scientific grounding in the universal patterns of connection between child and parent or other caregiver throughout the world. According to this research, there are four types of attachment relationships: secure, avoidant, ambivalent, and disorganized. *Secure* attachment between a primary caregiver and a child is associated with positive outcomes in many aspects of the child's development, including the growth of the capacity for emotional resilience, self-awareness, and engaging in mutually rewarding relationships with others.

In the field of interpersonal neurobiology we have synthesized the findings from attachment studies, neurobiology, and other scientific fields to come to this simple but powerful perspective: Integrated attachment relationships that involve children being honored for their differentiated nature and linked in caring connections—secure parent-child relationships—lead to the growth of neural integration in the children.

Our ability as parents to be open and present for our children enables them to be both *differentiated* from our own expectations and desires for how they should be and *linked* to us through compassionate, respectful communication, enabling the integrative circuitry of their brains to develop well. That neural integration in the brain is the fundamental mechanism for optimal regulation—of attention, emotion, mood, thought, memory, morality, and relating to others.

Nonsecure forms of attachment, the other three types of attachment—what in the research literature are called *insecure* attachment relationships—include patterns of a child's learning from their experiences in a way that can compromise these regulatory capacities. Attachment is a relational measure emerging from the experience of interpersonal connection, not an innate feature of the child. Children can learn to be disconnected emotionally with parents with *avoidant* attachment relationships, they can feel confused by parents with *ambivalent* attachments, and they can become fragmented because they are terrified of parents in the case of *disorganized* attachment. Each of these three patterns of insecure attachment can be seen as blocked relational integration, with avoidance being excessive differentiation without linkage, ambivalence being excessive linkage without differentiation, and disorganization arising with the intense experience of terror, a feeling of fearful abandonment that is the exact opposite of the foundations of attachment.

Because brain integration is the basis for the many forms of regulation—from attention and memory to emotion and thought—when we limit integration relationally we directly compromise the child's ability to develop neural integration and therefore cultivate regulation. In this way, various degrees of impediments to regulation can be seen with insecure attachment, with those with a history of disorganized attachment showing the most regulatory challenges. For those with disorganized attachment, significant compromises are found in the regulation of emotion, thought, attention, and even consciousness in the form of a process called *dissociation*—the fragmentation of consciousness in which usually associated processes such as emotion, thought, and memory become disassociated.

Recall that Mona was a forty-year-old mother of three young children who was having frequent experiences of shutting down and distancing herself from her children, or, in some instances, frightening her children as well as herself, as she'd have chaotic outbursts of sadness and anger. Such outbursts were likely an example of Mona experiencing dissociation under stress. As many overwhelmed parents may experience, there are moments when we "flip our lids" and lose control of our feelings, thoughts, words, and even behavior. In your hand model of the brain from part II, we can see this as the sudden lifting of the integrative prefrontal finger regions off of the lower limbic-thumb and brain-stem-palm areas, resulting in a loss of balance and the rigid or chaotic ways of interacting with such a temporary blockage of integrating the whole head-brain system. Now out of balance with the body and relational world, what emerges for Mona—or any of us—in such a nonintegrated state of "flying off the handle" or "losing it" is a terrifying way of being that temporarily ruptures her connection with her children. Knowing that such frightening experiences for her children can produce significant negative impacts on their growth, Mona urgently sought help. She did not want to pass on the legacy of terror from her own upbringing to her children.

We've seen that when integration is compromised, any of us can move outside that river of well-being, that sense of harmony and openness with the FACES flow of flexibility, adaptability, coherence (resilience over time), energy (vitality), and stability. Instead of that harmonious flow of integration, we move to the banks of chaos or rigidity. I know in my own life this can happen at times, and it feels compelling at the moment as it pulls you into its activated state, but also exhausting and often humiliating to feel so out of control. It is quite possible, as I know personally, to be aware of a reactive state of chaotic outbursts or one of rigid withdrawal yet feel helpless to make a change. Sometimes, in those moments, it even "feels right" and you can feel justified in your behavioral reactivity. But soon it can feel depleting, and at some other level, in some other state, you know you are not being your wisest self at that time. Most of the parenting books I've written reflect on this important realization for us as parents.

This is how Mona found herself feeling overwhelmed by the "burden," as she experienced it, of raising her children without much help from her spouse, and with no family or community of neighbors around to support her.

As we have discussed previously, Mona began to practice the Wheel of Awareness and it enabled her to build the internal resources that could help her become more present and aware, and offer a secure attachment for her children. In order to understand how this transpired, let's look at Mona's process from an attachment perspective. According to attachment research, a secure bond between parent and child involves patterns in which the child feels seen, soothed, and safe. When ruptures occur in these patterns—for example, when the normal stresses of life cause us to be quick, abrupt, or even angry with our children—in a secure attachment a repairing of the rupture reliably follows. In this way, children develop a sense of security in the world and learn that even when things don't go well, they can be repaired. When we are living from the hub, we inspire those around us to live from their hub as well. In the case of the parent-child relationship this is essential for a healthy bond, and the Wheel of Awareness can help us develop these specific parenting skills in the following ways:

1. *Seen:* A child's mind needs to be seen beyond only a parent responding to their behavior or seeing through the lens of their own expectations. Mindsight is the skill of being present for a child's inner life, of being attuned to their feelings, thoughts, and responses so that a child "feels felt." When a child is seen she is both differentiated and linked—she feels she belongs to something larger than her private, inner self. Harnessing the hub, accessing the plane, enabled Mona to be aware of her children more fully and freely.

2. *Soothed:* When a child is in distress, feeling that she is cared for and loved can help her move back to a calmer baseline state. When as parents we are able to be fully present with where our child is in any given moment, we can gently soothe our children and help them to redirect their experience to the wider view that is the hub. The plane is the portal through which parental presence arises and integration is cultivated. Instead of having fixed filters of rigid plateaus restricting what we sense and how we react, accessing the plane widens our perceptions and opens us to respond in more connecting and soothing ways.

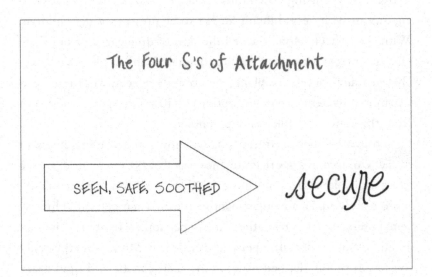

The Four S's of Attachment

SEEN, SAFE, SOOTHED ⟩ Secure

3. *Safe:* Our role as parents or other care providers is to protect our children from danger—to keep them safe, in very concrete terms. In a secure attachment relationship, we also need to make our children *feel* safe. If instead we are striking terror in them by behaving in an angry or unstable manner or becoming disoriented ourselves (children are extremely sensitive to our moods; they notice and deeply respond to our states as well as to our behavior), we need to recenter and recognize that the rupture must be repaired. By practicing the Wheel, we can operate in a more balanced way, accessing the hub to see our behavior from a bird's-eye view and, in turn, alter it to protect the atmosphere of safety that we hope to surround our child with. There is no such thing as perfect parenting, but by always aiming to maintain our connection to our children and reliably repair ruptures when they occur we allow them to feel seen, soothed, safe, and secure.

What the Wheel offered to Mona was harnessing the hub, accessing the plane of possibility, which became a sanctuary of relief from the chaotic and rigid peaks and plateaus of bursting out in rage at one extreme and shutting down in burnout at the other. This chaos and rigidity made it very difficult for her to be present for her children. With the Wheel, Mona learned the skill of disengaging from these chaotic or rigid patterns of her nonintegrated, above-plane activities. By learning to access the plane, she not only developed a more open expanse of awareness, but new options for how to respond could arise from this now accessible sea of potential.

From a 3-P perspective, Mona was now able to be more present for her children. It's not that presence was always there; it just became more available to her, and more familiar in her mind so she could more readily make a readjustment or repair when needed. This parental presence arises from the plane of possibility. Imagine this from an energy and probability perspective. Before, Mona was repeatedly lost up on rigidly defined plateaus and their chaotic and rigid peaks of reactivity. She was anything but present. Now in accessing the plane, Mona could rest in a spaciousness of time and choice, an inner vastness she never knew had always been available to her beneath all the chatter of her peaks and the filtering of her plateaus. What could now arise from Mona as a mother were peaks of interaction coming directly from this plane of presence. She could feel the difference, and likely so could her children.

There is no such thing as perfect parenting. In all of my books for parents I try to make this point by noting, sometimes to my own children's dismay, the many times I've messed up in my relationship with them. I also try to describe how in showing up for our kids, we express kindness not only toward them, but toward ourselves as well. This kind regard means being present for the reality that we, too, are simply human. From the plane of possibility, from the hub of the wheel, we can all find that love that empowers us to become our own best friend, our own support team. Naturally we need others as well, but the Wheel encourages us to begin the important journey of offering those same s's to ourselves. From this more integrated place, connecting hub to a more varied rim, plane to more flexible plateaus and peaks, we can see experience more clearly, soothe our own distress more effectively, and offer safety from both within and between. We can become our own secure attachment figure—an aspect of befriending ourselves that helps give us strength and resilience from the inside out.

THE WHEEL IN HEALING TRAUMA: TERESA AND THE TRANSFORMATION OF TRAUMATIC FILTERS OF CONSCIOUSNESS

Sometimes our attachment experiences in childhood do not provide the basics of being seen, soothed, or safe; as a result, we develop an insecure attachment. People with this form of attachment can find it challenging to feel at ease in the world and to connect with others.

Insecure attachment also seems to impose challenges to integration in our lives—both in our brains and in our ways of relating to others and ourselves.

Beyond the organized adaptation to suboptimal experiences that leads to the avoidant and ambivalent forms of insecure attachment, sometimes our attachment experiences are so extreme, as in the case of childhood abuse or neglect, that they are called *developmental trauma*. Sadly, developmental trauma is actually quite common in our human family. A range of studies has revealed that the outcomes of these and even less severe adverse experiences include challenges to our medical health, our mental well-being, and our relational lives.

In *Mindsight*, I offer a number of stories of how people with various insecure attachment histories, including developmental trauma, can transform their lives toward health. The important message to state here from the outset is that neuroplasticity studies, the research that explores how the brain remains open to growth and change throughout the life span, reveal how we can heal from prior assaults on the brain's healthy growth. If compromised integration is the outcome of insecure attachment to various degrees, with the extreme being developmental trauma, then the promise and hope would be that we can grow a more integrated brain in the future if this was our suboptimal experience in the past. Prevention of insecure attachment in general, and abuse and neglect in particular, is important, of course, but those who've had overwhelming early experiences need not despair: Repair is possible. What is repair based on? Integration. And integration is what this book and the Wheel of Awareness are all about.

A review of the impact of developmental trauma on the brain shows that these extreme experiences of nonintegrated relationships early in life impact the growth of the integrative fibers in the brain. Here is the simple equation: Integrated relationships lead to integrated brains; nonintegrated relationships lead to compromises in the growth of integration in the brain. Integration in the future—with interpersonal relationships in therapy or with friends and self-reflective practices like journal writing and the Wheel of Awareness—help promote more integration in your life at any age.

If you look at your hand model to map out the head brain we introduced in part II, we can visually review these findings now. Here are the names for the areas compromised in their growth with developmental trauma: the corpus callosum, the hippocampus, the prefrontal cortex, and the overall connectome of the brain. In your hand model, these would be the fibers connecting the left and right sides of the finger-cortex for the corpus callosum, the hippocampal region of the limbic-thumb's medial temporal lobe that links widely separated memory systems to each other, and the prefrontal-fingernail regions of your fingers, just behind the forehead and where your fingernails are in your model, that links cortex, limbic regions, brain stem, body proper, and the social world together. The connectome refers to the many differentiated zones of the brain and their linkages to each other, so that we might say, "That's an interconnected connectome," or not so interconnected, as in the case of trauma.

If you've observed that these four areas of integration compromised by trauma are exactly those that grow with mind training, you are detecting a consilient finding. Meditation studies are independent of attachment and trauma research, yet these disciplined pursuits of knowledge about how experience shapes the brain's growth reveal this common ground of neural circuitry integration. Secure attachment and mindful awareness seem to be cut from the same cloth. The way I like to think about it is that both are forms of attunement. Secure attachment is based on interpersonal attunement, and mindful awareness is a form of internal attunement—how we tune in and befriend our inner selves.

The great news about this consilient finding is that while the impaired integrative experiences of developmental trauma impede the growth of neural integration, mind training supports the growth of those same integrative circuits. What we need are focused studies of large numbers of individuals examining how those who've experienced developmental trauma as a group also develop integrative growth with mind training, in order to affirm that this consilient implication of mindfulness and attachment might also apply to a traumatized individual's neuroplastic changes with reflective practices.

Why is the abuse or neglect in developmental trauma revealing of a nonintegrated relationship? Recall that integration is made of differentiation and linkage. Is there differentiation of a child's needs when a parent's anger results in physical or emotional abuse of the child? Is there differentiation of a child's needs when a parent's sexual drives are imposed upon a child? The answer in both cases is no. These intrusions in fact reveal a lack of differentiation and excessive linkage. In the case of neglect, is there integration? Emotional and physical neglect are profound impairments to being linked, leaving the child isolated and excessively differentiated, comprising integration in the connection of parent and child. Abuse and neglect are extreme examples of impaired relational integration.

It is striking that even without this perspective on relationships, the findings are clear: The main impact on the brain with developmental trauma is impairment of integration in the head brain. Since all forms of regulation, as we've discussed, appear to arise from neural integration, we can see how developmental trauma sets the stage for a life of dysregulation within the body and its brain, and within relationships in the future—unless some concerted efforts are made to cultivate integration in the individual's life. Because our sense of self arises from our body and our relationships, we can see how developmental trauma is an assault on our sense of who we are in the world.

In some ways, we can view the impact of trauma as constructed plateaus of various kinds that keep the individual in a reactive survival mode of being. Recall that plateaus serve as filters of consciousness that shape who we are, and in this way, developmental trauma may involve the ways we've both been impacted directly by overwhelming experiences and how we've adapted the best we can to those terrifying experiences, including abuse and neglect.

Developmental trauma and other adverse childhood experiences may compromise integration and create social, psychological, and physiological impediments to regulation—but these outcomes of nonintegration may be responsive to interventions that create more integration in the future. Repair is possible even if we haven't yet empirically shown the exact mechanism of this healing. The Wheel of Awareness may prove helpful in this journey toward integration by enabling us to access the plane of possibility, with all its new potential ways of being that have lain hidden beneath the rigid and chaotic plateaus, the direct or adaptive learned filters imprisoning us in a self-perpetuating manner, away from the more harmonious flow of an integrating life.

Our basic foundational ideas are these: Integration is the basis of health. We grow throughout the life span. Harnessing the hub—accessing the plane of possibility—may be an important step in that journey toward freedom. If adverse experiences such as trauma compromise integration, perhaps they do this in part by blocking access to the source of new potentials that rest in the plane. Finding the resources to cultivate healing likely involves the growth of new integration to liberate and create a healthier way of living.

These are the ideas that were stirring inside me when I first met Teresa.

Let's look again at Teresa's experiences to dive deeply into one example of how such a process of healing and growth might unfold with a Wheel practice and our new perspective of the 3-P framework. While Teresa's specific story is one of significant developmental trauma, her experiences offer each of us, regardless of our own personal histories, an opportunity to not only deepen our understanding of others but also find general insights relevant to understanding our own lives.

Recall that Teresa was a twenty-five-year-old who came to me for therapy having experienced significant developmental trauma. In Teresa's history, periods of early neglect were followed later in her childhood by the terrifying rages of an alcoholic mother and the sexual abuse of a manipulative and sadistic stepfather, who, to this day, is still married to her mother. Teresa was a graduate student who was struggling to find rewarding relationships in her life that would last beyond a few months. She came to me to find some way of understanding what was going on in terms of her own contributions to these experiences, in hopes that she might someday not live in such an isolated way. Learning the Wheel of Awareness was at first quite challenging for her. In fact, she felt terrified, and, just as with other individuals I've observed, she had the impulse to run from the Wheel practice.

Why *run*?

An impulse to run is sometimes part of the brain-stem-mediated *reactive state* of fight/flight/freeze/faint that is created and then reinforced in the brain in response to a threat from outside the body, or even from experiences generated within the body, or from the workings of our own inner mind. This reactive state is the opposite of a *receptive state* that turns on what is called the *social engagement system* and creates a sense of trust in what we are doing and with whom we are doing it. Let's try to see how and why the Wheel practice might initiate this reactive-threat state of mind, creating in Teresa a sense of fear and an impulse to flee. The lessons we can learn about her reaction certainly may be specific to her experiences of trauma, but there also may be generalizations that reveal layers of response to the Wheel's components and illuminate more about how we experience the mind, with its memory, attention, and emotions, and, from the 3-P framework, the plane, plateaus, and peaks in our lives.

Several components of the Wheel practice directly place focal attention—attention streaming energy and information flow into awareness—on an aspect of a person's life that may be similar to an early traumatic experience. In the brain, cues from the present can trigger the recall of experiences from the past that then impact how things are unfolding in the present moment, including how we feel and act now, and how we prepare ourselves for the future. In other words, the brain and the experience of memory link past, present, and future.

With unresolved trauma, a layer of memory called *implicit memory* may be the primary form in which the terrifying experiences are now being stored in the brain. Implicit memory involves bodily sensations, emotions, images, thoughts, and behavioral impulses. When a cue arises, such as an external signal or internal condition, these elements of implicit memory may be activated as memory retrievals. A key issue in the brain's memory system is that when retrieved from storage, pure implicit memory is not tagged as being from the past. Instead, it can feel as if it is happening in the present moment. This essentially means that the past is not really the past with unresolved trauma, reflecting the brain's way of shaping our mental life.

A timing view can help clarify this important finding. When we have an experience, we *encode* the firing of neural networks at the present moment, which then alters the connections in the brain in the forms we've discussed—strengthening synapses, altering epigenetic regulation, laying down the interconnecting myelin sheath. These changed connections are the structural basis for memory *storage*. At a later time, an internal or external cue similar in some ways to the initial encoding experience can trigger the firing of those stored neural connections, and then we have memory *retrieval*.

In the case of pure implicit memory, studies reveal that the retrieval process makes the retrieved bit of information enter consciousness, but it is not tagged or labeled as coming from the past. Pure implicit memory when retrieved simply shapes our here-and-now experience—so we get on a bike and ride it without feeling, "Oh, I am remembering how to ride a bike." With trauma, one proposal suggests, we only encode some aspects of a traumatic experience in its pure implicit form within storage. As a result, the retrieval of pure implicit memory for past trauma can enter awareness in the present and feel like it is happening now, a likely mechanism of a flashback or intrusive emotions and sensations of an unresolved trauma.

Focusing on the second segment of the rim, for example, might bring up bodily sensations of being choked with a focus on the breath or the chest, or of being sexually violated when focusing on the genitals or mouth. If these bodily sensations that arise are indeed unresolved imprints from the past, embedded now in layers of pure implicit memory, then when retrieved from their neural storage as potential firing patterns, they are not tagged as having an origin in the past, as a "memory" as we usually know it to be, but emerge instead as a here-and-now sensory reality. Such a disorienting mix of past and present can be terrifying, as it confuses conduition for construction and can fill a person with terror and helplessness. With unresolved trauma, we can feel that we are sensing ongoing terrifying experiences, not assembling the pieces of memory for something that happened in the past.

After her initial experience with the Wheel, Teresa described her reactions to me in detail. She told me that while the second segment of the rim brought up overwhelming sensations, the focus on the space between mental activities in the third segment review and then the next step of bending the spoke into the hub gave her different kinds of distress. We've discussed earlier how resting in the awareness of the hub of our wheel, resting in the plane of possibility, may create a sense of uncertainty that, for someone with unresolved trauma, can feel very unsafe.

As we've seen in our earlier focus on attachment, our brain evolved to need the three *s*'s of being seen, soothed, and safe in order to develop the integrative neural state of security. Each of us has an inborn expectation that this security is what we are here for. In neuroscience we call this *experience-expectant brain growth*—we are genetically programmed to grow circuits that expect certain experiences. Examples typically include hearing sound or seeing light. I think they also can include being loved and cared for. In other words, we don't need to have experienced security for our brain's need and drive for security to genetically grow. These needs are a part of the attachment regions of our social brain and they lead to the innate expectation that we will receive the loving relationships we long for, in which our parents, caregivers, partners, and friends are present, attuned, resonating, and cultivating our trust.

If suboptimal attachment dominates our lives as children, we need to do two somewhat distinct things: We need to take on directly what we are being given; and we need to adapt to the absence of what our brain evolved to expect. This adaptation is how we learn a strategy, a coping mechanism or what some might call a defensive structure, that gives us a way to respond as effectively as we can to these suboptimal attachment relationships in a way that helps us survive.

When a suboptimal set of experiences includes the abuse and neglect of developmental trauma, then uncertainty can be terrifying. This sense of terror learned as a response to the unknown may come to shape how we react to the uncertainty of the plane of possibility. The plane's openness of awareness, a state of open potential that might be experienced by some as freedom, is also characterized as not knowing, resting in the lowest degree of certainty, and can be reacted to by others as if it's dangerous. Accessing the plane of possibility may evoke an implicit memory retrieval of a deeply held but nonconscious belief that what is unknown is bad. Such a state of unpredictability for these individuals can act as a cue and initiate a learned state of threat.

Developmental trauma can lead us to no longer rely on our hopes and expectations, and to instead find ourselves in a terrifying world devoid of reliable connections, ruptures that feel beyond repair. One direct impact of such traumatic early experiences is that those experiences are encoded into the implicit layers of memory. This makes the intrusions of bodily sensations and emotions, the feelings of betrayal and isolation more likely to arise, and arise quickly. In addition, we have our adaptations to help us survive. Many such adaptive consequences can occur when developmental trauma is our reality, and two of them include the experience of *dissociation*, in which a usual continuity of consciousness is fragmented; and the emotional state of *shame*. While these two adaptive responses to trauma are common with the experiences of abuse and neglect, they are also frequently present to various degrees in many of us who have experienced forms of suboptimal attachment that would not be called developmental trauma.

Dissociation

Let's first look at dissociation. When one neural motivational and social circuit in our limbic area (thumb in the hand model) initiates a state that if it could talk would say, "Go toward the attachment figure, the parent, to be protected when you feel threatened," and another equally potent but anatomically older and deeper area, the brain stem circuit (in the palm of your model) says, "Go away from the source of terror—escape!" you have a limbic drive *toward* and a brain stem drive *away from* at the exact same time. When the attachment figure is the source of terror, how do you solve this dilemma when you only have one body? How can one body go both toward and away from the same figure, the caregiver who is the source of threat? This is what attachment researchers Mary Main and Erik Hesse have termed "fear without solution," and it is a biological paradox in that the limbic drive toward and the brain stem drive away from cannot be resolved because you have one body. Careful research reveals that the result of such fear without solution is the mental response called dissociation.

Dissociation can take a variety of forms, including subtle experiences of feeling unreal or disconnected from the body, or more intense experiences of memory lapses or an isolation of parts of the self that may not communicate with one another, as in a condition called dissociative identity disorder. While it is a proven outcome of child-hood maltreatment, dissociation itself can become traumatizing to the individual, as it can lead to the experience of being unable to trust one's own mind to be reliable. This unfortunate cascade of ongoing adaptation-induced traumatic responses to the outside world, and then also to the world within, can be profoundly fragmenting, but fortunately quite open to growth and healing. Dissociation is a nat-ural response to trauma, and the mind can be supported in learning a new skill of dealing with internal and external challenges through a healing, therapeutic relationship.

The Wheel of Awareness can be a powerful tool in supporting ways to have an internal locus of awareness beneath the dissociative reactions that may be above-plane learned reactions to an unreliable world. Rim points may be dissociative elements of unresolved, implicit-only memory that the openness of the hub can help reflect upon and integrate into a larger, emerging, ever-more coherent nar-rative of a person's life. A 3-P perspective suggests that fragmented states of the self may be seen as ingrained plateaus that shape how we react to ongoing experiences and have different degrees of access to memory and knowledge of painful events in the past. Serving as fil-ters, such plateaus are adaptive attempts to keep the individual in survival mode by dividing up ways of being. The plane of possibility, while terrifying at first, can come to be a source of new freedom and insights as these plateaus shift their rigid ways of confining and de-fining the individual's sense of a fragmented self.

Shame

When we add shame to this mix of adaptations, we can see how challenging developmental trauma can be. Shame is an emotion that can create a feeling of heaviness in the chest, nausea in the belly, and a tendency to avoid gazing into the eyes of others. The mental belief that often accompanies this emotional state of shame is a sense that the self is defective. Shame in this way is very different from guilt or embarrassment, in which we feel we've done something wrong or are too exposed but then can correct those behaviors or exposures in the future. Shame, in contrast, comes along with a helpless feeling that if I am defective, if I am damaged goods, there is nothing I can do to change. I am powerless. Shame is not only present in those who've experienced trauma; it may also be a part of many forms of suboptimal attachment.

Shame is so painful in its helplessness, despair, and feelings of being trapped without the possibility of repair that it may be very difficult to even acknowledge its existence in a person's life. For this reason, shame as an adaptation to maltreatment or suboptimal relational experiences may fly under the radar of awareness, unavailable to everyday consciousness. Shame may also surface and shape a comedian's repertoire, as in the famous line of Groucho Marx quoted by Woody Allen: "Why would I be a member of a club that would have *me* as a member?"

The good news about dissociation and shame is that while they may be quite disabling, they are both treatable conditions.

Healing

For Teresa, the Wheel practice challenged each of these learned adaptations to her painful past. The dissociated memories of neglect and sexual and physical abuse led to anxiety and painful imagery during her initial practice. Isolated implicit memory is one example of a form of dissociation. While many may feel an initial drive to avoid being aware of the body, the representation of the body in the head brain is an important node in how we know our feelings, how we know ourselves. For this reason alone, difficulties with feeling any part of the rim, especially the second segment, may best be seen as invitations to explore what is going on and heal unresolved memory configurations that may continue to imprison an individual. The urge to flee and never return to these uncomfortable sensations that arise during the Wheel practice can be due to a person's patterns of adaptation and present skill set, learned mental patterns—ways energy and information flow is shaped—that continue to keep the person in that prison of the past. Rather than fleeing and avoiding the practice, imagine if, with support, a person like Teresa might learn to access that plane of possibility and become open to any plateaus and peaks that might be swept up into her awareness. Instead of becoming those plateaus and peaks—the points on her Wheel's rim—she now can learn to access the plane, to rest in the hub, so that new ways of being can arise. Such an invitation would reflect a kind of "bring it on" attitude that the resolving of trauma entails. I can sit in the hub of my Wheel and invite any rim element's knowns into the knowing of awareness. I can rest in the plane of possibility and open my mind to whatever plateaus and peaks of memory might configure themselves into being. These above-plane elements are the transient flows of energy and information; they are not the totality of my identity. With such a newly learned skill of accessing the plane, I become open and receptive rather than staying repeatedly closed and reactive.

The process of healing may involve the retrieval of any peaks, any rim elements, into awareness in the plane, experienced from the sanctuary of the hub, so that they can be reflected upon and new configurations of memory established. This is how resolution of trauma can involve both the unlearning of the understandable but no longer useful adaptations from a painful past and the new learning of the skill of being receptive and integrating one's mind.

Memory retrieval can become a memory modifier, meaning that in the right conditions, harnessing awareness of past events can actually free a person from their imprisoning effects when they are unresolved. Resolution involves the integration of the Wheel such that this bring-it-on attitude can be cultivated and you are open to anything that might arise from the experience.

In the brain, a process of cortical consolidation has been explored in which memories become stored in the highest regions of the brain. One component of this unlearning and new learning may involve the movement of pure implicit memory into its more flexible and integrated layer, called *explicit* memory. Awareness may be needed to activate the limbic hippocampus, which is required for taking implicit memory and weaving it into the two major forms of factual and autobiographical explicit memory. When we retrieve explicit memory in either of these forms, it has the tagging of an ecphoric sensation, the feeling that what I am recalling now is something from the past as a fact I know or an episode I experienced. *Ecphory* simply means "retrieval," and so now memories that arise can feel like they are something being retrieved, not something happening now. Resolving dissociated pure implicit memories may involve the hub of the wheel's taking in rim elements that may have been avoided for a long time.

In 3-P terms, the latent plateaus (mental models and beliefs) and peaks (particular sensations or images) of implicit memory may have been unactivated or excluded from entering awareness by not being connected to the plane. In other words, previously we would not know these were events from the past. Their intrusion into consciousness as flashbacks or other distressing implicit retrievals does not facilitate their resolution—it simply re-traumatizes us and makes us feel helpless and hurt all over again. What a painful cycle.

Teresa needed to befriend the hub of her mind to facilitate this process of resolution and healing. From our 3-P perspective, we can now understand this step in her growth as allowing her energy probability state to enter this near-zero certainty position of the plane. Yes, that is where awareness arises. And this is where memory integration needs to occur. So on one level, viewing this as the metaphor of the hub or the mechanism of the plane, the issue is the same— awareness of things that are overwhelming is, well, overwhelming, and they may be avoided one way or another. They may be blocked from retrieval, or they may be dissociated so that as they emerge into awareness we don't know they are events we actually experienced in the past.

Seeing the plane's maximal uncertainty of near-zero gives us new and expanded insights into this situation. One is that Teresa's reaction of fear of this uncertainty is understandable given her past terror in uncertain situations. What this means is that her fear of the plane may be a learned response embedded in a particular plateau filtering her experience and allowing only certain peaks to arise— such as those of fear or terror. A second important insight is that no matter what happens to us—whatever might create direct impacts or adaptations as plateaus and peaks—*nothing can take away our plane of possibility*. Nothing.

And so when I looked into Teresa's eyes, I could feel a connection with her plane of possibility. Your plane, my plane, and Teresa's plane are the same, as infinity is infinity. As the generator of diversity, as this sea of potential, this plane of possibility is the source of all that could be. So I am not exaggerating or trying to be dramatic when I say to Teresa that I believe in her, that I can sense there is an aspect of her, a place inside her, that is filled with possibility. I feel this in every bone and neuron in my body. And hopefully she can feel that from me—and perhaps you can, too.

The work is hard when trauma is unresolved. The fabulous news is that the plane of possibility is there for new combinations of energy configurations to arise. It's a resource, and it became a sanctuary for Teresa even if it wasn't comfortable at first.

At the beginning this openness and uncertainty can be terrify-ing. We can envision this terror as perhaps a low-lying filtering pla-teau defining Teresa's self in that adaptive state and trying to protect her from the unknown. In many ways, as we've discussed in the strategies of adaptations we use to survive, our default mode network likely generates this sense of who we are to enable us to adapt as best we can. The Adult Attachment Interview is an instrument that can directly reveal unresolved states of trauma and loss in the disoriented and disorganized aspect of the narrative that arises, identifying the crucial importance of making sense of these self-defining autobiographical stories we tell ourselves about who we are. To move beyond the prison of a constrictive self-defining and self-confining plateau into a freer experience is the journey that is needed—a process that is at the heart of how we make sense of our lives and heal these unresolved states of being.

Imagine how the avoidance of resting in the plane of possibility shapes Teresa's experience. Not knowing, being uncertain, activates implicitly learned states of terror that need to be avoided at all costs. Her emerging plateaus and peaks that symbolize these adaptive reactions become repeated so often that they become rigidified in a DMN pattern of filters. Her life then becomes more constrained as she grows, making her prone to rigidity.

Yet Teresa also has dissociative tendencies, her peaks and plateaus not only isolated from one another but also suddenly emerging with intrusive emotions or bodily sensations, implicit memories of unresolved traumatic experience. This chaos swings her mind toward the other extreme, now away from rigidity as she bounces back and forth along these banks and away from the FACES flow of a more harmonious, integrated life.

Moving toward the hub of the wheel in the practice is learning the important skill of resting in the plane of possibility—learning to not only tolerate but also to thrive with uncertainty.

When Teresa could learn to let go of the low-plateau filter that likely was giving her a sense of fear and dread at the open and vast expanse of the plane, something profound shifted. This view suggests that her panic is not in the plane, but is a reaction of a historically constructed adaptive plateau defining her reactions to the openness and uncertainty of that plane. What the work needed to do was not continue to avoid or to alter her plane of possibility, but instead to help her access the plane by supporting her in learning to open her mind to the notion that her past adaptations, while useful then, needed to be updated. It was time to download a newer version of her DMN protective sense of self. It was time for a plateau redo.

Teresa began to experience a sense, briefly at first, of relief and being at ease with the Wheel practice. She used this daily routine to give her a sense of mastery in the face of the prior frequent feelings of being out of control and of being master of nothing. As she continued to practice, she could feel a sense of joy, connection, and gratitude that at first she was scared to acknowledge for fear they would go away.

Exploring the Wheel was a grounding place for her work in reflecting on the experiences of the past and how they'd shaped her development up to this moment of her life. Now it was time to see how making sense of how this past impacted her could be a part of freeing her to live a new life. Reflecting on the past and building a more integrated mind with the Wheel practice go hand in hand. Learning new skills of integration is essential for the updating of "self-software," or "selfware." Given that mind may be an emergent property of energy flow, and that this flow entails shifts in probability as we've discussed, Teresa's ability to reclaim her mind is a powerful skill of learning new ways of monitoring and modifying those shifts in probability. Simply put, Teresa was revising the relations among her plane, plateaus, and peaks.

And reflecting on the past was important for her to unlearn the developmental adaptations she had from a past that before had made no sense. Making sense of a past that made no sense is opening to the sensations of the past and putting them together now to see how they impacted you then, and how you can free yourself to live the life you want now. That's why making sense makes so much integrative sense. We cannot change the past, but we can change how we understand the way it has impacted us and how we liberate ourselves in the present to free ourselves for the future. While in the past being open to uncertainty was understandably terrifying, now accessing that plane of possibility has made being open to uncertainty a pathway to freedom.

As we also began to work with Teresa's experience of shame, we could reframe what that emotional state was—a plateau of mood and belief that primed her mind to give rise to specific peaks of the emotion of shame and the thought that she was defective. She had been convinced that the core of who she was, her essence, was broken, was garbage, that she was a bad person. Now with the Wheel practice in her life and our therapeutic relationship unfolding in these reflective conversations, she could literally see, with the visual metaphor of the Wheel, that shame was simply an understandable adaptation to her painful past. Shame was a point on her rim, and not a quality of her hub—the core, the essence of who she is.

When we are children we *cannot* simply say, "Oh, my parents are not available to care for me well because they are distracted or disturbed. I know I have experience-expectant neural connections that are waiting for their love and are frustrated right now. So my parents are not able to keep me safe. No problem, I'll just find my need for being seen, soothed, safe, and secure elsewhere." If children could reason like that, they would feel completely at risk of dying without the protection of their parents. That incessant feeling of dread could drive a person insane. So instead of going insane, children tend to go to shame. I can survive if I say to myself as a child, "Oh, I have reliable parents who love me and care for me—*I am not receiving what I need because I am defective* and actually don't really deserve to have these needs I feel met." That is the likely developmental adaptive origin of shame.

All of this learned emotion and belief is plateau and peak material above the plane. *Trauma does not mar the plane of possibility.* Even with direct impacts of bodily sensations and interactions that are terrifying, and secondary adaptations like dissociation and shame, the plane remains the plane. What trauma does is shape our plateaus and peaks that define who we are, at least for the moment. Over time, the repeated activation of these above-plane energy configurations reinforces our belief that we are defective in shame or fragmented in dissociation. At the above-plane level, these are the survival adaptations of the inner processes that perpetuate the traumatized sense of self; at the plane level, there are unrealized potential ways of being, awaiting liberation.

Imagine Teresa's growth when she could now access this inner core of clarity and calm in her life. If we stayed only at the metaphor level, we might be able to say that somehow the hub of the Wheel became an avenue of her healing. Metaphorically speaking, her unresolved trauma was intrusive rim elements, which no longer imprisoned her. But with our deeper dive into mechanisms, with our 3-P perspective, we can see how trauma shapes these probability functions and how healing would need to confront the direct and adaptive patterns of energy that kept her from the very source of healing, that sea of potential inside her that trauma could not touch. The brain naturally participates in all of these adaptations with neuroplastic changes: Where attention goes, neural firing flows, and neural connection grows. That plane of possibility Teresa had to avoid in her young life and replace with a low-lying plateau of a DMN self-defining filter of shame could now be seen as something she could make sense of, an adaptation that kept her sane in the face of an insane family.

We can even make sense of things that didn't make sense by deeply sensing, literally, what happened to us and understanding how it has impacted us. In that making-sense journey, we need the sanctuary of the hub of the Wheel, the choice and change that come from the plane of possibility, in order to access new pathways to liberation. In that making-sense process, ultimately what often arises is a feeling of forgiveness—not a sanctioning of abuse or neglect, but, as my dear friend and colleague Jack Kornfield describes it in his own personal and professional work as discussed earlier, "a letting go of all hope for a better past."

Teresa could move into her plane of possibility and find the love that had been there all along, buried under plateaus and peaks of adaptation that were trying to protect her but ended up imprisoning her along the way. Now her own mind could become a source of what she had longed for all along. She could free herself from that prison, and open her plane of possibility to release all the magnificent joy and gratitude she could now experience in her life. She could *see* her own mind now with a bring-it-on state of receptive awareness, the essence of being present. She could *soothe* her own mind, with tenderness and care, offering the kinds of connections and compassion she now felt she deserved. She could keep herself *safe*, being open to real potential dangers in the world around her, and avoiding ways she experienced terror from her own unresolved implicit-memory world of the past. And all of this—being seen, soothed, and safe—enabled Teresa to grow a newfound sense of *security* in her life.

THE WHEEL, PROFESSIONAL LIFE, AND AN AWAKENED MIND: ZACHARY AND ACCESSING THE PLANE

In teaching the Wheel practice over the years, it's become quite clear to me that integrating consciousness does more than simply help people find calm and clarity in their lives. For many, there is an emergence of meaning and connection that some define as the essence of a kind of spiritual growth, an awakening of the mind. As a student of mine once said, "I feel whole now. I feel free in a way I didn't know was possible." His smile and the glow in his eyes spoke volumes as he shared with me these simple but profound words.

As you will recall from the beginning of our journey, Zachary attended one of my Wheel of Awareness workshops and ultimately had a similar experience to this student of mine. Prior to practicing the Wheel, Zachary was a real estate investor who felt a lack of meaning in his profession. He told me that something felt "off" in his life. Unlike the other life stories we've discussed here, in which there were issues with rigid or chaotic thinking, Zachary's narrative as he explained it to me was that his life seemed to be going as he thought it should. And yet, if there was one element of his life that might need some tending, it was that there was a dullness in his experience at work he could not quite name.

As Zachary progressed through the Wheel practice after that weekend, he told me later, he felt quite disconnected from the mission of the company where he and his colleagues worked, even though he thoroughly enjoyed working with them and felt great love and admiration for them. When Zachary initially tried the fourth segment of the rim, where we dive into our interconnectedness, he became filled with a sense of joy and elation that he was surprised to experience. These sensations were then followed, after the workshop came to a close, by feelings of longing and loss as he reflected on what was missing from his current life.

As he thought about his experience, he told me that he felt apprehensive about expressing his love and admiration to his colleagues, fearing that he would appear to them to be "too soft." I once heard virtually the same reflections from a government official participating in a different Wheel weekend workshop. Unlike Zachary, this elected official said that he would not share his experience with his fellow policy makers—in this case, what emerged with the hub-in-hub part of the practice—because they would see his experience of love as a sign that he was weak or that there was something wrong with him. When I told this public officer that while I understood his reluctance to appear weak in front of his peers, I wondered how he and his colleagues might be leaving love out of their policy planning for the communities they had been elected to serve. His eyes widened with these reflections, and he waved a knowing finger slowly toward me and went to speak with his colleagues. Let's hope that with his courage, together they might bring this sense of our interconnection and joy, this love, into their work on behalf of our shared communities.

(*Love* is a powerful word. Just as I am typing these words to you, my phone buzzes with an incoming text. I pause after typing "shared communities" and the text arrives from my daughter, our illustrator, Madeleine Siegel, who is babysitting for some family friends. Here is the photo she sent in the text of a drawing she had just created for the kids she is taking care of who asked her what love is: "Love is truly caring for an( )other and their well-being while caring for yourself and your own well-being." As I come back to the computer to continue typing, the screen saver has, naturally, a photo—one I've never seen scroll through before—of my daughter. Timing coincidence? Entanglement? Who knows? But I love it.)

Zachary's experience, similar to that government official's, about the word *love* led me to contemplate how in our professional lives, just as in the whole of our lives, it can be so challenging to approach our relationships with others from this source of love, the plane of possibility. We may have soaked in the messages in our schooling, perhaps from friends or family, or just from society at large, that the way to be in the world is tough and independent. In other words, we have received the message that there is strength in separateness and, as a result, we feel more at home—more familiar—in these above-the-plane states that may keep us from becoming aware of the sensation of the deep interconnectedness that the plane of possibility offers. This interconnectedness expands to our relations with others and also to our conception of ourselves in the universe—our purpose and meaning. As so many have suggested, meaning and connection are what they often mean when they use the term *spiritual*.

The meaning aspect of mind may emerge in unique ways in each of us. We can identity what we've seen as the ABCDE's of meaning in the brain in which *a*ssociations, *b*eliefs, *c*ognitions, *d*evelopmental periods, and *e*motions all can coalesce in differentiated ways, linking to create an integrated sense of meaning. Viktor Frankl wrote and spoke eloquently about how finding meaning in our lives can give us strength and purpose. For me, as a clinician and scientist, as a father and husband, as a son and friend, meaning emerges with integration. In this way, living with meaning is finding a way to have both being and doing that tap into our freedom of associations, linking them to beliefs we hold dear; cultivating related streams of thought we call cognition; weaving past, present, and future in our development across the life span; and opening to the full spectrum of emotional experience. That's living an integrative life of meaning—one that is never complete, never finished as in "integrated," but rather is a verb of unfolding, a version of "to integrate" we simply state as integrating or integrative. This is how we speak our truth, how we live with meaning from the inside and out, how we pursue our dreams with integrity, insight, and compassion. When I live from the plane of possibility, I am able to both *be* in relationship and *do* as behavior within relationship. I can work to differentiate and to link—I can live with meaning. Meaning emerges with both being and doing. In this integrative state, this state of just being and doing with presence that connects with others, the feeling of "yes" arises, a feeling of hope and clarity, one accompanied by something feeling right, feeling whole, feeling free, clear, and innately coherent.

Meaning and connection emerge in an integrative life.

Connection involves feeling the deep ways that our self is not as separate as the messages we've received in contemporary school and society may have taught us it should be. Our self is both inner and inter. Meaning arises as integration is liberated in our lives.

So much of our schooling involves knowing the correct answer. We are continually encouraged to learn facts, and are rewarded for determining which exact choice is the right one on exams, or which specific wording is best for our essays. These educational experiences reinforce a life above the plane of possibility. We choose a response on a test with a peak, we construct an essay with sub-peak thinking from a plateau of certain ways of approaching knowledge, and we write those sentences with specific peaks of actuality.

That's a lot of construction toward the goal of a correct way of actualizing things. There's not much value placed on the sensory flow of conduition.

In the plane, there are no previously existing right and wrong answers built into experience; there are no innate judgments about what ought to be, no shoulds that are preformed by prior experience. Much like the Rumi poem in which he describes a field beyond right-doing and wrong-doing: "When the soul lies down in that grass the world is too full to talk about." Yes, as Rumi writes, "I'll meet you there," in that field filled with the formlessness of potential beyond words, a field that we may now imagine is the plane of possibility from which awareness arises. Living from the plane is where we truly meet one another and find meaning in our lives.

If you've ever worked collaboratively with colleagues, you may know the energy of such a joining in which each person is respected for her or his point of view, and the synergy of the work gives rise to something much greater than any single person could have created. That's the synergy of integration, in which the whole is greater than the sum of its parts. That's the synergy of love.

Without integration, we are disposed to live lives of isolation that lack vitality, connection, and meaning. Yet we may simply have adapted, going through the motions without any knowledge that vitality, connection, and meaning are not being optimized in our everyday lives at home and at work. At fifty-five, Zachary was now at a point when his family life was full, his relationship with his wife and children was rewarding, and his real estate business was doing well. After attending that first workshop with his brother the prior year and experiencing the Wheel, he became aware of sensations that he had not been able to clearly experience before. He started to become aware that something seemed to be missing in his life that he could not articulate. Zachary returned for a second Wheel workshop with me a year later and it was fascinating to learn about how the Wheel was transforming his life.

This lack of meaning and connection may have been what had been plaguing Zachary for a while in his career before our first workshop. Earning money for his family was of course important for their survival and financial well-being. But having money as the only goal of his work life left something out of a large chunk of his waking hours. He had achieved that important financial grounding place for surviving. Now the question was one of thriving. When we are fortunate enough to have a choice in our type of work or to reflect on what our work means for us in the world, we are given a moment to pause and consider ways of transforming our professional lives. Not everyone is afforded that luxury—perhaps many people are not. Yet each of us can be aware that living with presence and being of service to others are research-established components at the heart of a life of purpose and well-being. Even if we don't change professions or organizations, we can use this sense of something missing, this longing for something more, to awaken our minds to a new way of living, one filled with more meaning, connection, and vitality. That's a more integrative way of living in the world that we can learn to create in our lives.

This sense of something missing led Zachary to begin to ask fundamental questions about meaning and connection in his working life. It was this set of questions that had inspired his brother to invite Zachary to our first workshop on the Wheel of Awareness, called "Soul and Synapse." The plane of possibility is our sea of potential. By fully accessing it, we are inspired to imagine inner and inter ways of being and doing that may be far beyond what we could ever have consciously imagined before. As we immerse ourselves in the Wheel and become more adept at differentiating the hub from the rim, we gradually move past the filtering plateaus that constrain our lives. We also impact the architecture of our brains by loosening up those DMN-constructed, restrictive notions of self and enabling new combinations of brain firings to emerge.

After the first night of our first Wheel workshop, Zachary began to question how his connections to others were supporting their well-being. How did collaborating with others help him become a part of a larger something, a larger whole that in isolation did not exist? How did the focus of his work make this a better world for all of us and for future generations? If integration is a natural emergence of presence, and presence is essentially the plane of possibility, then these questions about a more integrative way of living would be natural inquiries arising from this more awakened state of presence.

When we went further on the next day of the workshop into the more advanced Wheel practice and explored the hub itself, as you also have done along this journey, things began to emerge even more. Zachary had an experience between mental activities during the third segment review that gave him a deep sense of calm and clarity that surprised him, as his mind was usually filled with internal "monkey-mind" chatter, as he called it. When he then bent the spoke around and experienced awareness of awareness, he had what others have described, a sense of being wide open and at peace. During this hub-in-hub part of the practice, a new experience of being connected to everyone in the room arose. He could sense the others doing the practice, and then felt a connection to people he knew outside our workshop. That sensation was also new for him. Zachary at that moment had a feeling of timelessness—not so much that time had stopped, but that it was irrelevant, that it did not exist. He called this a "sense of eternity" and initially felt unable to say more about it during our sharing time in the workshop.

This sense of connectedness and of eternity was accompanied with a feeling of joy, an elation that stayed with Zachary long after the practice that weekend.

As we discussed earlier, doing the Wheel practice was accompanied by a dissolving of that long-standing pain in Zachary's hip, a diminishing of chronic pain that had been demonstrated in other mind-training practices as well. Each of these experiences impacted Zachary in a powerful way, motivating him to continue the Wheel on a regular basis during the following year. As his practice continued, clarity about what was missing in his work and then a sense of needing to make a change in his professional life began to emerge. He started to talk more intensely with people at his real estate office about the mind and relationships. The demands of the sales team's responsibilities, the focus on business transactions, and the primacy of income generation all made Zachary begin to consider changing the course of his professional career. If his priorities were changing and his job setting had no room for such transformation, perhaps it was time for him to make a switch.

Zachary began to discuss the meaning of his work with his wife, his brother, and his close friends. Fortunately, he had the wherewithal to consider trying out a new direction. But what would that tacking of his professional sailing venture be?

Have you ever experienced the feeling of becoming aware of something that, at the same time, you sense intuitively was something you already knew or felt? As British novelist Doris Lessing once said, "That is what learning is. You suddenly understand something you've understood all your life, but in a new way."

In this way, the Wheel of Awareness can enable you to "get out of your own way." Letting go means letting the state of presence emerging from the plane of possibility naturally arise. For some, this can be such a release and relief that it feels as if they've been waiting their whole lives to find it.

If we consider that Zachary's subjective experience in this open state of awareness had the texture of a vast, spacious quality, one he and others have used words such as *joy*, *God*, and *love* to describe, we can see how this changed his sense of not only who he was in those moments of practice, but who he might be for the rest of his life.

Zachary's mind was in a state of transformation. If you had been there to hear these descriptions at the workshop, or to hear him reflect on their impact on his life in the year that followed his first Wheel workshop, you, too, may have used the term that Zachary's brother used to describe what was happening: the *awakening* of Zachary's mind.

When the brothers left the workshop, Zachary felt that he wanted to "live these changes at home and at work." When he mentioned this to me, I thought of Khalil Gibran's statement "Work is love made visible." Zachary wanted to express that love within the work of a new career.

His brother felt calm and clear, but did not have these same transformative experiences. Each of us is in our own place in life when we begin the Wheel practice, and each of our experiences with it is unique. For some, finding new meaning and connection in their same profession can bring a fresh sense of freedom and vitality to their work lives. I have several students who've remained as mental health practitioners and find the Wheel has deepened their feeling of commitment and reawakened a sense of vitality in their work. For others, like Zachary, finding a way to develop a more integrative way of living in his family life, with his friends, and in his profession inspired him to move toward a new professional life. He wanted to enter some kind of work where he could share this emerging freedom with others. Zachary at this point has chosen to pursue a career in the field of mental health, where he can use this new way of being to support meaning and connection in the lives of those he can now connect with through a new sense of presence in his own mind.

Viktor Frankl's work on meaning describes the bodily sensations of feeling at ease, calm, and whole when one lives with meaning and purpose directing their actions. This was the feeling Zachary described, a sense of clarity in his mind that this new pathway for him would be guided by meaning, a journey whose direction was now taking concrete form as he learned to trust this awakened state and realize the importance of it in his life.

In the next and final part of the book, we'll reflect on these many ways of integrating our lives by returning to the foundational ideas of the mind that the Wheel of Awareness has enabled us to explore along this intricate journey you and I have been traveling together.

PART IV

THE POWER
OF PRESENCE

D o you recall how we began our journey with the analogy of a container of water and salt? When we harness the hub and access the plane of possibility, we expand that vessel of water and bathe in the beauty and expanse of eternity. We are fully present in our lives.

On our journey together in this book we have explored the science and practice of presence. As you go forward it will be up to you, and no one else, how you use these ideas and skills to continue to cultivate a life of being more present and aware. But please be gentle with yourself. Regardless of how much you deepen your Wheel practice, life itself can sometimes get in the way of showing up and being present for life.

In this final section of our journey, I hope to give you some insight into how you can navigate these moments with more ease and clarity.

As we have seen, obstacles to presence may come in the form of learned or innate patterns—the plateaus and peaks that sometimes dominate our lives and keep us from experiencing the openness of the plane. With each of the life experiences of Billy, Jonathan, Mona, Teresa, and Zachary, we've seen how both experiential and genetic factors can contribute to creating challenges to accessing the plane. Let's go forward and address the question of how such blockage happens and what you can do about it if it occurs.

As we have learned, often in our brains things happening now are deeply shaped by what happened before and what we anticipate might happen next. A colleague of mine, psychology researcher Jennifer Freyd, did a study, for example, in which a series of dots was displayed in an arc pattern. When the series stopped, subjects actually perceived the arc extending beyond the last dot. In other words, these *dynamical representations* shape our perception by how we sense a pattern from the past and anticipate and project that pattern into the future. Our present-moment perception is a construction of this past-future assembly of pattern detection and anticipation. What this means is that learned patterns of reacting that become ingrained as synaptic shadows of the past shape our experience in the present. What is this experience? It involves perception, yes, but also emotion, thought, mood, and states of mind that emerge as the learned filtering plateaus of life. However, the exciting and fortunate reality is that the path to freeing the mind is *not* in classifying or worrying about all the specific and varied ways predictive plateaus may create impediments that can rigidify your life or make you prone to chaos. The path to living a life more fully aware, a life of presence, is simple though not necessarily easy: accessing the plane of possibility.

Recall that a mind stretched to a new idea does not return to its original shape. For our purposes here, the notion that your hub and rim are distinct from each other is the transformational idea that has guided us on our journey from the beginning. You can learn to harness the hub—to access the plane—through the ideas and practice of the Wheel of Awareness.

But what does it really mean to harness the hub and access the plane? How can we use these skills to enhance our everyday life experience? This is exactly what we will be diving more deeply into throughout the remainder of our journey.

Living from the plane invites the presence of mind that enables us to make the distinction between knowing and known. The glimpses of the spaciousness of the hub that we have during our Wheel practice can be carried into our daily lives. We can use these receptive moments of dipping into the plane to more clearly sense our plateau filters with clarity—and not be fooled into thinking the peaks they create reveal the complete and accurate story of who we are, or even of who we can be. Living from the plane not only means becoming more wide awake and aware; it means tapping into the sea of potential from which new possibilities arise. It means being open to transformation and changes in ourselves—personal growth—that is possible at any time.

This view suggests a piece of advice we often hear: What you need you already have. The plane has been there all along, perhaps not in plain sight, but nonetheless there waiting for you with kindness and acceptance. As poet Derek Walcott reminds us to greet ourselves at our own door in his poem titled "Love After Love," "You will love again the stranger who was your self. . . ." The plane may get covered up by plateaus and their peaks, but this source of curiosity and wonder, this sense of gratitude and awe, rests there, a stranger, perhaps, waiting for you to gain access to the presence that it gives rise to. From this place of presence, you can then follow Walcott's advice to "Sit. Feast on your life."

The key to applying the Wheel of Awareness in your day-to-day life is to increase your access to the plane of possibility. That sea of potential has been with you from the moment you were conceived. Some would perhaps rightly say, from a physics perspective, that this quantum vacuum, the sea of potential that is your plane of possibility, existed even before the moment of your conception. The plane of possibility is your birthright, and it has been right with you, forever.

You do not need to create the plane; you simply need to access it and learn how to live from it.

CHALLENGES AND OPPORTUNITIES OF LIVING WITH PRESENCE AND BEING AWARE

Early this morning I went to my periodontist to have an intense dental procedure that involved surgery. I thought this might be a good time to see if I might walk the walk of the Wheel, reflecting on all of these things you and I have been discussing, and I elected to try to begin the Wheel of Awareness practice as the periodontist got ready to numb my mouth. When the time for the first injection came, I pictured the Wheel's hub and rim. I imagined that whatever sensation of pain that would arise in awareness would be one of many possible points along the rim. If I could harness the hub, if I could use the sanctuary of the plane of possibility as a source of serenity, I might be able to feel the peak of that pinprick in a wide-open expanse, just like we discussed in part I for the tablespoon of salt being placed in a now-accessible and very large tank of fresh water—the sea of potential. If this approach didn't work, my container would be more like that espresso cup; I'd be swept up into the peak of pain, the water too salty to drink, and I'd be lost on the rim of that sensation from my mouth. I was ready to give it a try.

I didn't tell my dentist anything, my mouth now filled with gadgets, but just gestured to him with a thumbs-up that I was ready for him to begin his work. I went to the image of the hub in my mind's eye, and imagined the range of rim points that could possibly become linked to it. This is the power of a visual image as metaphoric idea. One of those many points might be a sharp sensation in my mouth, and I welcomed it in. I could have an open, bring-it-on stance of not trying to push something away or cling to it once it came. I would be in the neutral spaciousness of the plane, welcoming anything in.

I went to the hub and waited. There in that moment, I felt quite peaceful. From a distance, I could feel a sensation in my mouth. I imagined under other circumstances I might focus intensely on that sharp, painful sensation of the needle, to the exclusion of all the other things going on, and then become quite overwrought with it. Instead, in this setting, with this mindset, resting in the plane, harnessing the hub, I was ready and felt fine.

As the procedure proceeded, I also continued with a very slow Wheel practice. At some point the dental surgeon checked in with me to see that I hadn't fainted because, he said, I appeared so calm. When I came home I further reflected on the ideas and practices we've been exploring on our journey together, and in this time of holding ice over my sore mouth and staying still as I recover, it feels clear to me that the Wheel has benefits—and it also has potential drawbacks. This ice against my cheek does make it challenging to type these words to you, but it seems to be working fiiiiiieeeene.

The benefit we can see in this example is placing pain in context, and finding a way to reduce anxiety or fear and replace that with a sense of clarity and calm. I remembered the ten-thousand-person study and the numerous people who had volunteered their experience that bodily pain had subsided during the Wheel practice. I recalled, too, that mindfulness research had found the same pain reduction, in subjective sensation as well as registration in the brain itself. A range of similar studies we've discussed, too, reveals that other benefits of mind training include enhanced immune function and an increased ability to heal with the reduction of inflammation, as well as an optimization of telomerase levels to maintain and repair the ends of chromosomes so vital to cellular health, as Elizabeth Blackburn and Elissa Epel have shown. That's great after a dental procedure, and in life in general. Meditation teacher and researcher Jon Kabat-Zinn even found that listening to a mindfulness meditation during ultraviolet light treatment caused psoriasis to heal four times faster.

All this supports the notion that mind-training, skill-building

practices that include the training of focused attention, open awareness, and kind intention, truly enhance bodily health. No hype, just
empirically proven reality. That is awesome.

One possibility is that these health benefits, in mind and body
and in relationships, have a mechanism of accessing the plane of possibility at their core. When Elissa Epel and I, along with two of my
interns, Suzanne Parker and Ben Nelson, tried to explain the science
of presence in an academic textbook chapter, we found it useful to
offer the 3-P perspective and the presence of the plane to propose a
mechanism beneath the research-established ways the mind can
transform the molecules of the body, including telomerase levels.

Following this surgery, my hope is that these practices we are
exploring, and the ones I am doing right now and that you may
choose to do as well, will support our body's ability to heal well and
recover from the challenges we face in life. That's the power of presence and the promise of living from the plane of possibility. Accessing the hub and learning to live from the plane is a pathway to
cultivating health and resilience in our lives.

In addition to these opportunities to promote well-being by being present for life, there are challenges that can become obstacles to
well-being. In development, periods of opportunity are also moments of vulnerability. There are potential downsides to reflective
practices, not often addressed, that also can be illuminated with this
dental immersion.

One risk of meditative practices, including the Wheel of Awareness, is something that has been called a "spiritual bypass," in which
a person aims for spiritual growth, a transformation toward more
meaning and connection in life, but instead avoids pain that needs to
be looked at, made sense of, and healed before that growth can actually happen.

If physical, emotional, and social pain are points along the rim,
then trying to live only from the hub will give an individual an es-

cape hatch from which to try to avoid the pain that feels intolerable. This is understandable, but healing pain may require we move toward it, not away from it.

Think of it like being bitten by a dog: When his teeth are clenched around your hand, if you pull away from him, he will tighten his grip and cause even more damage. Move your hand into the dog's throat and he will release his grip; your hand is less damaged and your body can more easily repair the wounds.

As I had this dental procedure, I realized that the sanctuary of the hub is both a powerful resource and a potential disabling escape hatch. What would happen if there were not only dental pain but also emotional and relational pain from the past or from ongoing interactions? Experiences of trauma or loss, betrayal or outright abuse can embed themselves as plateaus and their particular rigid or chaotic peaks in our lives that need integration, not avoidance. Might someone choose, if they've been learning these practices, to avoid the painful sensation of the rim and just rest in the hub? Would learning to live from the plane of possibility become a liability if someone were using this approach to avoid rather than integrate the painful peaks and plateaus of their life?

I once worked with a meditation teacher who was having trouble in his life. When he came for therapy and I suggested we do the Adult Attachment Interview to review how the early experiences in his family may have influenced his life, he said to me that he didn't "do the past." When I asked him what he meant, he said, "I am a teacher of meditation. This is all about living in the present. The past is an illusion. Thinking of your self, or thinking of your memories, is a part of dualistic delusion." I could understand the drive toward a "non-dualist" view of honoring our true interconnectedness in the world. But for me, integration invites us to live the reality that in fact we do have a body, that body has a history, and that history shapes the connections in the embodied brain now, even if they came from then. We do have a me, and we do have a we; we do have a past, and we do have a future—all of which can live in awareness and be embraced by living with presence.

If now is all that exists, I said to my new patient, then there are neural connections shaping his mind and relationships, *now*, that are shadows of a prior now, and he might want to live a freer now by making sense of those now-experiences, now.

When he agreed to try, and we did the attachment interview, what emerged were recollections of a very painful history of developmental trauma of both abuse and neglect, experiences he had not shared with anyone before, and had not made sense of in his focus on the present to the exclusion of his past. In our work together, he came to understand not only how the past had imprisoned him in the present when he avoided reflecting on it but also that this past in many ways had driven him to become an expert in meditative practices.

Finding a plateau that says, "Don't look at anything but now," helped this individual survive. The only peaks that were allowed to funnel into actualization by this filter of consciousness were those related to the here and now, and he could then effectively—at some level of his experience, at least—block from awareness any memories of the painful past. This plateau also could keep him from experiencing any new questions that might make those memories feel like real events. Such an adaptive but rigid plateau could create a mindset that even betrayal does not matter, as evidenced by his belief system about refusing to be a "dualistic thinker," in which he emphatically told me relationships and the past didn't matter.

For this individual, those meditative techniques that likely accessed the hub of his Wheel enabled him to *dissociate* from any rim points of pain from his traumatic past. We can understand the drive to reduce pain and survive; we can also understand the natural impulse to pull your hand away from a dog that is biting you.

If we learn to dissociate from the pain of our reality, we can survive a childhood of tremendous betrayal, sadness, pain, and fear. But dissociation—though a survival tool—if perpetuated, has its costs. Disconnection from pain is not selective; we inevitably disconnect even from the joy of being alive. *Unlearning* that dissociative adaptive skill is as important as learning to live a life of openness to what is.

For my patient, what he experienced for all those years could also be called a kind of emotional bypass, a way of avoiding living fully. The risk of unexamined emotional pain is that it comes back to influence our waking as well as sleeping life. Taking the time and putting in the energy it takes to feel and reflect on the painful realities of our lives gives us opportunities to make sense of these events and discover the meaning beneath the madness and the pain. No, we cannot change the past. But reflecting on it gives us a new possibility to make sense of how the past has shaped our development. By becoming aware of these recollections and experiences, we tap into both the sanctuary of wide-open awareness and the new possibilities from the plane. That's what being present and permitting integration to arise really means—not avoiding things, but welcoming anything into awareness. The plane gives us the capacity for a bring-it-on state of mind, in which we are open to anything—past, present, future, all welcome into awareness.

A related obstacle to being present can have historical roots as well. The helplessness and shame of difficult early life experiences can keep someone terrified and longing for the escape hatch of a hublike disconnection from the pain. These emotional challenges can occur especially when they arose with our attachment figures, as was true with this meditation teacher and as we've seen with Teresa's story of developmental trauma. I say "hublike" because this dissociation is an escape from receptivity, not an immersion in it. Yes, numbing from bodily or emotional pain by disconnecting from it is possible, but what we mean by harnessing the hub is not an escape; it's a receptive embrace. You are not avoiding the salt; you are expanding your container of water.

No matter what the traumatic past is, nothing can take your

plane away. The challenge for many with this history, as we've seen, is that the uncertainty of the Wheel's hub may evoke rim responses of terror that keep them from opening awareness to new possibilities. In this way, a plateau is a state of mind that may carry with it the response of fear of the plane. Dissociation may reinforce that feeling of terror-with-uncertainty, an automatic reflex to fragment in the face of stress or emotionally challenging situations. Sadly, the accompanying shame makes people lose faith in the goodness of who they are and lose hope in who they might become, feeling defective at their core. When we realize that this is simply the erroneous conviction that shame creates, pointing the finger of blame at the self rather than acknowledging the frightening reality of unreliable attachment figures, we can begin the journey to embrace the hub of our Wheel, the plane of possibility, which offers both the sea of potential as an expansion of being aware and the new diverse set of responses that help us embrace the reality of our being whole, being intact individuals, regardless of our developmental beliefs that imprisoned us before. We can learn to release the hold of plateaus of shame and the peaks of despair that arise from them. Those beliefs embedded in restrictive plateaus, filters of consciousness and adaptive states of mind that protect us at first, can become our unintended prison. Now we can drop beneath those imprisoning but previously helpful plateaus, changing the meaning of experience and the experience of self, opening to the plane and accessing new ways of being.

I avoided being flooded by pain from my dentist's needle. But I did not avoid all the frustrating steps I am taking to care for this body now that the procedure is over. I still have this ice on my face to reduce the inflammation in my gums, as painful as it feels to my skin. The whole of the experience is the way I can be present for this procedure and the healing it invites me to cultivate.

An emotional bypass can be how a mind-training practice, or even a way of living, is used to avoid living one's life fully, rather than achieving integration. You may find it helpful to reflect on ways in your own past or current life that being present has been or remains challenging. Meditation, or any other practice or way of being that offers access to the plane of possibility, does not by any means need to be a form of dissociation. Dissociation is simply a potential hazard, a vulnerability of any plane-accessing practice if we attempt to escape by living only in pure receptive awareness as a bypass.

Even without a history of trauma, when intense integration is the primary goal, for some the safety of the hub, that wide-open expanse of the plane of possibility, can become excessively differentiated within a regular reflective practice to the exclusion of feelings, memories, and thoughts. Some people say things like, "I love it so much there, and all I want to do is hang out in the hub!" I like to say that living with the presence of the plane, in Wheel terms, is being open to anything from the rim, not avoiding the rim. Blissing out in the hub is great, and great for you. But you don't need to be avoiding anything. "Bring it on" means integration—embracing the times when you can simply rest in the hub, and other times when exploring the rim is equally important, simply different. That's how we integrate the mind—linking these different ways of being with hub or rim, these different probability positions that are our mind's peaks, plateaus, and plane.

Whether we've had trauma or not, only focusing on the hub may be a vulnerability of the practice. Sometimes the feeling of peace of the plane is alluring and becomes the "goal" of meditation. In this way, the Wheel practice has become no longer integrative in that the hub is being preferred over the rim, which is thought of as "not as good." Instead, an integrative approach takes the stance that all are good; hub and rim are simply different and help us in unique ways.

The beauty of the Wheel as a practice is that you can learn to access the plane even by shifting your sweep-ratio to include more of the plane in your everyday experiences. The timeless nature of the plane gives an expansive quality to moment-by-moment unfoldings that can enrich your life, even when not in the formal practice.

Sometimes being sure to take care of any leftover issues, any rigid or chaotic plateaus and peaks from past experiences, will be a helpful starting place to open your access to the plane.

In plane of possibility terms, resolving trauma or living an integrative life of presence means being able to connect the plane of knowing within the sweep-ratio of consciousness to anything arising as the plateaus and peaks of the knowns. "Bring it on" means saying, from the expansive consciousness container of the plane, "I am open to anything that may arise—welcome!" This is the source of the notion of living with the ease of well-being.

Learning from the plane means letting everything be our teacher.

As Rumi's poem "The Guest House" reminds us, we can let every visitor to the house that is our lives be a guide to learning more in life.

FREEDOM: TRANSFORMING INTO POSSIBILITY

Living from the plane means acknowledging that we may have many plateaus and peaks that are part of self-states defining us and potentially confining us—meaning that they may be *confining our potential*. Growth is possible because we can tap into the plane, the source enabling new configurations to arise.

Plateaus and peaks create the proclivities of personality as they shape the probability values that arise. These are our tendencies that shape how we think, feel, and behave. Researchers might call these features of our personality; we might simply call them traits of who we are. Living from the plane frees us from the persistent patterns of proclivities of personality that recursively define our sense of self. We don't lose our personality; we expand its range and reach. This freedom is not simply an ideal; it is a way of living that feels fresh and alive.

Imagine it this way. If feeling, thought, and behavior are particular probability values that create a sense of self in the world, then living from the plane gives freedom to both awareness and the creation of an emerging sense of self. New combinations of plateaus and peaks may now arise from a freely accessed plane. No longer defined only by past and persistent plateaus and peaks, the presence of the plane lets new above-plane probability patterns arise, giving fresh life to ways of thinking, feeling, and behaving. Accessing the plane enables new plateaus and peaks to emerge and frees our personality.

As we've seen in the profiles in part III, the Wheel in idea and practice offers relief from habitual ways of being that may have initially seemed unchangeable. Personality traits can be viewed as particular proclivities of our nervous system, including the tendency to be conscientious, agreeable, and open, to have neurotic or emotionally intense reactions, and to be outgoing in our approach to the world. These "big five" personality traits have been studied and revealed to change over time with intentional effort, in processes of transformation such as psychotherapy. One way of viewing this empirically demonstrated change in our personality traits is that each of them may be a pattern of above-plane values that have become reinforced as particular traits in an individual's life. Personality is not fixed; these studies reveal how our tendency to be open or conscientious, for example, can be cultivated with effort. How could that be? By envisioning shifts in plateaus and peaks and perhaps tapping into the plane, we can see how new combinations may arise. Naturally such changes would have an impact on the brain as well as on our relationships with others.

Transformation moves us from ingrained personality proclivities as we open the doorway of possibility.

Personality can be seen as how our innate temperament interacts with our experiences to shape who we become over time. Sometimes aspects of what we imagine are unchangeable features of our temperament are actually learned tendencies of our personality, an amalgam of often genetically influenced neural patterns combined with how experience has molded our neural connections. Because of lifelong neuroplasticity, the brain is capable of changing its structure. This change can lead to alterations in how we behave, how we feel, and how we tend to think—in other words, changes in our personality and the experience of who we are.

Personality patterns can be envisioned as enduring traits from the interaction of genetics and experience that manifest as particular plateaus and their specific peaks of actualized thoughts, emotions, and behavioral outputs. Now that we've come to this place in our journey together, can you visualize how freeing yourself, opening your personality proclivities, may simply involve enabling new probability positions to arise in your life? You access these new possibilities from the plane of possibility. In this basic way, living from the plane is a pathway toward freedom in who you are.

When you practice the Wheel, you access the plane, which offers new variations in how plateaus may arise and even how peaks may come to emerge directly from the plane itself. This is what learning to live from the plane empowers you to create in your life—a freeing up of ingrained personality patterns that are now open to change with intention. This is how tenacious and potentially restrictive plateaus can be transformed in our lives with intention, practice, and opening to freedom.

This is your challenge: You can use your mind to shift the patterns in your relationships and in your brain. That's the secret sauce. You are not a captive prisoner to brain or relationships, even though the propensities of these inner and inter sources of your mind will tend to move you in old patterns. Getting lost in familiar places is a natural vulnerability we all have; using your mind and your capacity to be aware is the pathway to freedom from these ingrained patterns. Patience and persistence will be your friends along this path to the freedom of living from the plane.

PRESENCE BEYOND METHODS

I think one of the terrible dangers in spirituality and in trying to become aware is to privilege some particular method to take you there—because then I think the method becomes the end, not the means. I think that being here is it, and that ten thousand times a day you can slow a little and throw one savoring glimpse at the miracle of being around. I think that ultimately the test of even very rigorous practice over long years is actually to invest all of the non-practice moments with the presence. I think the presence is it.

John O'Donohue
Awakening the Mind Workshop taught by John O'Donohue and
Daniel J. Siegel, the Berkshires, Massachusetts, 2006

Whatever method we've found useful in helping us to become aware, there is a common thread shared by many modern and ancient practices: the freeing of the mind from filters of consciousness that keep us from being open to the present.

On this journey, we have been exploring one particular method called the Wheel of Awareness. This practice was created to integrate consciousness as it differentiates the knowns we are aware of from the knowing of being aware itself; then, with the systematic movement of the spoke of focal attention, it links these together. If this metaphor of the Wheel as idea and practice has been working for you, wonderful. And if the practice has been hard, and maybe not even your cup of tea, hopefully the ideas of potential mechanisms beneath the metaphor of the Wheel have been useful. Ideas by themselves can stretch your mind. You may be developing a prepared mind with these experiences and ideas that can build integration in your life in many ways.

As integration may be the fundamental basis of health and happiness, then integrating your life—with whatever methods you find that fit you—is a positive pathway as you move forward.

John O'Donohue's reflections may parallel our journey's view of the mechanisms of awareness—the presence we experience when the probability position is able to rest in the plane of possibility. How I wish John were alive for us to share this quantum view of mind with him and see how he might have responded to this suggestion that the presence he referred to, that "glimpse at the miracle of being around," possibly has the mechanism of the plane; alas, he died—or his body died—just the year before. Michael Graziano suggests, as we've seen in part II, that John's mind can be seen to live on in those of us who knew him well; and so John's mind in mine, and perhaps in yours if you've studied his works well, would be giving out a bellow of a laugh of agreement and excitement about the prospect of sharing a view from spirituality to science, dissolving their boundaries and sharing in laughter and light the insights from both fields of knowing.

The presence of being aware is the foundation of awakening the mind and freeing our lives.

The Wheel of Awareness gives you but one of many methods to cultivate access to the plane of possibility. Centering prayer in the Christian tradition, versions of mindfulness meditation, yoga, tai chi, qigong, compassion practices, and myriad other ways of training the mind may give access to this generator of diversity, this sea of potential. The Wheel simply offers one method to serve as a means to directly access the plane. With that state of awareness, we can develop the trait of living from the plane of possibility.

It can be illuminating and freeing to have some regularly exercised method, a focused, disciplined practice—even if it is not a formal approach, in the tightly controlled sense of a traditional form of "rigorous practice." A frequently engaged reflective practice that nurtures your capacity of "being here" can open your life to the presence of being aware from the open plane of possibility. For some poets, such as my friends John O'Donohue and Diane Ackerman, simply walking through nature with an awake mind, paying close attention to one's surroundings, was and is a regular rigorous practice—even if not a "formal" one. For others, a formal meditation that builds the mind's traits with focused attention, open awareness, and kind intention is a preferred pathway to presence.

Whatever the method, it is possible that glimpsing this miracle of being here, of accessing the power of presence, of being aware and celebrating your life is revealed by the mechanism of living from the plane of possibility. As Diane Ackerman concludes in her School Prayer, "I will honor all life—wherever and in whatever form it may dwell—on Earth, my home, and in the mansions of the stars."*

An integrative life emerges from integrating consciousness as a start, whatever the method or approach that works for you. In our 3-P perspective, this doesn't mean living only in the plane; it means differentiating and linking plane, plateau, and peak. John calls this state of being aware and glimpsing the "miracle of being around" *the presence*—and we can suggest that this "the" before "presence" has the universal quality that is signified in *the* plane of possibility. Your plane and my plane are virtually if not completely identical. Infinity in "your" plane is infinity in "mine." In "wherever and whatever form it may dwell" we are connected in life. We find our differentiated nature in our plateaus and peaks and we share this differentiated nature of our unique identities. And we find each other on common ground in our shared plane of possibility, as infinity is infinity: The quantum vacuum, the sea of potential is the mathematical space of wide-open possibility that is the generator of diversity, the source from which all that might be arises.

---

* Diane Ackerman, *I Praise My Destroyer* (New York: Vintage, 1998), 3.

MINDFUL AWARENESS AND INTEGRATION

We have been proposing that many methods, new and ancient, may be harnessing this common mechanism of accessing the plane.

In research terms, as different as these approaches may be from one another, they have a common ground of ultimately involving an attention to both intention and attention itself, and the opening of the mind to some way of being aware of awareness—of monitoring the contents and experience of being aware.

We've seen that three pillars of research-supported mind-training methods involve the cultivation of focused attention, open awareness, and kind intention. Although the Wheel of Awareness has a different origin than other practices, as it was created from scientific ideas and clinical experience to integrate consciousness rather than coming from traditional approaches, it does include all three essential components for a mind-training practice that have been empirically demonstrated to cultivate well-being.

Our proposal has been that one facet of the mind is a self-organizing emergent process that regulates energy and information flow within the body and within our relationships. Within and between is where this facet of the mind is. And as a regulatory process, this facet of mind includes two basic functions: monitoring and modifying. Strengthening the mind happens when we stabilize monitoring and then learn the skills of modifying toward integration. Mind-training practice, including the Wheel of Awareness, strengthens the mind by building both monitoring and modifying abilities.

In a mindful awareness practice that builds mental integration, we come to strengthen our ability to monitor energy and information flow as we repeatedly bring our wandering attention back to focus. That's focused-attention training. When we experience open awareness, we further develop the mind by sharpening our ability to differentiate the knowns from the experience of knowing—of being aware. This is how we modify toward integration. And kind intention practice furthers that integration by widening our sense of concern and care, enabling us to experience not a loss of self, but an expansion of how we experience what our "self" really is, or at least what it can become. As Naomi Shihab Nye states regarding kindness being the "deepest thing" in life as we come to realize the universal sorrows of life in our world, "Then it is only kindness that makes sense anymore" as it "goes with you everywhere like a shadow or a friend."*

In our relationships, being able to steady attention enables us to focus on the incoming energy and information flow from others and connect with them in a deeper way. As we become more open to the input others are directing toward us, we are able to better resonate with them and cultivate the experience of *feeling felt* within the connection. When we then add the ways in which care and concern for the well-being of each of us—the selves in other bodies and the self emanating from our own body—we see how widening our circle of compassion and concern, developing kind intention, hugely expands our relational integration. We differentiate and we link across perhaps previously more restricted senses of who we are to become a more integrated self, a Me plus a We, or a MWe.

Try it out in your daily life—sensing the hub of your Wheel, dropping into the plane as you connect in communication—and feel the difference now as you drop expectations and judgments, those fixed plateaus and peaks, and simply glimpse this miracle of being here, the presence of an openly aware mind.

Presence has the power to create not only the kind and compassionate connections of relationships and the happiness we feel in our mental lives but also the health of our embodied lives—our skin-encased bodies, including our brains.

Presence frees our *minds* and brings health to our *relationships* and our *embodied brains*.

---

* Naomi Shihab Nye, *On Kindness, in Words Under the Words: Selected Poems* (Portland, Oregon: Far Corner Books, 1995).

LINKING FROM THE PLANE

One feeling for me that has become even stronger as this journey has unfolded is a growing sense that our modern view of a self defined by the skin or skull alone has led to a feeling of isolation and dis-ease. The term *self* seems so natural to assign to the body, but in this journey of exploring awareness and the Wheel, perhaps you have also experienced that a new sense of identity emerges. At first I thought this was what we might call a "we identity," a feeling of belonging to a larger group. But then, with the encouragement of a student who was distressed at a lecture I was giving titled "From Me to We," I realized that there might be something else I was really trying to describe. She was right—we don't need to lose a sense of me to gain belonging to a we. Yes, we need to care for the body, know our body's own personal history, get good sleep, eat well, exercise, and enjoy our bodily experience. That embodied reality is the me of who we are. Belonging does not mean losing integration by letting this differentiation of me disappear. Within my relationship with this student, in our communication and with her concern, within our linking connection, emerged an integrated notion of how a self could combine me and we in the plural verb sense of a whole, integrative self, a *MWe*. Who we are is both me and we, a plurality. And who we are is continually emerging—a verb, not a noun. This plural verb of a selfing experience can be seen as an integrating way of ever becoming as MWe.

Around the same time, another student approached me and expressed confusion. She had been listening to one of my recorded teachings and never saw my name spelled out. Being from the Lakota tribes in the Midwest, she told me that she thought my name was Dan Siegel. That is my name, I said. No, she repeated, I thought it was Dan Siegel, I heard her say. I again politely repeated that this *was* my given name. Then she politely spelled out what she had thought my name was: D-A-N-C-E . . . E-A-G-L-E. Ah! When she told me that the course she had been listening to had included a story about my having quit medical school to consider becoming a dancer, I could see how her mind was primed both from her culture and from the personal story to hear my name in this creative way. Dance Eagle is now my family's nickname for me. I hope who I am will continue to be open and evolve as the many top-down filters of my inner mind are released from fixed nouns and names, those plateaus relaxed and released, and the open potential of the bottom-up freedom becomes realized as our collective and interconnected relational fields unfold.

At this moment of expressing this to you my body is filled with energy and excitement. The vision in my mind's eye is that our embodied brains can become more integrative, our relationships more receptive and connected, our minds more awakened and aware, as we live from this open space of presence. Fixed patterns of plateaus and peaks do not have to define us like nouns in a dictionary of top-down proclamations of who we are or who we think we should be. Together, MWe can make our lives more enriched, more supported, and more fun in ways an isolated self alone could never create. I'd lived my whole life without considering Dance Eagle as a linguistic label for a joyful aspect of my identity.

Living from the plane opens us to the freedom of taking on a new name.

In isolation, our self-filters try to project into the world an identity that can predict how we and our surroundings *should* be. These filters are the repeated patterns of plateaus and their peaks that may, for some of us, be reinforcing a sense of a separate me, connected within, perhaps, yet disconnected between. When we open to living more from the plane of possibility, we engage in a life without the prison of projective predictions of past perceptions, awakening now to the majesty of living fully in the moment, connecting in new ways within and between that no longer strive to control.

This is the fun and fascinating journey presence permits.

We shape one another, because we *are* one another. That's what

MWe entails, acknowledging our uniqueness in the above-plane peaks and plateaus we can enjoy, while also embracing the uncertainty and ever-changing possibilities of the plane. Linking the differentiated and recognizable plateaus and peaks with the freedom of the plane's wide-open potential, we emerge in this balance of the familiar and the novel within the integration of a life of presence.

When we drop down into the plane of possibility inside the inner mind, we become open and receptive to whatever arises inside us. When we bring that state of social engagement and receptivity to our relationships, the relational field created has the spontaneity and "yes" stance that invites each to simply be, and be simply respected.

Perhaps you can feel that sense of harmony and energy that comes from such a vital sense of joining. What often arises, too, is a deep sense of joy, belonging, and laughter.

LAUGHING, LIVING, AND DYING FROM THE PLANE

Humor is serious business.

I was once walking to dinner with my colleague and friend Jack Kornfield. The two of us had just finished the first day of a two-day workshop we were teaching together, and our mutual publisher, Toni Burbank, was taking us out for the night. As we were strolling down the streets of San Francisco toward the restaurant, Toni, walking between us, said, "Oh, now I think I understand the difference between the two of you." We walked along, Toni glancing first at me and then back at Jack. "You," she said, gesturing toward Jack, "you know how to tell a joke."

Ouch.

Toni was right. However the joke skill is passed down, whether it is genetics or learned or some combination, I didn't get even a modicum of it. This is a feature of my mind that my kids, when they were younger, would be happy to remind me of every time I'd try to tell a joke or even attempt to relate a funny story, with little well-placed timing or inducement of laughter. "That was *really* funny," I'd often sarcastically hear, with good reason. Jack, on the other hand, is a master jokester. Even after hearing the same jokes with all of our shared teaching in different settings, I still crack up. Why? Because I think Jack gets us to laugh from the hub.

Laughing from the hub is a way of setting the stage for dropping into the plane of possibility and then meeting one another there. The story or joke has you resonate with some shared predictable plateaus of expectation or peaks of particulars, and then, with impeccable timing, Jack blows your above-plane values out of the sky and wham, you're into the plane of possibility, wrestling with something you never saw coming (even if you've heard that story a dozen times before). Once you're in the plane, some new combination of things that seem to be arising from one direction—plateaus and peaks of one kind or another in the punch line of the joke or climax of the story—are then suddenly shifted and you become joined with Jack and everyone else in the room in an unexpected way. It feels as if top-down expectations are meeting bottom-up surprise. It's fabulous.

Laughing feels good and is good for you. Humor actually opens us up to new learning, it enhances neuroplasticity and makes learning last longer as the brain grows new connections in that open state, it builds trust, and it joins us to each other. Not bad for a good chuckle.

I am not sure why I can't really tell a joke, but I love to laugh. When I was feeling down after my father had passed away years ago, a friend invited me to join an improvisation class for nonactors—meaning it was for pure fun. The standard improv stance is "Yes, and," meaning we don't say to our partners in an improv skit, "No, but," when they come up with some line or action that moves the scene into a direction we didn't expect or want.

Yes, and is a great way to live from the plane.

Imagine all the combinations that are present in the plane of possibility. My improv teacher would remind us not to plan out how we would respond to our partner, but to be *present for connection.* At first I found that quite challenging. My top-down urge for control and predictability would come up with all sorts of scenarios ahead of time—some funny, some serious, but each of them preplanned plots that prevented presence. I was filled with plateaus of story ideas with their prescribed set of peaks designed to elicit specific responses. For example, if the setup was to enter an imagined room and take in the signals and sense of my partner and let the scene unfold from there, I might actually come with so many plateaus of ideas or peaks of specific things I wanted to say to be serious or funny or just interesting. That above-plane positioning kept me from being present. I was lost on the rim of my Wheel even before I began the scene. Being in the hub gives you access to all the diversity of the plane. When I'd get feedback from the teacher that I was "thinking too much" and should just be present for my partner, I used the image of the Wheel and my familiarity with the hub to reorient my approach. The shift into presence let the power of connection unfold. Sometimes it was serious and moving, sometimes goofy and hilarious, but always connecting and real.

When an emerging scene was belly-bustingly funny, sometimes it was hard not to lose the scene with our own laughter. Humor seemed to be moving along our 3-P diagram in a particularly free pattern, engaging our bodies, our minds, and our relationships. Laughter released from the plane of possibility enables us to embrace the spontaneous nature of life, riding the waves of expectation of plateaus and peaks, feeling the surprise, shock, or irritation when that wave shifts into a new direction, and then letting the energy of that surprise be released in the freedom of tapping back into the plane, the source from which laughter may truly come. Laughing is liberation from the prisons of probability that create our propensities toward expectation and proclivities for thought, and it reveals the freedom arising from the plane of possibility.

Humor is serious business.

When my father was nearing his dying day, having been quite ill and bedridden for eighteen months, he asked me if he was dying. I looked over his vital signs and sat close to him on the side of his bed as I affirmed that yes, it looked like it was nearing the end. I held his hand and we began a conversation I will never forget.

"What should I do?" he asked. I told him he should be sure that if there was anything more he wanted to say to anyone in his life before he left, this would be a good time to do it.

"And where am I going when I die?" he inquired.

My father was a very strong-willed, self-declared non-spiritual person who was an engineer by training and committed to a materialistic, science-based view of reality—his own words, not mine. He also had a way of having intense negative reactions to anyone in his family who might offer a different viewpoint than his own (my words), the correct view (his words).

And so you might imagine how nervous I was as I considered how to respond to his existential question at that moment, a time that might be our last. So I said that I certainly didn't know what happened to any of us when we die. Then he asked me what I thought might happen. So I told him what I thought.

I said that after a quarter of a century of being a psychiatrist, I had never had anyone come to me in therapy saying they were worried about where they were *before* they were conceived.

He looked intrigued, so I continued.

If you imagine that there were trillions of sperm and billions of eggs in the world that could have formed you, I told him, but only one egg and one sperm of that vast set of possibilities of gametes actually came together, then you are an actualization emerging from a sea of potential, a plane of all possibilities.

Okay, he said, listening intently.

And you get about a century to live in this body, this actualization of a form that arose from a formless sea, the source of all that was possible. That's your life; that's the opportunity you get to live in this body. When you die, you simply may go back to where you came from—that plane of possibility.

He looked at me, and a serene expression came over his face for the first time in a long, long time. Maybe for the first time I'd ever seen. And then he said, "That makes me feel so peaceful. Thank you."

We spent the rest of that time holding hands as he rested in bed, just talking about various things. It was the last time I saw or spoke to my dad.

Living from the plane is a dance of divine inspiration freeing us to rejoice with gratitude for this miracle of being here. Yes, we are born into a body that gets about a hundred years, if we are fortunate, to dance on this earth. But we also have a mind, one that is part arrow-bound and living in a Newtonian level of reality. That is a simple truth that my mechanical-engineer father could embrace. But we also live with a mind that is in part arrow-free, as we live in the timeless freedom of the plane of possibility.

To see the serenity on my father's face in those last hours of his life was a gift that makes me smile now, and even feel a laughter of delight arise from every facet of my being. That plane of possibility may tap into a joy of spontaneity and embracing the paradox of incompatible realities, time and timeless, body boundaries and infinity, form and formless. We may not be able to experience the joy of life without the reality of death. I know this all may not sound funny, but it is a funny reality that is *fun*-damental to our mental lives.

And why not laugh?

I once was teaching with my colleagues Diane Ackerman, Jon Kabat-Zinn, and our dear friend John O'Donohue. At that Mind and Moment gathering, none of us knew that John's body would soon have its last breath. Near the end of that three-day gathering, a participant desperately asked us to explain why we were helping her become more open and empathic while the world is so full of pain and suffering. We soaked in her question, and I offered this reflection: I once was at a meeting with His Holiness the Dalai Lama, who was asked by a participant how he could be so full of laughter and joy when the world is in such turmoil. The Dalai Lama's response was incisive and insightful. He said that it wasn't just *in spite of* the world's suffering that he laughs and finds joy in each day, but rather *because of* the suffering. If we don't cultivate our innate capacity for joy and laughter, then the suffering of the world will have won.

It is our privilege, and our responsibility, to find joy and laughter while fully aware of the wide array of pain and perils, as well as the vast possibilities for being of service on our precious planet.

In the face of life's challenges, if we don't find the humor in all that we confront, inside and out, we'll be sunk. If joy and laughter, gratitude and love emerge from the plane, then that's the path of life MWe can support MWeach other in cultivating in our lives. Let's find that plane of possibility together as MWe create a joyful laughter and love from the presence of our collective minds.

LEADING AND LOVING FROM THE PLANE

Living from the plane of possibility invites each of us to become leaders in life. Along with other scholars, Arthur Zajonc, a quantum physicist and former president of the Mind and Life Institute, which supports the scientific study of meditation, uses a term I love: *pervasive leadership*. I taught Arthur the Wheel of Awareness and we shared the excitement of the 3-P framework for the mind. And Arthur shared with all of us this powerful view of leadership and love. The notion is that how we approach guiding our inner lives can empower each of us to take responsibility for bringing change into the world. Coming from the inside out, we can lead the journey to a more integrative way of living that can be pervasive in our world as each individual takes on the responsibility and the opportunity for ethical and compassionate living.

When we imagine a life of being aware, of living from the plane, we can sense how each person can learn to access this hub of their Wheel and find the potential to live with presence from this place of possibility.

Collectively, we have many challenges. One of these is that we've inherited the survival trait of making in-group distinctions so that especially under threat we disregard those we assess to be in the out-group. Brain studies reveal how we shut off our circuits of compassion, restricting how we use our mindsight perceptual skills for insight and empathy and no longer respect the differentiated nature of our individuality or link with kind intention and caring action. We can lose our capacity for integration. The good news is that though our human family has this tendency to restrict our circles of concern to only those "like us," research reveals that mindfulness and compassion practices can widen those circles and reduce implicit biases that divide us. How might this happen? If we drop into the plane of possibility, we access our connection to each other that rests beneath the plateaus of prejudgment, our in-group versus out-group distinctions that can lead us to dehumanize one another. Living with presence, being mindfully aware, releases us from this ancient way of disregarding those not like us to embrace a larger reality of our interconnectedness as living beings on this planet.

When schools, society, and even science tell us that we are separate, we come to another challenge to well-being, as we believe those information patterns and embed them in our own persistent plateaus and peaks of identity. We've seen the mind is broader than the brain, the self bigger than our body—and in becoming aware of the reality of this inner and inter nature of our identity, we can grow toward clarity and freedom.

This wider view of who we are is sometimes challenging to

communicate—but it can be a matter of life and death. In speaking to a high school where a series of recent suicides had devastated the culture of that community, I tried to relate this notion of how a limited sense of a separate self can bring despair and hopelessness to youth and adults alike. Meaning and connection emerge when we embrace the reality of our deeply relational nature. Living in isolation can lead to life-threatening anguish. This is what I told the students, parents, and staff assembled at the school gathering.

Imagine that we are candles. If we think that we consist only of a clump of wax that is never engaged to give off light—that is never lit—then we have a sense of what it means to think of the self as only a body and a mind as only a feature of our head. On the contrary, each of us is capable of carrying a flame—and furthermore, of sharing our light. If your family and society, on the other hand, send you the message that you must be the most distinguished and unique candle in the bunch, any other candle that is shining brightly becomes a threat to your uniqueness. Your tendency might be to feel inadequate in the glow of other candles, and you might even feel motivated to blow out their wicks so that your flame will be the brightest.

Now imagine a different kind of world. What if who we are is not only the wax but also the light of our flame? And when we glance at another candle that is not lit, we lean over and light their wick—we share our light. You see, it takes nothing away from us to share our energy. And what does it do to the world? It makes the world a brighter place to live.

When we practice integrating our consciousness, when we harness the hub and access the plane of possibility, we become more deeply aware of our interconnected identities. Yes, we have a me that is the wax of the candle of our identity. But we are more than the wax of these bodies we get only about a century or so to live in. We are also the flame, the light we can generate together in this world MWe all share.

ACKNOWLEDGMENTS

Simple words of thanks for all those whose journey has joined the birth of this book: I am filled with gratitude beyond the linguistic symbols of these lines of appreciation.

In the reading of the manuscript in its various stages, or discussing some of the ideas related to its fundamental structure, many offered their helpful comments to make the book into what it has become, guiding me as its steward to appreciate what was working and what needed more expansion or clarification. Those individuals include Ed Bacon, Lou Cozolino, Richie Davidson, Elissa Epel, Bonnie Goldstein, Dacher Keltner, Jack Kornfield, Maria LeRose, Helen Liang, Jenny Lorant, Veronica Magar, Deena Margolin, Sally Maslansky, Deborah Pearce-McCall, Madeleine Welch Siegel, Elli Weisbaum, Caroline Welch, Elisheva Wexler, Barnaby Willett, and Suzanne Young. Thank you all for taking the time and offering your invaluable insights.

At our Mindsight Institute we have our meetings often around the table that served as the original inspiration for the Wheel of Awareness, and I am honored to share those circling seats with Jane Daily, Ryan McKeithan, Kayla Newcomer, Andrew Schulman, Priscilla Vega, and our chief executive officer, Caroline Welch. Having each of you supporting the mission to share the vision of interpersonal neurobiology and the mindsight approach to promoting more insight and empathy, compassion, and kindness in our world is a privilege. Collaborating with you as a team to bring these ideas out into the world for practical use in applying integration within and between is a gift for which I am deeply grateful.

Over the years, the individuals, couples, and families I've been privileged to clinically care for, the online and in-person students as well as workshop participants, all of who have immersed themselves in the Wheel of Awareness, have been vital in both its creation and development. I thank you all for the courage to try something new and to offer your feedback on how to improve this practical application of integrating consciousness into your everyday lives.

At Penguin Random House's TarcherPerigee division, it is a pleasure to work with the professional and efficient staff, including Heather Brennan and copy editor Kym Surridge. Since the days of *Parenting from the Inside Out* and *Brainstorm*, working closely with my publisher and editor, Sara Carder, has been a joy. Thank you for your keen eye, your delightful sense of humor, and your devotion to the readers' experience as we considered the structure and edited the words of the book into its final form.

Expressing these ideas about the subjective experience of consciousness in words alone is challenging. Along the journey of this book coming to be created, I had the privilege of working with a brilliant artist who is also a student of science and of meditation—Madeleine Welch Siegel, my daughter—whose creative ideas and deep understanding of the mind enabled the book to have illustrations that are instrumental in visualizing the concepts and practices of the Wheel. Maddi helped me to think through many of the challenging concepts and explore how to articulate them more clearly; she also came up with the title *Aware* when I was told that my original suggestion for a book name was not going to fly. The title and the images are just what the book needed, and I thank you for your essential presence on these pages.

My family is the deepest source of my support and inspiration in the writing of this book. With Maddi now in New York, various other family members in Los Angeles have been crucial in feeling the clarity of mind in my life to write. We are blessed that our son, Alex, whose life in music inspires us each day, can have his path cross with his parents' journey still. We have a pretty great time finding movies to share when we're both in town. My mother, Susan Siegel, is fascinated with the mind and continues to challenge me with questions about what all this means. My brother, Jason, provides thoughtful reflections as well as humorous anecdotes about how mindsight plays a role in his busy life. Caroline Welch, my life and work partner, is an insightful reader and thoughtful practitioner of meditation and mindfulness. Our discussions about the ways we can cultivate a healthier life using the power of presence and the training of the mind infuse our discussions with passion, focus, and fun. Thank you, Caroline, for being such a supportive and pivotal presence and for helping me to prioritize and pace myself in our shared personal and professional life.

SELECTED REFERENCES AND READING

A bibliography with background reading and scientific references for this book can be found on my website, DrDanSiegel.com/pdf/Aware_DanielJSiegel_References.pdf. I've organized the listings by topic so you can find further information that might be of special interest to you. Topics include telomeres and compassion, or more general areas such as neural function and structure or the impact of meditation on mental processes, our relationships, and the brain. If a specific quotation was used in the text itself, then a footnote is available at the bottom of that page to indicate the exact source from which the quotation was drawn.

As mentioned, this book is not intended as a comprehensive review of scientific research but rather as a practical guide to a scientifically inspired tool for cultivating awareness, focusing especially on one particular approach, the Wheel of Awareness. The references listed should be considered a starting place from which you may dive more deeply into the research, and not an exhaustive listing of empirical studies. Also, familiarity with these resources that serve as the scientific underpinnings of *Aware* and the Wheel of Awareness is not in any way necessary to fully utilize the practices and discussions along our journey in the book. This book is a comprehensive, self-contained guide to a practice that stands on its own. My hope is that having this set of resources available to you will simply offer an inspiring sampling of the diverse work that is the interdisciplinary science underlying our journey.

For a general background on how the mind develops and its connection to our embodied brain and our relationships, please see my first book, *The Developing Mind*, an academic textbook now in its third edition, which offers thousands of scientific references on mental processes such as attention and memory. The field of interpersonal neurobiology outlined in that book offers a way to focus on the nature of the mind and mental health built upon this way of connecting a wide range of disciplines into one framework. As the founding series editor of the Norton Professional Series on Interpersonal Neurobiology, I have worked hard to make available more than sixty-five textbooks primarily authored by others for further study in this exciting area. If you are inspired to dive into any of these books or the abundant resources you'll find on our website, please enjoy and remember to differentiate and link your direct experiential immersion with the Wheel practice with the scientific knowledge of these references to integrate your experience!

Enjoy!

Dan

INDEX

Page numbers in *italics* indicate illustrations.